TARAHUMARA

OF THE

SIERRA MADRE

Seledonio

TARAHUMARA

OF THE

SIERRA MADRE

SURVIVORS
ON THE
CANYON'S EDGE

JOHN G. KENNEDY

ASILOMAR PRESS • PACIFIC GROVE, CALIFORNIA

© 1978 by AHM Publishing Corporation.
Tarahumara of the Sierra Madre: Beer, Ecology and
Social Organization (First Edition)

© 1996 by John G. Kennedy (Second Edition, revised)
All rights reserved
Printed in the United States of America

LIBRARY OF CONGRESS CATALOGING IN PUBLICATION DATA
Kennedy, John G.
*Tarahumara of the Sierra Madre: Survivors on the
Canyon's Edge*
1. Tarahumara Indians. 2. Northwest Mexico.
3. Tarahumara environmental adaptation. 4. Tarahumara
religion. 5. Tarahumara social life. Bibliography included.
ISBN number: Second edition 0-964 7877-3-3, paper
Library of Congress Catalog Card Number: 77-044

This book may be ordered from Asilomar Press by mailing
a check or money order for $17.95 plus $4.00 for shipping
and handling. For each additional book add $1.50 for
shipping. U.S. funds only.

ASILOMAR PRESS
1199 Forest Avenue, #321
PAcific Grove, California 93950

Photographs—John G. Kennedy
Cover and book design—Wendy J. Utsuki

To the memory of

Tomás Hinton
Francisco Plancarte
Venancio Gonzales
&
Guadalupe Fierro

CONTENTS

FOREWORD

Among the Tarahumara Indians of Chihuahua, Mexico, are some who have steadfastly refused to subordinate themselves either to the secular or the religious authority of the national society. The price of this intransigence has been their restriction to a remote and difficult terrain high in the western Sierra Madre. Or, perhaps one should put this the other way about—only those Tarahumara who are protected by such a formidable bastion can withstand the pressures of priests and politicians. They are not, of course, entirely uninfluenced by the Mexican national culture, economy or social institutions, yet their daily lives are little touched by these influences.

Tarahumara of the Sierra Madre is an examination of the patterns of life among these *Gentiles*, these pagans, whom their more acculturated cousins call *Cimarrones*, wild animals. Their lives are lived on narrow shelves; one, two, or perhaps a half dozen homesteads on each, and each separated by deep gorges from the others. They cultivate these narrow ledges, and have learned to use livestock to transform the forage that grows deep in the barrancas into corn, beans and squash by a unique pattern of fertilization. Though they keep the animals more for this function than for their meat, hides and wool, the herds and flocks are nevertheless an important measure of a man's worth and social influence. For, though these Tarahumara are all poor, they are by no means all equal.

The scarcity of natural resources is perhaps a less important factor in shaping the social institutions and cultural characteristics than are the dangers of the precipitous landscape and the social isolation that it creates. It is an environment that cannot sustain rigid and stable social units above the household, but requires flexibility and adaptability in social relationships.

To understand the social organization of these Tarahumara and to penetrate the necessary adaptations in attitudes and sentiments, Kennedy has rightly focussed his attention on what he calls the *tesgüino* complex. *Tesgüino* is a mild nourishing maize beer that is the center of all major productive labor, all important social activities, all ritual performance; it is both the leaven in all social intercourse, and the anodyne that lessens the tensions inherent in their isolated, hostile world.

The *tesgüino* complex is necessarily central to a sophisticated approach to cultural ecology. The more standard input-output orientation of an ecology that focusses attention too narrowly on the utilization of the biomass is inadequate for an understanding of the social institutions and patterns of interaction. These require an appreciation of the psychological effects of the environment as well as an appreciation of the economic forces. Kennedy has taken steps toward what Bateson has called *the ecology of the mind* and married it appropriately to the more usual material ecology environmental adaptation.

—Walter Goldschmidt

ACKNOWLEDGEMENTS

The research for this book was made possible by grants from the Grace and Henry M. Doherty Charitable Foundation for Latin American Research, and the George C. Barker Memorial Fund of the University of California, Los Angeles. I gratefully acknowledge their support.

My friends at the Instituto Nacional Indigenista, Centro Coordinador Tarahumara were of invaluable aid in ways too numerous to describe here. Their assistance began when the late Professor Francisco Plancarte put his knowledge and the facilities of the Instituto at the disposal of Tom Hinton and myself on our first trip through the Sierra Tarahumara in the summer of 1957. The encouragement he gave to some neophyte anthropologists played an important part in my decision to go on and do a study of the Tarahumara. On the later 1959 field trip which culminated in this book, Professor Agustín Romano, Director, and Professor Maurilio Muñoz, Subdirector of I.N.I. assisted me in every way possible. The entire staff of the Instituto were friendly and helpful, and Professors Silvino Espino and Fulgencio Gutierrez introduced me into several Tarahumara communities personally. Dr. Armando Trigo and Professor Guadalupe Fierro also provided invaluable support and help when it was urgently needed. Without the assistance of these and many other I.N.I. people, I would have been slowed down immensely and perhaps would not even have survived.

I owe a profound debt of gratitude to the teachers who most inspired and guided me in my quest to become an anthropologist. I had many great learning experiences at UCLA, but here I can only single out those teachers who had the greatest impact on my professional development. These were professors Walter Goldschmidt, Ralph Beals, Council Taylor, Pedro Carrasco, William Lessa, Joseph Birdsell, Harry Hoijer and George Barker.

I am also happy to have an opportunity to express my appreciation to Father Luis Verplancken S.J., for his unceasing helpfulness, and for his encouragement to rewrite my dissertation for publication. He should be commended for his nearly four decades of service among the Tarahumara, and particularly for the hospital he founded in Creel.

I wish to express my special gratitude to my wife, Wendy Utsuki, who has worked tirelessly and patiently in many of the roles necessary to bring this book about. Without her energy, design capabilities, computer understanding and psychological support it is very unlikely that this project would have culminated in publication. I would also like to thank Flor de María Oliva-Hennelly for coming to my aid in her careful proofreading of the manuscript.

All field workers are ultimately dependent upon the people with whom they work: the people who so patiently coach them in the nuances of their cultures. In this regard, I am particularly in debt to Venancio Gonzales, my interpreter-guide, and to Seledonio Inápuchi a man whose inner strength and wisdom would be recognized in any culture. Additionally, I must express my undying appreciation to all the good humored people of Inápuchi, Aboreáchi, and Yehuachíque who, despite the cultural gap between us, graciously and patiently instructed the unexpected stranger in their midst.

_John G. Kennedy
Santa Fe, New Mexico
1996

Preface To Second Edition

One century ago Carl Lumholtz, the first ethnologist to work with the Tarahumara, was in the midst of his nearly four years among them. At that time the general feeling of educated people in the Euro-American world was that many, if not all of the native peoples of the world, were on the edge of extinction, inevitably destined to be destroyed or assimilated by the technologically advanced countries. Lumholtz expressed this belief, with specific reference to the Tarahumara:

> "Luckily, withal, the Tarahumare has not yet been wiped out of existence. His blood is fused into the working classes of Mexico, and he grows a Mexican. But it may take a century yet before they will all become servants of the whites and disappear like the Opatas. Their assimilation may benefit Mexico, but one may ask: Is it just? Must the weaker always be crushed, before he can be assimilated by the new condition of things? Future generations will not find any other record of the Tarahumares than what scientists of the present age can elicit from the lips of the people and from the study of their implements and customs" (1902: 420).

It is now clear that this judgment was far too pessimistic. The process of mexicanization has certainly continued, and the Indians have not completely escaped the ever accelerating impacts of influences from the outer world. Nevertheless, when I returned to the area again in the late 1980s, I found that these same influences still differentially affect them. In the remoter regions, particularly those where roads do not yet reach, the Tarahumara are carrying on their customs and traditions in the same ways they did in Lumholtz's time. It is true that in the more accessible areas men now wear machine made clothing, that modern pots and pans are displacing the native pottery vessels, and that around the growing Mexican towns in the Sierra many more Indians have gone to school long enough to achieve a working knowledge of Spanish. However, such changes are often superficial. Appearances notwithstanding, most of the Indians in the region of greatest density of Indian population still preserve a strong Tarahumara identity. This is especially true for the *Gentiles* (unchristianized Tarahumara) described in this book, but in general, native customs and beliefs have remained strongest among those Indians farthest removed from modern Mexican society.

However, despite the fact that in many areas Tarahumara culture has survived nearly four centuries of threats to its existence and is still viable, the present situation cannot be viewed with complacency. During the past twenty years international drug interests have entered parts of the region, reeking havoc in their wake. Powerful lumbering companies have devastated much of the Indian timber resources, and hordes of tourists inundate those Indian communities nearest new transportation and lodging facilities. This is not the place to discuss these important events. The purpose here is to provide a descriptive analysis of native Tarahumara cultural adaptation in a region which so far has avoided full confrontation with the forces of modern social change. This work, along with those of Lumholtz, Bennett and Zingg, Pennington, Merrill and others, helps to establish the baseline which is necessary for any study of sociocultural change. This does not mean that we should ignore the serious problems that some of the Indian communities of the Sierra Madre now face, but only that these issues must be dealt with elsewhere.

The Tarahumara have become more generally known outside Mexico since the original research reported here was done. Since the mid-1960s, when the railroad between Chihuahua City and Las Mochis was completed, daily trains full of tourists have been traversing the spectacular canyon country which is their homeland. The remarkable running feats of the Tarahumara and the magnificent grandeur of the Copper Canyon, have been extolled regularly in magazines and in the Sunday supplements of newspapers during the last three decades. In spite of all this, most of the information generally available on these Indians is very superficial.

This book is written for those who are not satisfied with a few scattered facts and opinions about "the cave dwellers of the Copper Canyon." It is for the educated reader, or the college student, who wants an overview with some substance, which is at the same time comprehensible. Some moderate demands are made on the reader, but I think that meeting those demands will yield the pleasures of knowledge and understanding gained.

Most of the changes I have made in this second and revised edition of the book are clarifications of meaning, eliminations of mistakes, some amplifications of ethnographic facts, and the addition of a new Appendix on Tarahumara running. This last was included as a response to the curiosity stimulated by numerous reports in the mass media concerning Tarahumara running abilities and their traditions of racing. Because most of these reports are vague and incomplete, I felt that the addition of a more accurate discussion of this topic would be interesting and useful, not only to those people who have a desire to know more about this little-known culture, but also to the many sportsmen and sportswomen who are interested in learning about great endurance runners who approach training and performance from a very different perspective than our own.

In this revision of the book my understanding of Tarahumara culture has been augmented by several reports of more recent research. I am especially indebted to the work of William Merrill. His careful ethnographic work as displayed in *Rarámuri Souls*, and several articles, has provided a number of new interpretations of cultural meaning, particularly in the domain of religion. Some of these have served as sources for some of my own inquiries on recent short trips to the Tarahumara. Though the community in which Merrill worked is a Christianized one, I have been able to verify that some of these meanings are the same in Inápuchi. Where they do not coincide we have more evidence confirming the high degree of intracultural variation which is typical of Tarahumara culture.

My understanding of Tarahumara culture also has been significantly increased by several doctoral dissertations, particularly those of Francis Slaney, Jerome Levi, and Martha Graham. Slaney used her research in the Christianized pueblo of Panaláchi as a basis for a highly original reinterpretation of the existing data on Tarahumara ritual and belief. Levi utilized research in a remote community of unchristianized Tarahumara to develop new ways and means to analyze processes and concepts of ethnicity, and through these to propose some interesting hypotheses regarding the history and behavior of this Indian group. His work is additionally valuable because, other than the book you now hold in your hand, it is the only study in the literature which focusses on an unchristianized, or *Gentile*, Tarahumara community.

I also want to express here my admiration of the Tarahumara people. One of the themes of this early book, as well as much of my later work, has been to challenge what I feel is Anthropology's promulgation of an oversimplified doctrine of cultural relativism. I used examples from my first significant research endeavor, which happened to be among the Tarahumara, to illustrate some of my ideas on this subject, and this has been taken by some to be a negative evaluation of the group. Such a conclusion is a misreading of my work. I have always admired the Tarahumaras' serene sense of self, expressed in their dignified composure, their quiet shyness, frequently coupled with a humorous attitude, and their independence, which reflects a kind of freedom we cannot know. They are profoundly individualistic, yet respectful and generous to others. They are a strong and practical people. I do not want to seem overly romantic here, but when my antirelativistic arguments are encountered in later chapters, I urge the reader to keep in mind that I freely admit holding positive emotional values towards the Tarahumara. The antirelativistic concepts which I propose might be better articulated than I was able to manage in this early work, but they are meant to be applicable to **all** societies. I think that when our own society is analyzed in a similar manner, it emerges in many ways more negative and more dangerous to its members than is that of the Tarahumara, or in fact, than those of many nonliterate societies. In my view, though they are obviously adaptive, all cultures are also makeshift, haphazard, historical constructions, many of whose attributes may be more counterproductive than otherwise. Yet many irrational beliefs and practices are doggedly held by their members as "truths." My early attempt here was only an initial start on the difficult task of divesting a few potentially useful evaluative concepts of as much of their surplus meaning as possible. My intention in this was only to begin the creation of a basis upon which more accurate and honest judgements could be made. We must admit that the expression of value judgments is fraught with hazard and can easily lead to unexamined prejudice, self indulgence and arrogant ethnocentrism, but on the other hand, claims of complete impartiality are simply inane. To some degree value judgments cannot be avoided; true objectivity is beyond human reach. Yet, I believe that continuous striving for that elusive goal in a highly conscious, analytical and self critical way still promises the best results.

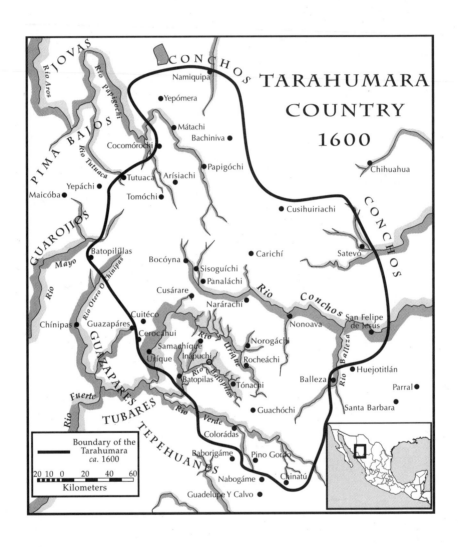

TARAHUMARA
COUNTRY
1600

Boundary of the
Tarahumara
ca. 1600

20 10 0   20   40   60
Kilometers

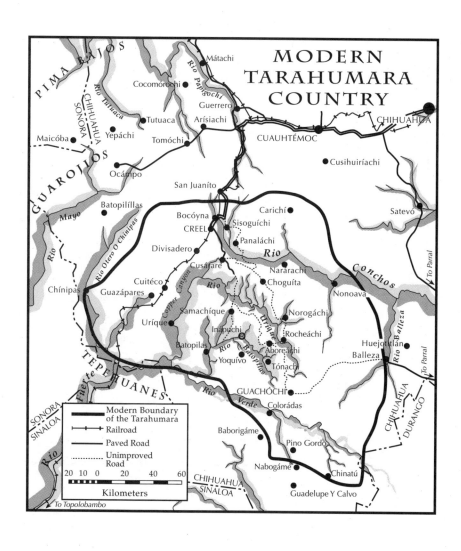

MODERN
TARAHUMARA
COUNTRY

Mátachi

Cocomórochi

Guerrero

Tutuaca   Arísiachi

CHIHUAHUA

CUAUHTÉMOC

Maicóba   Yepáchi

Tomóchi

Cusihuiríachi

Ocámpo

San Juaníto

Batopilíllas

Carichí

Satevó

Mayo   Bocóyna   Sisoguíchi

CREEL   Panaláchi

Divisadero   Rio

Cusárare

Nararachi

Cuitéco   Choguíta

Chínipas   Guazápares   Nonoava

Samachíque   Norogáchi

Inapuchi   Rocheáchi

Batopilas   Huejotitlán

Uríque   Yoquívo   Aboreáchi   Balleza

Tónachi

GUACHÓCHI

Colorádas

Baborigáme

Pino Gordo

Nabogáme   Chinatú

CHIHUAHUA
SINALOA   Guadalupe Y Calvo

Modern Boundary
of the Tarahumara

Railroad

Paved Road

Unimproved
Road

20 10 0   20   40   60

Kilometers

To Topolobambo

PIMA BAJOS

GUAROJIOS

TEPEHUANES

SONORA
SINALOA

CHIHUAHUA
DURANGO

To Parral

To Parral

Conchos

Rio Papigochi

Rio Tutuaca

Rio Otero O Chínipas

Copper Canyon

Rio Urique

Rio Batopilas

Rio Verde

Rio Balleza

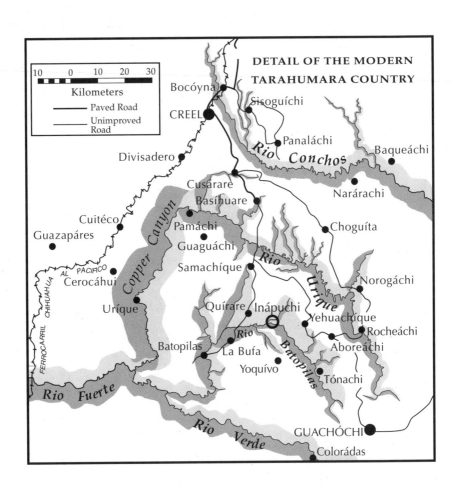

DETAIL OF THE MODERN TARAHUMARA COUNTRY

10 0 10 20 30
Kilometers
Paved Road
Unimproved Road

Bocóyna
Sisoguíchi
CREEL
Panaláchi
Rio Conchos
Baqueáchi
Divisadero
Narárachi
Cusárare
Basíhuare
Cuitéco
Pamáchi
Choguíta
Guazapáres
Guaguáchi
Samachíque
Rio Urique
Norogáchi
AL PACIFICO
Cerocáhui
Quírare
Inápuchi
Yehuachíque
FERROCARRIL CHIHUAHUA
Uríque
Rocheáchi
Copper Canyon
Batopilas
La Bufa
Aboreáchi
Rio Batopilas
Yoquívo
Tónachi
Rio Fuerte
GUACHÓCHI
Rio Verde
Colorádas

INTRODUCTION

This book describes the social life of Inápuchi, a community of Tarahumara Indians living in the western Sierra Madre mountains of northern Mexico. The Tarahumara, who number between 35,000 and 40,000, are the largest tribe of Indians north of Mexico City, apart from the Navajo. They are also among the least known and the least affected by modern society. The ability of the Tarahumara people to preserve their cultural integrity derives chiefly from the circumstance that their environment is among the least hospitable in Mexico. It has been extremely difficult to build roads through the precipitous canyon country they call home, and the relative scarcity of tillable land has deterred would-be settlers from invading the region in large numbers.

Tarahumara country occupies the southwest corner of the present Mexican state of Chihuahua. Their territory used to be much larger, but through processes of encroachment and displacement by members of the dominant Mexican society, along with the mestizoization of Indians, it is now restricted for the most part to the most inaccessible fastnesses of the western Sierra Madre mountain chain. The core of this region, where most of the Tarahumara preserve their indigenous culture, is notable for its magnificent canyons—the great *barrancas* of the Urique, Batopilas, and Verde rivers, which wind westward, and the slightly lesser canyons of the Concho, which flows eastward. The first three of these rivers, which have carved gorges comparable in size to the Grand Canyon of Arizona, constitute the main arteries of the Río Fuerte drainage system. The tributary streams of all four of these river systems criss-cross the north-south stretching mountains with a maze of arroyos, valleys, and canyons. Cool pine-covered slopes of the plateaus and uplands are found in proximity to the warm semi-tropical recesses of the larger *barrancas*, some of which descend sharply more than 6,000 feet.

Most of the Tarahumara regard themselves as Christians. Their ancestors were "converted" to Catholicism when they accepted baptism along with many beliefs and practices of the Catholic Church of Spain. However, some of the Indians refused to become Christians, or later renounced their conversions and became apostates. It was with a community of these *"Gentiles"* that most of the research reported in this book was carried out. The *Gentiles* are those Tarahumara whose ancestors rejected the efforts of the early Jesuit missionaries to convert them. They never adopted the mass, nor the full official community organization introduced by the Spanish priests. They did not allow churches to be built in their communities, or else moved away from areas where churches were being built. Furthermore, the *Gentiles* continued to bury their dead in caves in the *barranca*, while those accepting Christianity were persuaded to inter their deceased in cemeteries. They did, however, adopt many agricultural practices and tools and absorbed some Christian beliefs and practices, which they modified and incorporated into their own religious system. On the other hand, the majority of the Tarahumara accepted baptism and became "Christians." They retained most of their aboriginal beliefs and customs, adding the new set of practices onto the older set.

The group here designated the *"Gentiles"* usually refer to themselves simply as *Rarámuri*, but this term does not distinguish them from the Christianized Tarahumara, who also call themselves *Rarámuri*. Originally the word *Gentile* meant "Pagan," and was a label applied by the Catholic missionaries to native peoples outside the fold of Christianity. It designated the yet "unsaved" or "unbaptized" ones, since baptism with water became the symbol of identification with the Christian system of beliefs and practices. It took on negative connotations because it referred to the recalcitrant resisters, or those who did not accept the new "enlightened" beliefs and life-style proffered by the invaders of their homelands.

Cimarrones and *Broncos* are two other terms much less commonly used by people of the Sierra to refer to those whom I, and all scholars before me, have called *Gentiles*. Both of these appellations mean "nonchristians," but both also have the added connotations of "wild ones" or "savages." I have preferred the term *Gentiles*, not only because it is the most common term applied to them in the region, but also because it contains less of the prejudicial overtones imbedded in the terms "*Cimarrones*" or "*Broncos.*" Additionally, I have occasionally heard the people of Inápuchi refer to themselves with such phrases as "*Somos Gentiles,*" whereas they never refer to themselves as *Cimarrones* or *Broncos*. Finally, as Levi has noticed, "As a noun, the Spanish word *gentil* means gentile, pagan, heathen. As an adjective its homonym, gentil, has the strange effect of connoting the opposite image of that which is stereotypically 'heathen'—namely, elegant, graceful, handsome, in short, genteel" (1993:67). Since these latter three adjectives seem particularly apt in describing the nonchristians of Inápuchi, I find the designation *Gentiles* to be especially appropriate.

I have devoted some attention to this question because Levi has recently written a fine dissertation on Tarahumara ethnicity in which he favors the term *Simarroni* for the unbaptized Indians. He bases this choice on the argument that they are mostly descendants of runaway Tarahumara slaves during the early colonial period, when the word *Cimarrone* meant "fugitive" (Levi, 1993:114-143). Many of his ideas are interesting and persuasive. However, this is not the place for an academic discussion of the subject; I only want to make clear the reasons for my own choices.

The *Gentiles* are a conservative minority but they do share many of their traditions with the Christianized majority. Most of the Indians of the pueblo of Aboreáchi regard themselves as *Pagótome* or *Bautizados*. Both of these terms mean "Baptized Ones," or "Christians." To the Mestizos of the area the *Gentiles* of Inápuchi are unbaptized heathen. In addition to the differentiation due to differential acceptance of Catholicism, the life patterns of the Christians of the pueblo of Aboreáchi also vary somewhat from those of the *Gentiles* because of microenvironmental differences between the two communities and their adaptations to them. My description supplements previous ethnographic work in Christianized communities and it also provides glimpses of the considerable subcultural variation which characterizes Tarahumara culture. From this point on, I will use the term *Pagótome* to refer to the Christianized Tarahumaras, since their version of Catholicism is quite specific to the tribe.

FIELD METHODS AND CONDITIONS

My wife and I with our nine-month old daughter arrived in the Tarahumara region in early November 1959. The initial problem was to locate a community with a sufficiently large concentration of *Gentiles*, and also one in which I could find a suitable guide-interpreter. These apparently simple goals proved much more difficult to meet than I had expected.

The 1957 survey had suggested that Guachóchic would be a likely base from which to start, since both the Instituto Nacional Indigenista and the Asuntos Indígenas, organizations of the Mexican Federal Government for dealing with indigenous peoples, have headquarters there. What scanty hearsay existed about the location of *Gentiles* also indicated Guachóchic as a place I might safely leave my family while I conducted my searches for their isolated communities. Luckily, we found that, following the death of Professor Plancarte, two congenial and competent men had been assigned to take charge of the Instituto headquarters in Guachóchic. Professor Agustín Romano and Professor Maurilio Muñoz, Director and Subdirector of I.N.I. respectively, were both trained in anthropology. They immediately understood my aims and always stood ready to assist me.

Despite this generous help, a number of circumstances prevented intensive work in a single community before early spring. Several times I was unable to make reconnaissance trips because of alternating snow and rain. Also slowing our progress was the scattered distribution of *Gentiles*; they are the most isolated of the notoriously isolated Tarahumaras. My worries increased when I found it difficult to find an Indian who knew Spanish well enough to interpret, and who could and would afford the time to work.

However, in this initial exploratory period I was able to move widely throughout the canyon country, and I made several mule trips to the deep gorges where *Gentiles* were occupying their winter caves. Between these trips I witnessed the winter cycle of ceremonies in the *Pagótome* pueblos of Norogáchi and Samachíque.

The community which I finally selected for the study was named Inápuchi after the largest of the *Gentile ranchos* in the vicinity. At first we were not welcomed by the Indians, so we did not force ourselves into one of their *ranchos*. Instead, we located our field camp in close proximity to a number of them. This had the advantage of allowing equal time to be devoted to several *ranchos* so that a larger sample of behavior could be observed. Unlike a village situation, the scatter of the small Tarahumara *ranchos* and hamlets is such that no concentrated body of happenings is occurring each day in any one place. Thus, on any given day we would select one of many places to visit, basing our decision on our estimates of whether individuals were likely to be at home, or whether group activities would be occurring.

My general schedule was to walk daily to one of the *ranchos* in the vicinity (*ranchos* vary in size from one to twenty households). If possible, a one to three hour interview was conducted, and daily activities were observed and photographed. Usually I returned to our cave in the evening, though on many occasions when a beer party was in progress I stayed at a Tarahumara *rancho* overnight. This schedule required from two to four hours in hiking daily, in addition to the several hours necessary for observing daily life and for conducting interviews. The fieldwork routine was varied by occasional trips to *Pagótome* ranchos in the vicinity for *tesgüinadas* (drinking parties), ceremonies, and other special events. Longer trips were made to witness the Easter ceremony at Aboreáchi, an interpueblo race near the Norogáchi area, and the September 17 fiesta at the pueblo of Samachíque. This routine was so strenuous that I usually found it necessary to rest one day after each four days of work. Some longer rests were needed to recover from various illnesses, and once five days were lost due to the severe effects of a poisonous mushroom, which I foolishly believed to be identical to some I had seen Indians carrying when passing by our cave.

Participant observation was used in numerous *tesgüinadas*, working parties, and fiestas. We gained a feeling for the isolated character of Tarahumara life through the circumstance that we resided in a cave, far from any Mestizo ranches or towns. Visits to our cave by passing Indians were daily occurrences, and our food was mainly a semi-Tarahumara diet of tortillas, *pinole*, beans, and varied greens, with an occasional addition of eggs or meat.

Our guide-interpreter resided with us and proved a constant source of information. Venancio Gonzales, a man twenty-nine years of age, had been taken from his home at the age of six to the Jesuit school at Sisoguíchi, where he had remained until the age of eighteen. He had then defected from the missionaries, who had hoped to keep him in the service of the Church, and worked a year as an agricultural laborer near Ciudad Delicias in Chihuahua. He had returned to his native *rancho* of Yehuachíque, had married, and for the prior nine years had worked a piece of land in close proximity to his relatives.

In the field some difficulties arose from unscheduled absences of Venancio, who sometimes remained away unexpectedly for two or three days at a time. Usually these absences were caused by his own farming requirements or by obligations to other adult members of his family, but a good part of our trouble came from social pressure exerted on him by nonfamily members of his own *rancho* of Yehuachíque.

Unable to understand my motives for being in the area, suspicions were aroused among some Indians that I was gold hunting; others surmised that I was after Tarahumara women. One man felt that I was going to cause sickness with my camera. The search for gold and the lust for Tarahumara women are common motives among the Mestizos with whom the Indians are most familiar. Several times at *tesgüinadas* Venancio was threatened by his enemies with magical reprisal should any mishap occur as a result of my activities. He was genuinely afraid of being attacked by a sorcerer using *híkuli* (peyote), which is considered to be the most powerful of malevolent magical weapons. Because of these pressures he almost quit my employ on more than one occasion.

These brief comments may be enough to indicate some of the difficulties we encountered. Some Indian women shunned me.

Many Tarahumara girls are taught that anytime they are caught alone with an unrelated male they are likely to be sexually assaulted, and that cohabitation with Mestizos will cause disease and perhaps death. Though there are many confident and fearless Tarahumara women, it is not uncommon for an elderly female to break into a run when approached by a stranger.

Through constant visits I was able to build up friendly relationships with most of the men, but even near the end of my stay, surprising incidents occurred. Once, at a beer party Juan-Tasio, an unpopular member of the community, began a long harangue aimed at Venancio and myself. He claimed that we were buying Tarahumara and selling them in Chihuahua at a profit, and that we should be expelled from the community. I finally understood that he was referring to the genealogies I had previously taken from many people, for which, as for other interviews, I paid two pesos (the only method for motivating a person to sit and answer questions). He thought I was somehow transferring the souls of the individuals to the paper along with their names, and further generalized that, like other goods taken from Indians by Mestizos, these souls must have commercial value. Fortunately, the leaders of the community, who were by then trusted friends, scoffed him into silence.

I collected information from many people, but Seledonio Inápuchi was my principal informant. He never showed any fear or suspicion of us, and was helpful on numerous occasions. His major asset, as an informant, was that he was very near to being a living contradiction of the venerable anthropological adage that no person can know all of his own culture. Seledonio commanded nearly all of the skills of the Tarahumara. He was a ritual specialist, an official, and one of the wealthiest men in the community, as well as a weaver, violin maker, and potter.

An Ecological Approach

This research was undertaken as a study in cultural ecology. I was impressed by the theoretical concepts of Walter Goldschmidt regarding the role of technology in socio-cultural evolution (*Man's Way*), and by the work of Julian Steward, which was suggestive of how ecology and culture could be studied in particular

7

situations. Ecology, in its broader sense, is the study of the interrelationships between populations of living organisms and their environments. In the work of biologists and botanists, studies of the adaptations of species and communities of plants and animals to particular sets of habitat conditions have been fundamental to understanding evolutionary processes, distributions, and many other problems. Anthropologists and other social scientists in recent years have adopted many of these ideas, as they have studied human communities in their environments as "webs of life."

One reason that human ecology has become popular among anthropologists is that the people they study generally have simple technologies, and their ways of life are more obviously linked to their environments than are those of peoples with complex cultures. Earlier notions that features of the environment such as climate *determine* the specific forms of social and mental life were long ago rejected. However, studies of hunters and gatherers, horticulturalists and pastoralists in the more isolated and peripheral environments of the world show that societies at each of these economic levels have many functionally similar cultural and social features. These similarities are clearly related to the close relationships to the environment which are characteristic of groups with simple exploitative techniques.

A major difficulty with ecological interpretations arises from the condition that any given environment can support a range of cultural forms depending on the types of technology and the attitudes and interests of the people involved. In cultural ecological studies this has fostered "possiblism," the notion that the physical environment plays only a "limiting" or "permissive" role in the production of cultural forms.

The possibilist position has sometimes led to a complete emphasis upon historical factors such as diffusion and invention to account for cultural forms. Julian Steward, however, reoriented this field by asking the empirical question—just what is the role of environment in any given case? Thus, it may be allowed that at a given level of technology a number of options are open in a particular environment, but causality may still legitimately be hypothesized with regard to some environment-culture

8

relationships. He showed, for example, that the fragmentation of Shoshonean Indian society into self-sufficient nuclear family units without higher levels of social organization was related to the unpredictable occurrence of all principal foods, along with the absence of technical skills in a collecting economy for harvesting and storing amounts of food sufficient to sustain larger and more permanent settlements.

Steward took us beyond the conception of the environment as merely permitting a number of possible adaptations by demonstration that under some conditions, environmental factors can be shown to cause certain cultural features. The ecological search then became one of showing the influence of such factors within the total complex of conditions (including historical accidents) which together operate to produce any particular cultural system.

It seems useful to think of two major more recent directions of ecological studies in anthropology: macroscopic studies, and microscopic studies. Macroscopic studies are those which look at human communities and areas in much the same way that animal and plant ecologists look at communities of flora and fauna. Patterns of population distribution in space and time are searched for, and correlated with environmental variables. In such studies there is scarcely any interest in human motivation or human perception.

A good example of macroscopic studies is Birdsell's Australian work showing how aboriginal groups formed demographic units which he calls "dialectical tribes"—stable units of approximately 500 individuals of both sexes and all ages, which were ranged in cellular fashion across the landscape. Their populations stayed in homeostatic balance with the environment under conditions of hunting and gathering economies (Birdsell, 1974).

In contrast, the microscopic, or ethno-ecological, approach as represented by the studies of Frake (1972), Conklin (1954), and others, tries to construct models of the "cognized environment" of a group. The focus is descriptive, and "emic," being focussed upon a people's own classificatory principles and mental constructs rather than directed to large questions of adaptation or evolution.

The older "cultural ecological" approach, as laid out by Julian Steward, in many ways falls between macroscopic and microscopic frames of reference, and still seems to be useful, since meaningful work can be done by an individual or, preferably, a small research group. An example of the latter is an interesting strategy pursued by Goldschmidt and a number of colleagues in the "Culture and Ecology project" in East Africa (Goldschmidt et al., 1965, and Edgerton, 1971). The present study also falls in this intermediate category and was carried out by a single fieldworker. It might best be viewed as an ethnography of a segment of the Tarahumara tribe, which was oriented by attention to environmental variables.

Though the principal emphasis in this book is upon ecology, I also have found it useful to consider historical events and the uniform effects of alcohol produced by the institutionalization of beer drinking among these Indians, as contributory to the development of social and cultural form. Since the term "ecology" in its human sense necessarily includes within its meaning the adaptation of existing knowledge of the group to the specific environmental features which exist, many historical considerations are automatically subsumed in an ecological analysis. In the same way, any institutionalized behavior such as beer drinking among the Tarahumara is also subsumed. However, some historical changes which affect the shape of a cultural system have little to do with ecology and their formative influences may be best assessed in their own right—apart from ecology. I have in mind such important events as the withdrawal of the Jesuits from the Tarahumara region in 1767—a decree by the king of Spain, thousands of miles away, had a profound impact on Tarahumara culture, an impact still evident today.

In a broad sense, this impact might be considered ecological—a significant part of the human "environment" was altered. However, considering it in this way does little to assist our understanding. It seems better to view this kind of event, and there are many of them, in simple historical terms. Similarly, the beer-drinking complex should be seen as ecological in one sense—a psychological and social response to the isolation imposed by the mode of life in the rugged Sierra Madre. Again, however, because of the special circumstance that alcohol universally produces similar physiological effects, it has been fruitful to view this complex as another set of attributes which, like aspects of the ecology, plays a determinative role with regard to some features of Tarahumara social organization. While the *tesgüino* complex is certainly ecologically shaped in itself, it has produced independent effects upon Tarahumara culture and history. It is my thesis that a similar institutionalization of alcohol use in any *similar* ecological context would tend to produce many of the same kinds of cultural and psychological effects. This approach certainly does not avoid or deny the profound ecological involvements of historical events with the alcohol complex. I try to point out these involvements in many places, and in fact stress them. I only want to demonstrate that in this case, the addition of these other considerations has assisted an understanding of the shaping forces of Tarahumara culture.

An outstanding feature of Tarahumara life is the remoteness and isolation from contact with non-Tarahumara, and from the centers of trade and influence in Mexico. A related feature of their life is the relative family isolation within the Indian society. The extreme mountain topography and historical contact events were the important forces bringing about these characteristics. In such a context, their herding-agricultural economy with its necessity for physical movement has created a rudimentary and flexible socio-political organization, and encouraged a basic personality structure characterized by independence, patience, shyness, stoicism, pride, passivity, evasiveness and dignity, as frequently encountered features. The presence of the institutionalized beer-drinking tradition has further reinforced the ecologically created uncertainties of life and enhanced the flexible aspects of the social system. The institutionalized beer party, as a major motivational force towards grouping in the society, has significantly contributed to the production of the unique "network" type of social organization among the Tarahumara *Gentiles*, and has provided the stimulus for development of a set of special social behaviors which contrast with those of daily life.

CHAPTER 1

HISTORICAL BACKGROUND

The Tarahumara share with Mestizos the southwestern quarter of the state of Chihuahua, Mexico. On their northwest are enclaves of two other tribal groups, the Pima Bajo (between 100 and 200 members), and the Guarojío (around 1,000 members). On their southern border are the northern Tepehuáne (between 3,000 and 8,000 members, Pennington 1969:25).

The Tarahumara fall within the culture area called the Greater Southwest, forming a distinctive subarea which generally is called northern Sierra Madre, or the Sierra Tarahumara. The Greater Southwest extends from central California across the Great Basin on the north and includes all of Arizona, New Mexico, western Texas, and all of northern Mexico to the Sinaloa and Panuco Rivers. The Tarahumara language belongs to the Uto-Aztecan stock, the distribution of which, with a few breaks and enclaves, extends from Mexico City to Utah. Today the Tarahumara call themselves *Rarámuri*, and linguistically they are most closely related to the Yáqui and Mayo, who live to the west of them in Sonora, and to the Opata and Guarojío who border their northwest corner. When the Spaniards arrived at the edge of Tarahumara territory in the late sixteenth century, they encountered several other peoples speaking variants of the Tara-Cahitan subgroup of Uto-Aztecan languages. Most of these groups no longer exist.

After the Spaniards' first historic contacts with the "peoples of the Indies," and the subsequent successes of Cortez early in the sixteenth century, they began the awesome tasks of exploring these vast new lands, exploiting their treasures and "civilizing" the strange inhabitants of "New Spain." One of the last areas to be completely explored, and one of the most difficult to incorporate, was the region comprising what are now northwestern Mexico and the Southwest of the United States. Today this area is culturally split by the international boundary, but at the time the Spanish arrived there was a continuous series of interlocking culturally related ethnic groups extending from the Valley of Mexico as far as the Pueblos, Utes and Shoshones of the western United States. Because of the relatively greater cultural richness of both the extreme southern (Aztec) region, and the extreme northern region (the Pueblos), as well as the harsh conditions of life and geography in the zone between them, this huge region has been quite neglected by historians and social scientists.

Although letters and documents of missionaries and officials have been preserved from the early contact period in northwestern Mexico, we still know little about the culture and life-styles of the Indian peoples of the area during that time. These tribes had no writing systems and were regarded as savages by the Europeans, who, except for a few of the Jesuit missionaries, felt that the customs and beliefs of the indigenous peoples were not worth recording. Along with this attitude went a lack of concern about what the Indians thought about the Spaniards (Spicer, 1962:21).

Archeology has provided us with even less information concerning the cultures of this mountainous region, particularly in the remote part of it where the Tarahumara live. The fragmentary archeological evidence available suggests that the earliest peoples in the Sierra shared the simple culture called Basketmaker, which preceded the Pueblos in the American Southwest. This culture, probably dating from about 1000 B.C., combined hunting and gathering with corn cultivation. Some evidence indicates that in a later phase, between 1000 A.D. and 1500 A.D. the people of the region had attained a slightly more complex culture than existed later. This is shown by findings of stone dwellings and storage houses, blankets of agave fiber, woven mats, pottery, *metates* and *manos* for grinding, and extensive use of cultivated gourds.

Most scholars have assumed that these sparse archaeological remains were left by the pre-contact Tarahumara, but there is really little evidence for this. On the contrary, the speakers of Uto-Aztecan languages may well have come into the region fairly recently, archaeologically speaking. The relative homogeneity of cultures throughout the area and the great similarities of the languages suggest this, since with time divergence tends to take place (Spicer, 1969:782).

It was only after the coming of the Spaniards that we began to have a reliable record of northwestern Mexico. Coronado's expedition passed through the region in its search for the Seven Golden Cities of Cibola, but significant contacts between the Spaniards and the Indians began to occur near the end of the sixteenth century, when the gold and silver mines of Santa Barbara were opened. Meaningful interaction with the Tarahumara began between 1607 and 1611 when the Jesuit missionary Juan Fonte set up a mission at San Pablo de Balleza.

Whatever may have been the prehistory of northwestern Mexico, when the Spanish arrived they found an area thinly populated, but completely occupied by tribes of slightly differing cultures and languages. It was also an area in flux; that is, many of the tribes were expanding at the expense of weaker neighbors, who in turn put pressure upon others or moved to unclaimed territory. Some, like the Seris, Tobosos, and Apaches were nomadic hunters and gatherers who raided and traded with the more settled farmers of Uto-Aztecan stock. These tribes were also continuously in flux, expanding their own territories or withdrawing at various points throughout the region.

The Spaniards' principal motivations to settle in this part of Mexico in the early seventeenth century were the search for precious metals, which were rumored to exist in great quantities in the remote Sierra, and the drive to save the souls of the "savages" dying in ignorance of their possible salvation. Closely following the missionaries and miners came people with less visionary motives. These were the farmers and ranchers who were needed to occupy the newly claimed lands, and to provide food for the growing communities. Accompanying them were the soldiers of the king, who were sent to secure the conquered territories and to protect the colonists from the resistance of the indigenous groups who believed themselves to be owners of these lands.

The Spanish settlement eventually brought about a stabilization of the Indian populations, though some shifts of peoples continued during the first century of the Spanish advance. Many groups, among the latest of which were the Opata, became hispanicized and ultimately transformed into the Mestizos which are found throughout the region today.

The Jesuit Era (1607-1767)

At the beginning of the seventeenth century, as far as can be constructed from early records, the Tarahumara occupied much of the same area they inhabit today. However, their territory was much larger. On their southern boundary were the Tepehuáne, a tribe known to be more warlike than the Tarahumara. They occupied the territory below the Río Verde in Chihuahua and probably extended as far south as Durango City. The Jesuits established the first missions among the Tepehuáne in 1596, even though the Franciscans had already been in the area since 1560 (Pennington, 1969:19).

In Tarahumara country meaningful contact did not begin until between 1607 and 1611, when Father Fonte first entered their territory, after having worked among the Tepehuáne for ten years. Fonte made his first trip to the Valle San Pablo de Balleza, and a few years later he established the first Tarahumara mission there. This valley was then an unoccupied no-man's land between the two tribes, and the mission helped in the establishment of a peaceful border there. Fonte accomplished this by inducing several hundred members of each tribe to settle in the valley.

Most of the Uto-Aztecan-speaking groups, (like the Tepehuáne, the Concho, and the Tarahumara) were semi-sedentary agriculturalists, who depended significantly upon hunting and gathering. However, within this vast belt of related groups were several of more complex culture (Acaxé, Xiximé, and Chínipas), while all around the fringes at lower elevations were more warlike, nomadic, hunters and gatherers (e.g., Tobosos and Apaches on the northeast, Seris and Guasaves on the west). The process of adaptation to the intruding Hispanic culture by each of these groups was affected by its level of culture, its military interference capabilities with regard to Spanish aims, and its proximity to land and resources desired by the colonists. The Tarahumara area was a region with few apparent resources in the eyes of the Spaniards, and they were discouraged by its extraordinarily difficult terrain. This inhospitable territory was with few exceptions of little interest to them, and its canyons have remained a sanctuary of retreat for the Tarahumara over three centuries.

The Jesuit era has special importance for understanding Tarahumara culture because it was the time during which many of its major patterns were set. Another generalization which seems inevitable when reviewing the history of this region, is that though prior to contact with Europeans there were continuous movements of peoples and considerable inter-tribal strife, the appearance of the Spaniards on the scene brought about major cultural disruptions and ignited a chain reaction of changes which were of enduring and momentous significance. These processes were most catastrophic during the seventeenth and early eighteenth centuries, but they have continued up to the present on a much lesser scale.

After the establishment of the first Tarahumara mission in the valley Balleza between 1607 and 1616, the missionaries made a steady advance into tribal territory during the rest of the 17th century. They established a series of missions along the eastern lowland edge of the Sierra, and then penetrated into the mountains by the Concho valley to Sisoguíchi. By the end of the century they were well established in the valley of the Papigóchi river and had fanned out from Sisoguíchi, which is still their center of influence, to several other parts of the mountainous *alta* region. They continued to work in the area until 1767, when the Jesuit Order was completely expelled from the New World by the King of Spain. During their period of influence the priests learned the Tarahumara language, worked industriously, and built numerous churches. They had a tremendous economic influence, particularly through introducing domestic animals and the plow, and by the time they withdrew they had established fifty pueblos and had nineteen missionaries working in the area (Dunne, 1948:220).

Meanwhile, early in the seventeenth century, mines were discovered in Parral and other parts of the region, bringing gold-hungry miners and protective bands of soldiers from the governors of Nueva Viscaya, as this northern province was called. Since the miners and officials had to be supplied with food, many Spanish farmers and stock raisers also appeared on the fringes of the Tarahumara country. Much Indian land was usurped during the seventeenth and eighteenth centuries by these people. Many Tarahumara worked for the Spanish, both voluntarily for wages, and through impressed labor practices. Tarahumara are reported as working in mines as early as 1645, and some of them were slaves. The first mines affecting the Tarahumara were the one at Santa Barbara, established in the 1560s and those near Parral in 1580 and 1632, thirty miles to the northeast.

One of the common features of the life of the Uto-Aztecan speakers of northern Mexico was their dispersed settlement pattern. They farmed the Native American triumvirate of corn, beans, and squash, but did not generally live in villages. Their community settlements were called *rancherías* by the Spaniards, since they were not gathered into villages, such as the invaders were accustomed to; instead their houses were scattered along river valleys or on hillsides wherever somewhat level plots of cultivatable land could be found. The missionaries and political administrators found this dispersion very inconvenient and much effort was devoted to programs of "reduction," that is, bringing the Indians together in compact settlements where they could be "civilized" more efficiently, and, of course, more effectively organized as a labor force. In many parts of Mexico the reduction method worked quickly to turn Indians into "Mexicans," but in the wild mountains of the north it did not work well at all. The Tarahumara resisted reduction more effectively than any other Mexican Indian group.

As was the case with many tribes, the Tarahumara who lived on the Eastern spurs of the Sierra and toward the plains of Chihuahua at first were very accepting of the Spaniards, and particularly of the Jesuits. Early Jesuit records often speak of the Tarahumara as being much more pacific and friendly than the tribes around them. However, it was not long until disillusionment with the intruders became widespread. During the rest of the seventeenth century there was intermittent unrest, and a general withdrawal of the Tarahumara toward the west. However, at first they did not give up their homes and lands easily, and several of the bloodiest revolts that took place among the tribes of northwestern New Spain were unleashed by the Tarahumara.

The first important uprising involving them came in 1616 in the valley of Balleza at San Pablo. This revolt was primarily driven by the Tepehuáne who were living there with some Tarahumara under the administration of Fonte's mission. Just 10 years after entering the valley, Fonte and his assistant Father Moranta, on their way to a religious celebration, were ambushed and killed by some Tepehuánes. During the subsequent two years of turmoil several hundred Spaniards and probably more than a thousand Indians were killed.

The Tepehuáne rebellion was led by Quantlas, a charismatic Indian who received his divine orders from a small stone idol which he always carried. A God speaking through the stone figure promised resurrection from death for anyone who died fighting the intruders. Quantlas also preached that the Indians would drive all Spaniards from their territory. Before the Tepehuáne rebellion was put down by reinforcement troops of Spanish soldiers in 1618, six of the Jesuit missionaries in the territory were killed and more than 400 ranchers and miners were wiped out. Tarahumaras did not participate much in this rebellion, though two of their chiefs took advantage of the confusion stirred up the Tepehuánes to make some raids. However, this revolt provided a model for later uprisings of the Tarahumara.

In the following thirty years Spaniards continued to pour into the region, especially after the large silver strike at Parral in 1632. Many Indians were hunted down in the Sierra to serve as forced laborers in the mines, and many children were kidnapped and brought up as family servants of ranchers and officials on the pretext that they could be raised and educated as Christians.

Several more missions were opened during this period, and Padres Figueroa and Pascual took over the Jesuit leadership for Nueva Viscaya. The Order continued to introduce the Indians to new agricultural techniques such as irrigation. They planted fruit trees shipped over from the old world, and brought in goats and sheep for breeding new flocks. In 1646 the Jesuits recorded that they had baptized nearly 4,000 Tarahumaras, mostly in the lowlands, an area which came to be known as the Baja Tarahumara.

By 1648, the Indians again had become very restive due to the miserable conditions in the mining towns and to epidemics such as smallpox, which decimated the population. Many of the "Christians" decided to leave the mission communities, renounce their faith, and join the *Gentiles*, their pagan relatives farther back in the Sierra. Leaders arose who blamed the widespread death from epidemics on the Spanish God, and they, in turn, were branded "witches" by the Fathers.

The culmination of all this unrest came when several hundred Tarahumaras, along with members of some other tribes, joined in a march toward some of the missions. This uprising was quickly subdued when Spanish soldiers from Durango captured the four leaders and executed them. However, when the Jesuits opened another mission at Villa de Aguilar in the Papigóchic valley near the northern frontier of the Tarahumara, they unwittingly moved into another region near the point of revolt. Several well-known Indian leaders were there organizing resistance against the Spaniards, the most famous and dangerous of which was a literate former Christian known as Tepórame (sometimes called Tepóraca). This leader had gained the support of several hundred "apostates" who had renounced Christianity after suffering various injustices at the hands of ranchers and miners. Even the missionaries had produced some dissidents by doing such as things as publicly whipping Indians who failed to come to mass. Thus, not only the Tarahumara leaders, but also most of their followers were the products of culture contact; they knew the Spaniards well and deliberately rejected what they were offering.

The dissidents finally arose in 1650 and attacked the mission at Villa de Aguilar, crucifying the Father together with a soldier sent to protect him, and burning down the mission. We do not know whether the report is accurate, but at one point it was claimed that Tepórame commanded two thousand warriors. He had several successes against towns in the eastern slopes before Spanish soldiers with their horses and superior weapons were able to crush the uprising and to capture and execute him in 1652. Though the Spaniards were successful in finally putting down the revolt, the Jesuits were forced to give up their efforts to colonize the Upper (mountain) Tarahumara for the next 21 years.

Then in 1673, Jesuit Fathers Tarda and Guadalajara led a movement to establish a line of eight new churches linking the Baja Tarahumara with the missions in Sonora among the Opatas and Chínipas. Silver was discovered in 1685 in Cusihuiriáchic, and again miners and ranchers poured in, taking possession of Indian land, and pressing Indians into labor in the mines. In 1690 another rebellion occurred in the northwest corner of the Tarahumara country, opening almost a decade of hostilities and bloodshed. After a few years of apparent peace, a tense situation was again compounded by epidemics of measles and smallpox in 1693 and 1695, which resulted in many deaths and consequent retaliations against the Spaniards.

In 1681, a dynamic Jesuit, Father Neumann, took charge of the missions and was stationed at Sisoguíchi. This vigorous priest worked unceasingly during his entire 50 years among the Tarahumara. He was a courageous and dedicated man, but it is evident that his attitudes toward the Indians exacerbated the problems leading to bloodshed in 1698. For example:

> One afternoon Padre Neumann discovered a group of Tarahumaras near Sisoguíchi having a party in which they were drinking their traditional corn beer. Furious at the fact that they were disobeying his orders against indulging in this wicked behavior, he charged in among them on his horse, upsetting fourteen huge jars of the beverage. The group dispersed but they were furious and swiftly went to another house where they might continue their party. Neumann, knowing that they would do this, disguised himself in Indian dress, and under cover of darkness went unsuspected to the new party. When it was in full swing he threw off his disguise, kicked over all the beer *ollas* and delivered a sermon on the sins of drinking and deceit (Dunne, 1948:165).

Neumann's writings reveal his predjudices:

> These Indians are by nature and disposition a sly and crafty folk, from whom sincerity is not to be expected. They are accomplished hypocrites, and as a rule, the ones who seem most virtuous should be considered the most wicked of all… In fact, I cannot deny that with these stonyhearted people the result does not repay the hard labor of the valuable seed… They show no

aversion to sin, no anxiety about their eternal happiness, no eagerness to persuade their relatives to be baptized. They show rather a lazy indifference to everything good, unlimited sensual desire, an irresistible habit of getting drunk, and stubborn silence in regard to hidden pagans, and so we cannot find them and bring them into the fold of Christ (quoted in Spicer, 1962:311).

By 1696, various Tarahumara "witches" among the renegades from the missions as well as from remoter groups who had never accepted the new religion were again calling for ouster of the intruders. In that year, near Yepómera, the missionaries discovered a cache of maize and poisoned arrows on a cliff and near this cache they found an unusual gathering of people.

In answer to a plea from the missionaries, a Spanish Captain Retana was sent quickly from Parral to stop what was felt to be an incipient revolt. He took swift action, capturing about sixty of the Indians on the cliff and beheading thirty of them immediately. With the approval of Father Neumann he posted the heads along the road near Cocomórachic.

Retana's uncalled-for violence set off a general rebellion throughout the whole northern Tarahumara country. The fighting went on for two years but Retana and his troops were victorious at last. Father Neumann captures the quality of events, the temper of Indian-white relations, and the Tarahumaras' attitude about the new religion. He describes the attack on the church at Echoguíta:

> They then surrounded this group of buildings, battered upon the doors of the church, and with wild and furious yells rushed in. They climbed upon the altars, tore from their places the images of the Mother of God and of the saints, rent them asunder, and cast the pieces into the river which flowed close by. They smashed the altars and the baptismal font, which was carved of stone; pillaged the sacristy; tore to ribbons six chasubles and all other vestments, and scattered the fragments; beat the chalice against a rock and broke it into three pieces; and laid sacrilegious hands on everything else, destroying and ruining all (Dunne, 1948:181).

Retana retaliated, beheading 33 more men and placing their heads on poles near Sisoguíchi. The suppression of the uprising of 1698 permanently ended effective Tarahumara military resistance to Spanish rule. With a few exceptions, their mode of resistance from the beginning of the eighteenth century until the present has been chiefly one of avoidance of confrontation and withdrawal into the deep canyons and isolated highland forests.

They continued to resist Jesuit efforts to force them into villages and in 1744, Father Albée recommended that military authorities round up the Indians and force them to settle in the pueblos, proposing that their houses be destroyed and their granaries burned if they refused to go. Fortunately, these measures were never carried out, but Indians were still being pressed into mine work around Temóchic. Thus, though the Sierra was relatively peaceful after 1700, more of the Tarahumara people withdrew from Spanish-dominated settlements, and there was a hardening of anti-Spanish sentiment among them. Though by the early 18th century the Tarahumaras' typical mode of response to the continuing invasion of their lands was passive resistance and retreat, there are also accounts which report that numbers of them joined forces with the Apache bands which were, by this time raiding the growing Spanish settlements (Merrill,1988:35).

In spite of the generally negative attitude which the Indians held towards the Church during this period, one last influential burst of Jesuit activity occurred before the forced withdrawal of the missionaries, and by 1763 many new churches had been established throughout the Sierra.

A very important economic change during this period was the growth of Indian animal herds. The integration of sheep, goats, and cattle into their economic life, was to have profound effects on their culture, which still persist. The herds multiplied, stabilizing the food supply, as well as furnishing a new way of accumulating wealth in the Indian economy. Sheep now provided wool for clothes and blankets, and woolen cloth replaced the old material made of *pitaya* fibers.

By 1767, when the King of Spain issued the final decree, totally expelling the powerful and vigorous Order of Jesuits from the New World, the foundations for what came to be the syncretistic core culture patterns had been established. For the most part this set of characteristic customs, beliefs and practices persists virtually intact.

The removal of the industrious and influential Order was an historical event of profound importance. Though miners, ranchers, administrators, and soldiers continued to transmit selected aspects of Spanish culture and to disrupt Tarahumara life, the motive power of Catholicism largely was diminished to a maintenance effort. The Franciscans, charged with taking over the Tarahumara missions, were already overextended in other regions of New Spain and they introduced few significant changes into the lives of the Indians of this part of the Sierra Madre.

The Jesuit era brought a profound demographic shift in the region: an overall population decline. There are no accurate figures so it is impossible to determine the precise extent of this but, as I have mentioned earlier, new European diseases brought several great epidemics which contributed to the population loss.

The historical demographic picture is complicated by two change processes: migration and mestizoization. In the eastern part of what had been Tarahumara country the villages and towns took the concentrated "reduction" form that the padres had wanted. It is not known what percentage of the Indians left this lowland area or "Baja Tarahumara" for the highlands, but it is clear from the records that many did so at various times. Others opted to stay with the padres or to remain around the mining towns, and by the time the Jesuits left, many of these had adopted Spanish culture. A great deal of intermarriage and other interracial gene-mixing took place in this area, not only between Spanish and Tarahumaras, but also involved Conchos, Salineros, Tobosos, and others. This mixing process was assisted in the plains area by the silver strikes at Chihuahua in the eighteenth century, and by the rapid growth of that city into the Capital of the province of Nueva Viscaya.

However, there were, as was mentioned earlier, many Tarahumaras who chose to continue the old free and independent life which was still possible in the Sierra. These came not only from the eastern Baja Tarahumara region, but from its northern frontier when the missions moved into that area. A general movement by traditional and disaffected Indians was toward the west and south, into the more rugged canyon country, and the Tarahumara began encroaching into the territories of other tribes, even as these were being decimated in wars and rebellions. Some Tarahumara also moved farther westward into what had been

Tepehuáne country south of the Río Verde canyon, where they still remain.

A second series of critical changes in Tarahumara life effected by the Spaniards was the introduction of domestic animals into the basic subsistence pattern, reinforced by the introduction of peaches, oranges, apples, and quinces from the Old World, as well as new methods of farming. The Jesuits and early colonial farmers also introduced the Spanish wooden plow and methods of preparing fields which the Indians still use. They brought the axe, which soon became the most important tool in the wooded environment of the Sierra. As I have been arguing, the basic structure of the Tarahumara economy for the next two hundred years was established during the Jesuit era of Spanish contact.

A third sphere in which profound change was effected during the early period was the religious one. We do not know the percentage of those converted to Christianity among the Tarahumara at the time the Jesuits withdrew, but we do know that there were 29 missions and at least 55 *visitas* in Tarahumara country. A mission report from 1725 indicates 4,258 families under mission control, or about 20,000 Indians out of a Tarahumara population estimated at over 32,000 around 1784. As there may have been at least 10,000 uncounted Tarahumara, it seems reasonable to suppose that about half the members of the tribe were still unbaptized when the Jesuits withdrew.

Baptism, signifying identification with Christianity, apparently has continued to grow, for I estimate that probably not much more than five percent of those identifying themselves as Tarahumara are *Gentiles* today. Introduction of Christianity created a social cleavage of great importance between baptized and unbaptized Tarahumara. Rejection of the Spaniards' religion was not simply a matter of rejecting the theology; it was a most effective way of repudiating Spanish political control and the whole way of life identified with the foreign intruders.

A final point here: many Catholic religious concepts and many features of ritual became mixed with aboriginal beliefs and practices. This will be discussed in more detail later. Suffice it to say here that this penetration of native religion by Catholicism affected the beliefs and practices of the resisting unbaptized

Indians too, but not nearly to the same degree that it did those of the professing "Christians." The Christian Tarahumara, on the other hand, retained nearly as many of the aboriginal religious customs and beliefs as did their more rebellious counterparts, the *Gentiles*.

In assessing the major changes wrought by Spanish impact, I want to make two observations. First, a profound psychological change seems to have been effected among the Indians, and it became crystallized in a typical personality structure which still persists. In contrast to the frequent belligerence and rebellions of the first century of Spanish contact, since that time the prevailing Tarahumara mode of coping has been a strategy of withdrawal and passivity. It may be that this group originally had been the most peaceful and receptive one encountered in this region, but nonetheless, they engaged in continuous sporadic warfare with neighbors on all sides, and some of the bloodiest rebellions of northwestern New Spain took place among them. It also seems clear that there was a shift of outlook and implicit policy. In my opinion, though other factors are also involved, the present day Tarahumara traits of passivity, withdrawal from confrontation, avoidance of aggression, introversion and evasiveness are, at least partially, the effects of the responses to their punishing contact with the Spanish in the seventeenth century.

Another historical factor affecting their adaptation is that the Tarahumara country never took on vital importance to the major economic and political elements in Mexico. While gold and silver were discovered in some quantities at various places and times in the Sierra, the mines never yielded the great bonanzas of Durango, Parral, and Chihuahua. Additionally, the area was not an inviting one for farmers and ranchers, and until the present era, such resources as timber were not needed or exploitable by available technology. Hence, the region became a backwater. For the next 150 years the Tarahumara were left to work out their own integration of the legacy of new elements of culture. They used the cultural amalgam, or what I have called the syncretistic cultural core, formed by this legacy to create a more complex level of adaptation to the stringent demands of their mountain environment than had been typical in pre-Hispanic times.

The Post-Jesuit Era

Little is known of the period after the removal of the Jesuits until the 1890s, when Lumholtz and Schwatka recorded their travels through the Tarahumara region. The Franciscans were given the charge of continuing the missions to save the Indians' souls, but were never able to put as many priests into this area, and their approach was less vigorous. They had no explicit policy of learning the native languages, as had the Jesuits, and they introduced few technological innovations. The undermanned, caretaking approach of the Franciscans was not so much the result of their policies as it was a function of the political and military disorders going on all over Mexico. This was a time of the revolutionary changes which led eventually to independence of the country from Spain in the early nineteenth century.

Thus, from 1767 until after 1825, the Tarahumara of the Sierra were left relatively alone by the government and were little affected by missionaries. Their minimal contact with farmers, ranchers, and miners went on in the pattern already established, and without many incidents of violent friction. In 1781 decrees by Teodoro de Croix, the Governor of Chihuahua, officially banned forced removal of Tarahumaras from their settlements to work on Spanish haciendas, and prohibited impressing them to work in mining operations (Pennington, 1963:20, 23). This indicates indirectly that these practices were probably still common, and from what we know of law enforcement in the mountains, we may assume that such a proclamation did not stop such exploitative practices.

However, in addition to the difficult terrain, political turbulence, the lack of new silver strikes and the fading of the old ones, there was another condition which inhibited larger numbers of Mexican settlers from moving into this far corner of Nueva Viscaya. This was the increasing raiding in the early 1800s by bands of Apaches from the north. They raided all the way to Durango, throughout the region previously ravaged by Tobosos and Jumanos, and they did not spare the Tarahumara. The state government offered bounties for Apache scalps, and large retaliation raids were mounted against them, but these did little to stop their depredations. This situation made the area very unattractive to settlers for many years.

After independence came to Mexico in 1821, laws were promulgated in the 1820s and 1830s to encourage settlement in what became at that time the state of Chihuahua. These laws attempted to abolish the status "Indian" and recognize only "Mexicans," who were all to have equal rights. It was not possible from a legal standpoint for people to take clear and free title to plots of land around "depopulated towns," while uncultivated public lands were opened for general colonization to anyone who would settle them.

Most Tarahumaras had no knowledge or understanding of the laws, and the great proportion of them were uninterested in returning to the mission towns which had been vacated by them during the Jesuit era. Thus, though one of the purposes of the laws was to help Indians gain title to lands in areas where they could be "civilized" by their Mexican neighbors, the net effects were to induce more Mexicans to penetrate into Tarahumara country, driving the Indians away from much of the fairly good land which they still held.

As the nineteenth century wore on, the mestizoization process also continued on the fringes of Tarahumara country, but probably at a much slower rate. The pattern of avoidance and withdrawal into the mountain fastnesses had become the dominant means of handling contact with the encroaching culture.

Until the beginning of the twentieth century Indians of the remote regions enjoyed a period of relative peace and isolation. They were spared directed attempts to alter their life-styles, and for more than a hundred years, retaining their Indian identities, they were able to control their contacts with the Mestizos. They integrated the animals, agricultural methods, religious ideas and rituals, and many other elements of Spanish culture into a stabilized syncretism which still persists. The degree to which the Tarahumaras of the interior regions were able to effectively isolate themselves from Mexican influence is shown by the degree to which their language maintained its vitality. As Spicer notes:

> The Church had entirely disappeared as a bridge between Indian and Mexican cultures and did not reappear until 1900. In this situation the Tarahumaras, rather than learning an increasing

amount of Spanish, began in fact, to forget what they had learned during the days of the missions (1962:432).

As the twentieth century began, the plans of Church and State for renewing their campaigns to "civilize" the Tarahumara, and to incorporate them into Mexican life, were already in motion. In 1899 a state boarding school was set up at Tónachi, and in 1906 Enrique C. Creel established the colony of Creel which, being principally for the purpose of assisting the Indians towards betterment of their lives, was to consist of 75 percent Tarahumaras and 25 percent Mexicans. Each family was to have 10 hectares of land. He also proposed a "Law of Betterment and Cultivation of the Tarahumaras" which was to congregate, educate, and economically better the Indians' lives. However, though the town of Creel was established and today is a major Mestizo center of the Tarahumara area, the laws and program for Indian betterment never went into effect.

The return of the Jesuits to the Sierra in 1900, after their 123 year absence, was inaugurated with a new catechism in the Tarahumara language and the opening of boarding schools at Sisoguíchi, Carichí, Nonoava, and Tónachi. The Order also opened some orphanages and has continued to expand its programs. The Revolution of 1910 and its aftermath inhibited the efforts of both Church and State to deal with what they regarded as the "problems" of the Indians of the Sierra. Despite the continuance of Jesuit activities on a minor scale after the Revolution, the Tarahumara again had a brief period of freedom from interference by governmental and religious institutions. This was not all to their benefit, for ranchers and mining interests gradually increased their steady infiltration of the mountains.

A few small "cultural mission" teams began working in the Tarahumara region in 1926, but real governmental interest in these Indians was not aroused again until the mid-1930s. In 1934, in a meeting of officials with Tarahumara "little governors" acquainted the Chihuahua state government with the Indians' complaints regarding the ever-increasing Mestizo encroachment onto their land. In 1937 two more cultural missions were sent into the area, and the Department of Indian Affairs (Asuntos Indígenas) set up four boarding schools in the southern part of the Tarahumara territory. The program of these schools was ambivalent since, on the one hand, there was an effort to teach reading and writing in the Indian language, while on the other, the content of what was taught and the values expressed were the alien ideals of Mexican nationalistic lower-middle-class culture. Our observations of some of the graduates of these schools in 1957-60, led us to conclude that their effect was often to produce partially acculturated individuals who remained in servile positions around the Mexican cities and towns. Exploited, poor, and miserable, they are yet unable or unwilling to return to their home communities. *(For useful historical summaries with different emphases see Spicer 1962, Pennington 1963, González Rodríguez 1982, and Merrill 1988.)*

THE PRESENT SITUATION IN THE SIERRA

Population

Early estimates of the Tarahumara population are probably totally unreliable (see Pennington, 1963:23-24 for review). Bennett and Zingg (1935:vii), quote an estimate of 40,000 Tarahumaras in 1929. The general census of 1940 listed only 25,962 Tarahumaras, while a special Indian census five years later in 1945 found 44,142 (Plancarte 1945:101-2), a figure closer to Bennett and Zingg's estimate. The census indicated that the ratio of Mestizos to Tarahumara was almost three to one (87,230 Mestizos, 30,916 Tarahumaras). However, Dr. Plancarte told us that at least 10,000 partially acculturated Indians were counted as Mestizos and that perhaps 3,000 were uncounted. Thus, the best estimates in the early 1950s were around 45,000 Tarahumaras and nearly 80,000 Mestizos (personal communication, Professor Plancarte, 1957).

In 1970, 22,243 Tarahumaras were counted in the National Census, (González Rodríguez, 1994:69-70). However, again the figures are underestimates because only monolinguals were counted, while the Indians in the canyons were just as hard to reach as they had been in the previous census. Probably, those with the Tarahumara life-style are between 35,000 and 40,000.

Perhaps more significant than the population figures themselves are the distributions of the two ethnic groups. Much of the Mestizo population is in the larger towns, and it is clear to anyone passing through the area that the Mestizos are much more favorably placed as regards arable farmland. Some smaller valleys such as Aboreáchi, Yehuachíque, and Choguíta still remain in Tarahumara hands, but generally the Indians tend to live on plots of land too small to provide year-round sustenance. This situation forces them to find land in other places. Although there are also many poor Mestizo families in the Sierra, they generally have enough ground in one place to support themselves, and often they are able to raise a surplus for the market.

In the early 1950s a new organization attempting to alter Tarahumara life entered the Sierra, the Instituto Nacional Indigenista. I.N.I. is an agency which has been run by anthropologists. They established coordinating centers in all the major Indian enclaves in Mexico. In the Sierra of Chihuahua, the Centro Coordinador de Tarahumara was established at Guachóchic in 1952 by Professor Francisco Plancarte, who labored there on behalf of the Indians until his death in 1958.

The Instituto Nacional has been a more dynamic organization than the older Asuntos Indígenas. It has attempted to further the goals of the Mexican Revolution: land, schools, and medical care. Among the Tarahumara the land program has had to be pushed vigorously because of the recent exploitation of the timber resources in the Sierra. When timberland suddenly became valuable due to new roads and development by large companies, wholesale exploitation of Indians began to increase. It is into this situation that the Instituto stepped, and though there was resistance through pressure at both state and federal levels, I.N.I. managed to salvage something by creating *ejidos* in many of the Tarahumara pueblos. This strategy legally shifted the control of the land to the majority, which in some cases is the Indians, and has resulted in a more equitable distribution of land. The Instituto also has aided the new *ejidos* economically.

Though the principal legal efforts of the Instituto on behalf of the Indians have been directed toward land disputes, there are also endeavors to represent them in other conflicts with Mestizos. They have intervened in many cases that were unfairly ruled, or more often, never were adjudicated by corrupt local authorities.

The educational side of the Instituto program has differed in method from that of the Asuntos Indígenas. Instead of bringing the children into permanent living centers (*internados*), they have pioneered a system of training to make Tarahumara boys *promotores* (teachers) of day schools located in the communities. This program often has had a much greater effect on the *promotores* than on the students they are sent to teach. Many *promotores*, lacking the requisite knowledge to teach effectively, have become marginal within their own communities, fluctuating between seeking the company of Mestizos and wholeheartedly participating in the traditional Tarahumara beer-drinking parties. This often results in abandonment of their teaching responsibilities. Because of their abilities to speak and write Spanish, these young men find themselves in the ambivalent position of mediating the necessary contacts between the two cultures, but are sometimes rejected in their own communities because of their assimilation of disapproved Mestizo traits.

The Instituto Nacional Indigenista still has a great distance to go to accomplish its aims of equality, civilization, and citizenship for the Tarahumaras. Indian communities of the central area remain intact, autonomous, and distinct, except for those in close proximity to Mestizo towns.

At present the Church influence is strongest in the northeastern part of the area occupied by Tarahumaras, though Jesuit missionaries also have an outpost in Chinatú, to the south of the Río Verde. Their center of operations is in Sisoguíchi where there is a large *internado* for both boys and girls, and where Jesuits have created a community of "graduates" who are trained in various trades. There are also several Jesuit priests, neophytes, and nuns at Sisoguíchi, Norogáchi and Carichí. In these centers, where priests are resident, Catholic doctrine and practices are orthodox. However, even now the priests only occasionally find time to visit the more isolated churches, where they encounter resistance in spite of the generally high regard in which they are held by the Indians. As has been their tradition, many Jesuits are fluent speakers of the Tarahumara language, but they still find it difficult to interfere in the Indian "Catholic" rituals. The offices of the priest are mostly for baptismal ceremonies in the *Pagótome* communities, for which they are regarded as indispensable. Marriage and death ceremonies follow more traditional Indian patterns in which a priest is not only unnecessary but felt to be a hindrance.

The priests now have more mobility than previously, moving about in jeeps and landrovers on roads which have often been built by new lumber interests in the region. However, there are still many places where jeeps cannot go and many pueblos are rarely visited. Two Protestant missionaries affiliated with the Summer Linguistics Institute proselytized among the people of Samachique for 30 years. They translated a number of books of the New Testament into Tarahumara, but they have had little success in converting the Indians to Protestantism.

One of the major recent forces making change more rapid than ever before in the Tarahumara region has been the construction of a road from Creel to Guachóchic around 1950. Subsidiary roads were built to Tónachi, Norogáchi, and La Bufa, the American gold mine in the Batopilas canyon. These dirt tracks, which become impassable during the rains, were financed partially by the federal government through the Instituto. After 1972 a program to pave some of them was begun, but by the mid-1990s the main road between Creel and Guachóchic was still less than half paved.

Roads, even when unpaved, have brought an entirely new mobility into the region. Trucks are owned by many Sierra Mestizos who had never seen one before the building of the road. The combination of lumbering and new mining has increased the population and stimulated many small merchants to open stores. Many ranchers have made considerable fortunes from lumber and storekeeping while radios, ballpoint pens, carbonated beverages, cigarettes, manufactured clothing, galvanized buckets, and other mass-produced goods are now commonly used throughout the Sierra. Money has increased greatly in use and significance, even in the almost 40 years since I first started visiting the region.

Some Tarahumaras have been hired by commercial interests (road construction, sawmills, mines) because they accept lower wages, but the Indians never form a significant percentage of the labor force. Those who participate in the Mexican economy tend to be the same few acculturating Indians again and again, rather than a majority of the tribe. The usual pattern is for one of these men to leave for a month or two while his crops do not need tending or when he can find a relative to care for his affairs. The motivation is not usually the accumulation of capital, and indeed there is little chance for this on the minimal wages paid for unskilled labor. The individual is more likely to be interested in accumulating enough cash to buy a few pieces of inexpensive cotton cloth and perhaps a pocket knife or an axe head.

Other intermittent contacts between Indians and Mestizos occur in the numerous small stores throughout the Sierra. A common sight outside of a store is a group of Indians wrapped in their blankets, silently sitting or standing around watching the animated activities of Mestizo customers. For most people such contacts are relatively infrequent because of the scarcity of money among the Tarahumara. Corn, the staple food of the area, sometimes is bartered for desired items, or credit may be extended against forthcoming crops. Commercial contacts are generally confined to the contractual aspects of the transaction only. There are relatively few close intergroup friendships.

Another kind of interaction is with the itinerant Mexican traders who take several burros loaded with cloth, denim jackets, cigarettes, salt, axe heads, knives, and other goods, on journeys through the Sierra. Usually the objective is not so much to sell the goods or to collect money, but is to establish debts of corn from the coming crop. Traders generally come when the Indians' stocks of food are depleted, and they make a considerable profit by obtaining the manufactured items cheaply and trading them at their higher Sierra value. Through such advance trading the Indians not only become indebted to these traders but to Mestizos in the region. When they must pay at harvest time they deplete their own food supplies and must then later in the season of scarcity again buy maize or mortgage their own crop against a higher cost. It is the familiar exploitation pattern which has been typical in the Third World.

Present day Tarahumara communities are largely autonomous. They have their own sets of officials which govern their internal affairs, and which are guided by a set of rules and procedures differing from those more or less standard Mexican laws and practices common to the Mestizos. This system works for all cases and disputes between members of a community, except cases of murder or serious injury from attempted murder. In these the guilty party is taken to the state authorities so that he may be brought to the *municipio* center for incarceration under Mexican law.

All transfers of cattle from members of one group to another must be registered with a Mexican *municipio* official, and all births of children should, in theory, be recorded with him also. Aside from the infrequent occasions when such registrations occur, the only other official contact of the government with the Indians is an annual tax of a few pesos on all heads of households. This still negligible amount is regarded as a means for introducing the idea of government taxation to people with no allegiance to a wider system. These contacts with the state government are rare and sporadic, and many Tarahumaras never come into direct contact with any governmental agent. Yet, there is apparently a growing trend throughout the region toward placing more and more legal affairs in the hands of the government, and there is increasing government control over the affairs of the Indians.

With the exception of the school situation, the kinds of contact between the members of Mexican and Tarahumara cultures are intermittent and one-dimensional. Cases of legal action, trading situations, and other contacts, are of brief duration and centered upon the goal to be accomplished. In situations of wage labor, Tarahumara workers generally are segregated from Mestizos, and the points of contact are really only between the one or two Spanish speakers among the Indians and the Mestizo foremen. In most of these types of intergroup interaction (with the exception of some of those involving I.N.I.) relationships of superordination-subordination exist. It is probable that the degree of choice possible in these transactions has acted as a brake against cultural disorganization. Such limited one-dimensional contact has been a factor in the Tarahumaras' ability to retain most of their traditions.

There are a few kinds of occasions and circumstances when Indians and Mestizos of the Sierra meet in less impersonal or contractual ways. Sometimes Tarahumaras work for short periods as domestics or provide seasonal help for ranchers and store owners. Mestizo men also enjoy attending Indian beer parties when they chance upon them or find out where they are taking place. There are also occasional matings and even a few marriages of Mestizo men to Indian women, although the prohibitions against this are strong among members of both groups.

Thus, a situation of social and cultural cleavage still exists in the Sierra Madre of Chihuahua. The Mestizos call themselves *los de razón*, (those of reason) reflecting the self-image of superiority remaining from Spanish Colonial days. Animal qualities, laziness, filthiness and "simple" mentality are believed to be innate to the Tarahumara. As in most parts of Mexico, Mestizos value light skin and associate it with intelligence and civilization.

The Tarahumara call the Mestizos *orí*, or more commonly *chavóchis*, a term with derogatory implications. Lumholtz reports that the word *chavóchi* referred to the "bearded ones" or "sons of the devil." *Chavóchi* still connotes these meanings, along with the general notion of "disliked and envied outsider." In the words of one of my informants:

> *Chavóchis* do not go as high up into the sky when they die as do Tarahumaras, because they are sons of the Devil and do not make *wirómera* (animal sacrifice). *Chavóchis* love *centavos* (money) more than agriculture, and they do not let the Tarahumaras have land to work. Tarahumaras do not understand money or that other kind of work, only agriculture.

However, coexisting with their negative attitudes, there also exists among Mestizos a patronizing friendly feeling. This is consistent with the Mestizo opinion that the Tarahumara are not *muy bravos* (fierce), but are peaceful and acquiescent in contrast to the Tepehuánes or Yáqui. Such attitudes have recently been giving way to hostility in many parts of the region. The Tarahumara found, for a short time, a champion in the Instituto, and to a limited extent, have again begun to challenge those who are pressing upon their last resource, the valuable forests of the uplands.

The Tarahumara situation appears to differ from that of other Indian groups in Mexico in that within its central stronghold their distinctive culture is still relatively intact. In this region many of their communities are almost completely independent of outside control. As a group they are distinguished from the Mestizos who now share the region, by linguistic, cultural, racial and basic personality characteristics. As we will see, their culture is still a viable solution for the context in which it exists, but the question remains—can the survivors on the canyon's edge withstand another century of threats?

CHAPTER 2

ENVIRONMENT & TECHNOLOGY:
THE ECOLOGICAL BASIS

The majority of the identifiable Tarahumara now live in the narrow zone of pine forest along the ridge of the western Sierra Madre mountain chain; others inhabit the valleys of the Concho river system draining eastward and in the canyons of the Fuerte river drainage system leading west. The elevation of Creel, a major town of the northern Tarahumara area, is 7,775 feet while Guachóchic, a growing commercial center in the south, is 7,624 feet. Lying between these, the valley of Aboreáchi is approximately 7,000 feet, while the altitude of Inápuchi, in the upper Batopilas canyon country to the west of Aboreáchi, is approximately 5,000 feet.

The northern part of the range called the Sierra Madre Occidental is the region of interest here. Pennington (1963:25-38) has classified the environment of the area which has been occupied historically by the Tarahumara into five physiographic types, which are helpful in describing it. Moving from east to west we find: 1) *Basin and range country*, in which historically, there have never been many Tarahumaras.This region averages somewhat over 3,000 feet in elevation. 2) *Plains country*, which has a general elevation of about 4,000 to 5,000 feet. It contains Lago Toronto and rivers of the middle river basin of the Conchos, and most of the smaller rivers; Río Parral, Río Minas Nuevas and Río Valle de Allende. 3) The *foothill country* comprises a narrow strip from 10 to 40 miles in width running from northwest to southeast along the edge of the mountains. This band is characterized by rugged arroyos in the east and low rounded slopes in the west. Forms of juniper and acacia are typical, along with rare clusters of pine, and several varieties of grass. Indians retaining Tarahumara culture no longer live in either of these two regions. 4) *The uplands*, which contain most of the population of this region, both Indian and Mestizo, has an average elevation of over 6,000 feet with a number of peaks between 8,000 and 9,000 feet. The uplands consist of a rolling plateau dissected by many stream and river valleys and it is the region of fairly heavy pine growth. 5) *Canyon country* embraces the drainage systems of the Río Otero, Río Chinipas, Río Urique, Río Batopilas, and Río Verde. It also includes a portion of Río Fuerte, into which all of these other rivers empty. This is the country of immense and inaccessible *barrancas* (e.g., the famous Copper Canyon) so often extolled in wonder by travelers. Within the extremes of elevation found in the canyon country are a number of ecological zones. Descending to the west from the highlands into one of these *barrancas*, one quickly moves from pines and cedars through *madroños* and oaks, down to *nopal* and *agave* cacti and thorn forests.

The Kansas City and Oriente Railway, was built in the early part of this century, but until the 1960s it extended only from Chihuahua city to the town of Creel. It was finally completed all the way to Los Mochis and Topalobámbo on the coast of Sinaloa. Now tourists and travelers have an opportunity to glimpse some of the vistas previously known only to Tarahumaras, local Mestizos, and rare mule back travelers.

The following succinct description may aid the reader to picture the environmental zones described above.

> As the traveler winds his way westward across the central plateau of Chihuahua, before him rise ridge upon ridge, marking the higher rim of the plateau. As he climbs gradually towards them, the high elevation is evident in the cooler climate, the low hanging cloud formations, and the more luxuriant grasslands and open hills covered with massive pines and oaks and punctuated by red-barked madroña trees and red stemmed manzanilla bushes; the cacti of the lower and drier plateau to the east have all but disappeared. These hilly plateaus of the Sierra range from 6,000

to 8,000 feet in altitude, with a few rounded summits over 9,000 feet.

One cannot, however, travel very far through the Sierra Tarahumara before striking severe and breathtaking topography. Suddenly the traveler finds himself confronted with deep canyons whose precipitous slopes descend into the gorges of secondary streams. But these minor canyons are only a prelude to the mighty chasms carved by some of the principal rivers. These huge barrancas, as much as 6,000 feet in depth extend to the distant horizon and plunge downward in cave riddled tiers of delicately tinted strata of volcanic ash in innumerable shades of yellow, pink, brown, tan and white to the tropical shores of the brown, silt-filled rivers more than a mile below, where citrus trees, cacti, and bamboo crowd one another in the struggle for survival (Gajdusek, 1955:19).

At the time of contact by the Spaniards in the early seventeenth century the Tarahumara were distributed in all five of the described topographic zones of southwestern Chihuahua, but now those retaining their indigenous culture are concentrated only in the southern part of the upland region and in the canyon country. Inápuchi, the particular community of concern here, lies well within the canyon country, being situated on a plateau in the upper Barranca Batopilas.

The yearly rainfall for the upland parts of this region averages from 600 to 800 mm, or 24 to 34 inches. Creel, the closest weather station to the site of study, averages approximately 28 inches per year. The distribution of precipitation is largely in two rainy seasons. More than half of the annual rainfall comes in the months of June, July, and August, while up to one-third of the total falls in the lesser rainy season from late October through January. This lesser rainy season coincides with the colder months of the year.

The mean temperature in this part of the Sierra averages between 40° and 70° F. for the year, staying between 40° and 50° in the months of December, January, and February, and between 59° and 70° F. from May to October. According to the Koeppen system of climatic classification this region of the Sierra Madre is "cfwb," or temperate humid forest climate (Tamajo, 1949). This type of climate is characterized by hottest temperatures of less than 22°

C. (72° F.) and by dry winters with rainy summers (rainfall in the wettest months is ten times that of driest months).

The climate in Tarahumara country is not extreme. The Mestizos in the region and some writers on the Tarahumara have tended to exaggerate its harshness. It often freezes at night in the coldest months, yet snow is rare and lasts only two or three days, except in shaded spots. Persistent and biting winds blow throughout the cold months. The climate is well summarized by Gajdusek:

> The weather in the mountains is usually pleasantly cool and clear. During the summer sudden torrential downpours occur, and in January and February, light snows fall, but there is never any heavy snow. As the snow melts, the arroyos, usually dry, carry off the water. The rest of the year is dry. In the barrancas the climate is more like the warm subtropical climate of the Pacific coast, and for that reason many Indians migrate down into the caves in the cold winter. In the spring they leave the "unhealthy" barrancas to return to the cooler mesa tops (1955:20).

Within this mountainous environment, however, there is considerable variability, which necessitates adjustments in living. As mentioned, differences in elevation, slope, temperature and rainfall are encountered within comparatively short distances. There are corresponding differences in the amount of land available, and its relation to firewood and drinking water, as well as differences in distribution of grazing resources. These variations bring about a range of possibilities from the standpoint of desirability and value, and they have given rise to mixed strategies of exploitation of the potential resources.

INÁPUCHI

Inápuchi is the name which I have given to the group of *Gentile ranchos* where my study was concentrated. These include Urárari, Sumárachi, Awírachi, Yipó, Pisáchi, Sopilíchi, Rejóvachi, Dieciocho, and Rynárachi, as well as Inápuchi itself. The selection of Inápuchi as the central focus is arbitrary since, unlike the *Pagótome* pueblos, there is actually no center of this community. I have used Inápuchi as the name for the community because it is the largest and richest of the *Gentile ranchos,* and it was also the one which, at the time, served as a focal point of influence in the area. Some of the *ranchos* of this community are separated from one another by canyons approximately 1,000 feet deep, but many of the fields are visible from Inápuchi *rancho* and from each other. Dieciocho and Sopilíchi are actually within the boundaries of Yoquívo pueblo. Rynárachi is within Samachíque pueblo, and the others mentioned officially lie within the boundaries Aboreáchi pueblo. However, official *municipio* boundaries have little bearing upon the lives of the *Gentiles*.

Figure 1. Distances in Foot-Time

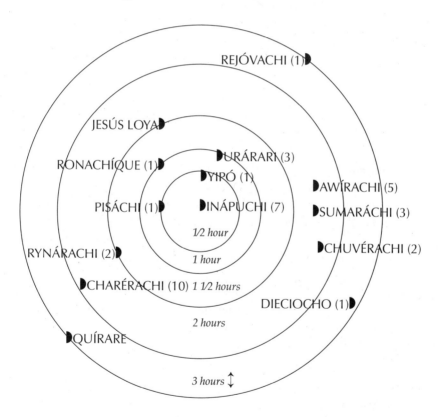

▶ denotes *ranchos*

The total population of this group of *Gentile ranchos* at the time of study was one hundred forty-two people, seventy-two males and seventy females. Inápuchi *rancho* had thirty-nine people living in seven households and is the largest of these *Gentile ranchos*. It is located on a small plateau where three canyons converge and open out into the wider and deeper Batopilas *barranca* descending to the west. East of Inápuchi, over the last ridge lies Aboreáchi and the large nearby *rancho* of Yehuachíque, both about five hours foot-time away. I estimate that Aboreáchi is about 1,500 to 2,000 feet higher in elevation than Inápuchi.

A little more than a day away and slightly to the northeast of the *Gentile* area is Norogáchi, the nearest pueblo with resident Catholic priests, and one of the oldest missionary centers. To the north at slightly more than half a day away lies Samachíque, the central point of research for Bennett and Zingg's well known study.

Another two days foot travel in the same direction will bring one to Creel, the lumber and trade center of the northern Tarahumara region. Directly to the northwest from Inápuchi, across a narrow canyon, is Rynárachi, on a similar narrow plateau with cliffs dropping off on two sides. If one faces a few more degrees west of north from Inápuchi *rancho*, he looks in the direction of Quírare, another *Gentile* community which is linked by kinship to Inápuchi. It also is more than three hours away.

About half a day's hike from Inápuchi down the Batopilas *barranca* directly to the west is the La Bufa gold mine. This is the site of an American-backed venture which had closed down two years prior to the study. Guachóchic is a comparatively large Mestizo town where I.N.I. is centered. A hub of lumbering and commerce, it plays a role in the southern part of the area similar to that which Creel and San Juanito play in the north. It is a two day hike to the southeast of Inápuchi.

The *Gentiles* of Inápuchi live in a world ringed by rising ranges of mountains on their east, north, and south, while below their small plateaus and canyon shelves, deep gorges wind down toward the west. In contrast, the *Pagótome* of Aboreáchi, five hours away over one of these rising ranges to the east of Inápuchi, live in shallow valleys with rocky bluffs and pine forest reaching down to the edge of their corn fields.

Yehuachíque

Barranca Batopilas

Both areas are exploited by the same basic technology, but there are many implications of the micro-environmental differences. For example, most of the year the people of Inápuchi must descend every day into the deep canyon below and trudge back up with a precious pot of water. By contrast, in the valleys of Aboreáchi and Yehuachíque water runs all year round in arroyos not more than 200 yards from any dwelling.

In Inápuchi, children must be kept under much greater surveillance because of the dangerous canyon walls dropping away at their very doorways, and the goats must often be taken down into the deep *barrancas* for daily foraging. In the Aboreáchi area, the hills above the valleys, on which the goats graze, have much less severe slopes.

These two areas represent the extremes in the topography of habitation in the alta Tarahumara region (not counting the somewhat larger plains occupied by Mestizos). Between these topological extremes is the intermediate cleared spot in the forest, which only allows from one to five households. Habitation locations vary in an almost infinite gradation of difficulties and requirements between these extremes.

The greater part of the northwestern Sierra Madre cannot be cultivated, and except for the larger plains and river valleys, largely inhabited by Mestizos, the small patches which yield to agriculture are for the most part from one to several hours distant from one another. Even these plains and valleys are small and poor in comparison with the large grazing and farming plains of the Chihuahua lowlands.

The microenvironmental differences between the higher and lower parts of Aboreáchi pueblo are not confined to differences in the brokenness of the topography. Differences in elevation (from 4,000 to 7,000 feet) with consequent variations in temperature and rainfall create differences in vegetation and different timings in the agricultural cycle. Rain is more dependable in the higher region, and the cold is more predictable and penetrating. In Inápuchi, on the other hand, drought is the greatest threat to the crops, while up the valleys of Aboreáchi and Yehuachíque an ever-present worry is the possibility of an early autumn freeze, a danger which is not usually a threat to the people of Inápuchi.

Herding Yehuachíque

Herding Inápuchi

Unfortunately, there are no detailed statistics available on the rainfall and temperature of this subregion, but from a cultural standpoint, the differences recognized by the Indians, and their adjustments to them provide a useful ecological comparison.

The Physical Community

The Tarahumara live close to nature and have devoted little attention to the elaboration of material culture. Their traditional housing reflects their mobile life and continuing lack of concern with many of the amenities felt to be important by the Mexicans. For example, the Indians of the area studied do not have stoves in their one-room dwellings, despite the fact that cheap iron models could be obtained fairly easily. They have not concerned themselves with any kind of latrine facilities, except in the community centers near churches, where the influence of the Padres is strong.

In pre-Colombian times the dwellings of the Indians in this area seem to have been stone huts chinked with mud, or constructed of mud and straw. They also had their caves in the *barrancas*. These house types, with the exception of the straw huts, have persisted up to the present. However, the introduction of the axe in the seventeenth century provided a means of realizing the potentialities for exploiting the wood resources of the area. Axes, and to a much lesser degree, metal knives, became indispensable Tarahumara tools.

Travelers in the Sierra are always impressed by the Indians' ability with the axe. Every Tarahumara boy learns to use it safely and skillfully at an early age, and the highly prized steel axe heads are passed from father to son. American-made axes are common, and many have been worn down to half their original size by several generations of users. The original handles have long since been replaced by a succession of hand-fashioned ones. Machetes are more common in the canyons, where they are used to cut dense brush.

In Inápuchi and Aboreáchi most houses and other structures are made almost entirely of wood. The grain storage structures are the finest buildings constructed; the Indians pay more careful attention to building their granaries than they do to their houses.

The disproportionate care that they lavish on these storage structures indicates the high value they place on maize, their most important food, and the basis of *tesgüino*, the beverage which is fundamental to their social life (see Chapter 4). These granaries are usually about eight feet square, and eight feet high, and are built of hand-hewn planks which are notched near the ends and carefully axe-planed. The boards are fitted so tightly that neither light nor rodents can penetrate.

To insure security the floor is raised off the ground about 18 inches by setting it up on flattened boulders under each of the four corners. The ceiling is constructed of fitted boards in the same manner as the sides and floor, and over it an interlocking slanting roof of *canoas* is placed. *Canoas* are logs which have been stripped of bark and hollowed into a V-shape. They are interlocked in the manner of roof tiles, and are a fairly efficient means of keeping out the snow and rain. The door of the grainhouse is usually about two feet square and made from hewn boards fitting into a frame in the center of one wall. There are no windows or other openings. The door generally swings inward on wooden hinges or thongs from above, and is secured with a wooden lock.

Corn dried on the cob is stored in these granaries, along with beans and articles of value: animal hides, cloth, balls of yarn, and so forth. Stored between the ceiling and the roof are baskets, horsehair ropes, wooden mallets for pounding *mezcal* (to make *meki*), and other articles. Less valuable items may be kept beneath the granary. Most families have at least two grain storage houses of this type, and many have three or four. Sometimes they are all placed together in the same compound, but one or more may be located at one of the family's other fields. In the *barrancas*, grainhouses are made of stone chinked with clay, and fitted with a wooden door.

The dwellings of the Inápuchi region are mostly single-room structures fashioned from peeled and axe-planed logs. These are notched, and chinked with mud, while roofs are of slanted *canoas*. Smoke exits from under the eaves or from an opening in the roof.

In the Aboreáchi-Yehuachíque upland area houses are of more tight and careful construction than are those of the Inápuchi *Gentiles*. This seems to be partially a result of their being closer to

Mestizos, from whom they have taken some ideas of house construction. However, it may be more related to the fact that these highland Indians have much more permanent households than do the Inápuchi people. Since they have more available land near their settlements and are distant from the *barrancas*, they move less during the year and they do not migrate in the winter.

Another probable reason for the differences is the ancient Tarahumara custom of abandoning or destroying a house when one of its inhabitants has died. The *Gentiles* still adhere to this custom, but it is not the onerous task it might seem. They simply dismantle one of their simple dwellings, and move it a few hundred yards away. In the *Pagótome* communities the custom has largely been abandoned, as the priests have convinced most *Pagótome* that the spirit of the dead has immediately left for other spheres. Nevertheless, even in the uplands a "curing" ceremony of native type is necessary in order to keep the dwellings habitable after a death.

Many of the Aboreáchi and Yehuachíque compounds have two or more log living structures, which, though separated, constitute a larger inside living area than is common among the *Gentiles*. In Inápuchi, the houses are more like those seen in old photographs, e.g., Lumholtz, 1902, and Bennett and Zingg, 1935. As I have mentioned, the climate is not as severe at this elevation and there is much more movement throughout the year due to ownership of fields in other *ranchos*, and to the yearly winter descent into the gorge below. Thus, though the same general type of log house as in the uplands is found, there is generally only one dwelling for each elementary family and less attention is paid to making it proof against the elements. Some families in Inápuchi have houses with walls formed of loosely piled stones with *canoa* roofs, which are more like those of aboriginal times.

An interesting housing feature typical of the *Gentile* community, but also often found in the uplands, is a kind of movable room created on one or the other side of a house by simply leaning axe-hewn boards at a steep angle from the roof to the ground. Families always keep a number of boards lying around which may be used for this purpose. They may be leaned either against the house or against one of the granaries. Children or guests may sleep out in this shelter when the weather permits. People also use it as a kind of porch to sit in the shade on hot days, and child-curing ceremonies are sometimes held there. The enclosure also forms another place to sit during beer parties. This flexible and useful means of creating extra living space can be altered to suit needs or weather, and is eminently suited to their life-style.

All houses have simple tamped earth floors; no one in the area studied had adopted the idea of wooden floors from the Mestizos in spite of long contact with Mexican culture. The same holds for house furnishings, which are extremely minimal and simple. Mexican houses of even the poorest families have glass windows and doors with metal hinges and locks. Mestizos make an attempt to assemble the basic European model of house and furnishings. For example, one finds tables and chairs, beds, shelves for storing things, a stove of some sort, pictures and calendars on the walls, chests, trunks for keeping precious belongings and religious objects (such as crucifixes, pictures of the Virgin of Guadalupe), and a collection of manufactured dishes and utensils.

Tarahumara houses have very few of such Western accoutrements. A few items, such as enameled metal cups and plates and galvanized buckets have become popular, but the interior living quarters has a much different, non-European atmosphere. The house is quite dark; in the absence of windows, light must enter through cracks, the doorway, and the flue. The only articles of furniture are some crude hewn benches by one wall and some small stumps scattered around to sit on. Over near one wall is a *metate* and *mano* for grinding, some half gourds, four or five clay bowls, a larger wooden bowl, and several *wári* baskets partly filled with dried kernels of corn or ground *pinole*. At one side near the open hearth may be several cow or goat skins which are used to sleep upon. A homemade violin or guitar and perhaps a blanket or two and some pieces of cloth may hang from the eaves.

The Mestizos have adapted some features of aboriginal Indian culture too; no Mexican house is without a *metate*, and on their beds they have heavy Tarahumara blankets. Notwithstanding some similarities, the overall difference between two groups is remarkable, and the life-style of the *Gentiles* is even farther removed from that of the Mexicans than is that of the *Pagótome*.

The differences in house furnishing reflect wholly different concepts and values. Mestizo houses reveal implicit assumptions about permanency, privacy, values upon accumulating material things and the notion of a family group carrying out indoor activities as opposed to outdoor ones. The Tarahumara style, particularly as exemplified by the more aboriginal Inápuchi, is a mode resembling some pastoralists in others parts of the world. These is little emphasis upon a rigid dichotomy of warm indoor versus cold outdoor spheres. The Indians' uses of space are much freer, and this is one reason I earlier remarked that they live closer to nature. Under most conditions, all the warmth that is necessary for sleep is provided by their blankets and the small hearth fire. If weather permits, most activities take place outside the house. Tasks are carried out anywhere in the environment that is convenient or appropriate. In this economy most people do most things on occasion, and they can perform most tasks in almost any location. There are only a few activities, such as weaving or grinding, which require the craftsman to remain in one specified place.

The Tarahumara of Inápuchi has a favored house at one location, which generally is on the *rancho* with which he identifies. However, he also has houses or lean-tos at other fields, and a cave or rock shelter in the *barranca*. After a drinking bout he may sleep in his neighbor's yard or lean-to enclosure, and when tending the goats far from home he will sleep in the most convenient rock shelter or hut he can find. Like nomads in other parts of the world, he accumulates little in the way of goods, and values the interaction and conviviality of his social activities much more than the setting in which they occur.

In addition to the dwelling house or houses, and a grain storage house or two, a living compound also contains some other structures made of wood. For example, there may be a crude chicken coop four or five feet square made of small notched logs, usually set up some five or six feet above the ground on four poles. There is frequently a corn drying structure, some six or seven feet square built roughly of interlocking logs and raised off the ground on stones. Near each house lie extra logs to be used for the movable corrals which are kept rotating in the fields in order to utilize animal fertilizer.

The Subsistence Economy

The earlier ancestors of the Tarahumara were maize horticulturalists who depended almost equally upon hunting and gathering. Because of greater dependence on hunting, their lives were much more mobile than they are now. They were spread out over some of the lowlands of Chihuahua east of the Sierra and in the canyons to the west. In the high country, the rigorous climate along with their limited technology, kept them more closely tied to the *barrancas* than they are today. Their garments were made of spun agave fiber, wild cotton, and animal skins.

Maize, called *sunúku* by the Indians, is the basic crop, and this was true in pre-Colombian times before they possessed any of the tools (except the digging stick) which are now necessary to their mode of existence. There are many varieties of this grain in the area and most of them are pre-Colombian (see Pennington, 1963: 39-42, for a good discussion of the ethnobotany). In Aboreáchi and Inápuchi the ancient *maíz azul* (blue corn), *maíz amarillo duro* (hard yellow corn), and *maíz blanco* (white corn), are favorites.

The Tarahumara still engage in hunting and gathering, and these activities contribute a small but still significant proportion of their diet: perhaps 10 to 15 percent in Inápuchi and 5 to 10 percent in Aboreáchi. Inápuchi is lower and closer to a *barranca* where there is access to *mezcal* (a type of *agave* which is cooked and eaten as a sweet), and to the edible *nopal* cactus. The Inápuchi people also catch the larger fish from the river in the *barranca*. Game in the Sierra has declined greatly since guns have become fairly common. Squirrels, birds, and occasionally deer are rare delicacies nowadays. There is no official hunting season, and all wild animals are slaughtered on sight. The Mestizos all own firearms, and they have been largely responsible for the present scarcity of wildlife in most parts of the Sierra.

Foods

The principal foods cultivated by people of the Aboreáchi-Inápuchi area are maize, beans (*muní*), *maquásori* (a species of mustard green), and squash (*bachí*). Wheat, oats, potatoes, peaches and a few oranges and sweet potatoes are also grown in small amounts in or near Inápuchi, while at the higher elevation of

Aboreáchi only apples and a few potatoes are cultivated to supplement the basic diet. I estimate that these foods make up 90 percent or more of the diet of the Tarahumaras in the region studied. The only other cultivated plants are chiles and tobacco. They possess fairly extensive animal herds, yet meat probably constitutes less than five percent of their food.

Maize, the major food, is prepared in a variety of ways. The form most basic to their diet is *pinole (kovísi)* a flour made by roasting the dried kernels in a special small clay *olla*, then grinding them twice or three times on the *metate*. *Pinole* can be kept for long periods of time without spoiling and is ideal to carry on the trail. One dips a gourd dipper or enamel cup of water, sprinkles a handful or two of *pinole* into it, stirs for several seconds with a spoon or twig and then drinks it before the flour settles. It is an excellent refreshment. Following the advice of my Tarahumara companions, carrying *pinole* on long hikes became routine for me, and it invariably gave me added strength to persevere.

Esquiáte or *keorí* is a variation of *pinole*. The major difference is that while parched corn is being ground, water is poured over the metate with one hand every few seconds. The result is a white thin soupy substance which is mixed with ground herbs or corn flowers. It is kept in the liquid form in an *olla* and dipped out at meals to be drunk along with beans, greens, or whatever else may be served. *Esquiáte* is even more refreshing than *pinole* in hot weather, and there is usually a jar of it in any Tarahumara house.

The more traditional Mexican foods such as tortillas, *atole*, and tamales are also made from maize by the Tarahumara, but these play a much smaller part in their diet than they do in the Mestizo cuisine. Tortillas (*reméke*) are usually made by the Indians in the typical Mexican manner. They cook dried corn with lime for several hours (natural or from wood ash) to make *nixtamál*, then after rinsing it in a basket, they mash it on the *metate*. The dough is shaped into balls, patted into flat cakes and heated upon a flat clay disc called a *remeráka*. When they are fairly crisp, they are set on edge against a rock near the flames of the fire for the final browning. Though they are made in several thicknesses, the favorites are made of blue corn and are thick (about 3/4 inch); these are called *nísi* by the Indians, or *gordas* "fat ones," by the

Mestizos, and two or three of them make quite a substantial meal. In contrast to the Mexicans, the Tarahumara generally make *nísi* only for ceremonial occasions or for long trips. Green corn tortillas, which are made from fresh corn ground on the *metate* and then baked on the *remeráka*, are among the most delicious of their foods, but are available only in season.

The simple unfilled tamales made by the Indians are formed either from green corn or from *nixtamál*. They are then wrapped in corn leaves and baked in a pit. Some variety is given to tortillas and tamales by grinding various wild seeds, herbs, and even figs and adding them to the dough (see Pennington, 1963:78-9 for details and botanical names).

Atole is the common Mexican name for cooked corn gruel, which is usually drunk while hot. The Tarahumara of this region have a variety which they call *watónari*. Dried corn is boiled, rinsed, mashed, and boiled again usually with sugar, or some ground seeds or fruits. One especially good variation in the canyon country has small pieces of *nopal* cactus boiled with the corn.

Another not uncommon use of corn is for preparation of a kind of succotash. The dried corn is boiled with lime and rinsed as for tortillas, but then it is simply boiled a little longer with salt or with meat if available. Like tortillas and tamales, this is popular for the *tónari* feasts for which an animal is sacrificed.

Where wheat is grown it is treated much like corn. Generally very stunted in this region, wheat is usually kept in small bundles unthreshed. When it is wanted for food, the bundle is rolled by hand on a metate and then winnowed in a basket. After roasting and grinding, a kind of *pinole* or small tortilla-like wheat cakes are made from it. Wheat flour may also be added to corn tortillas, *pinole,* or *atole*.

Beans supply most of the Indians' protein because meat is primarily ceremonial food, and eggs are scarce. One of the most popular ways of preparing beans is to treat them like corn. Dried beans are roasted in a small *olla* with sand, then ground twice on the *metate* before being boiled with water. This *oríki* is drunk as a hot soup after it thickens or eaten cold when it congeals. Beans are also simply boiled in an *olla*, but this form of preparation is less popular. Cold beans prepared in this way are sometimes put into a split thick tortilla which is eaten cold or heated by propping it against a rock near the fire. *Oríki* may also be mixed with boiled and mashed leaves of the *nopal* cactus.

Mustard greens and squash are the two other important foods in the region studied. Greens such as *maquásori* (or *quelites* as the Mestizos call them) are the third most common food of the Tarahumara of the Aboreáchi-Inápuchi region. *Maquásori* and other greens, such as oregano, are boiled with water and salt, like North American spinach. Usually this is eaten cold. Like chiles, greens provide a very welcome contrast to the ground starchy foods which constitute such a large part of the Indians' intake.

Our hosts nearly always brought us out a gourd of *esquiáte* or one of water with a bowl of *pinole*. Along with this came a bowl of cold salty greens to pick at with the fingers, and perhaps some *chilipiquín*, the peppery dried berries which are so popular a spice among the Indians. This combination is nutritious, refreshing and satisfying, but not heavy on the stomach. *Masquásori* greens are grown in large patches during the rainy season in both Inápuchi and Aboreáchi. They are carefully collected and dried, providing an important source of vitamins and minerals throughout the year.

Squash of several varieties is relished by the Tarahumara, but usually it is only eaten in season. The people of Inápuchi know a method of cutting it in strips and drying it, but little is preserved this way. Squash is usually cooked with water and eaten either cold or hot, and it may also be baked in a pit. The seeds are dried and eaten, or roasted and added to *esquiáte*. In season, squash flowers boiled with water and salt are also quite delicious.

Potatoes and wheat do not constitute a large part of the diet, but they are important because they are harvested during the annual famine period (June and July, wheat; August and September, potatoes), aiding the people to stretch the dwindling supplies of corn. In the highland *Pagótome* area of Aboreáchi a few potatoes are grown among the corn, but they are negligible, and wheat is even rarer.

Though, fruits are not a significant part of the Indians' diet, they do offer a welcome change from corn, beans, and *masquásori*. They also have some social importance because they provide one of the motivations for the yearly invasions of the Inápuchi area by

Mestizos, who exchange a few packs of cheap cigarettes or pieces of cloth for large amounts of fruit, stripping the peach trees of many Tarahumara *ranchos* in short order.

Apples of two varieties are grown in Aboreáchi, but none are grown by the *Gentiles* of Inápuchi. One kind, called by the Spanish term *corrientes,* is an inferior cooking apple evidently introduced by the Jesuits a very long time ago. *Corrientes* were probably better at the time of their introduction, but they have degenerated until they are barely edible. The other type, called *finas*, is a modern eating apple which was recently brought in by the Instituto Nacional Indigenista and planted in a communal orchard for the *ejido.* These are picked and divided equally among the people of the *ejido* once a year, and the *Gentiles* also get a share of them if they appear at the distribution *junta.* Each family receives only half a bushel, so it is clear that apples cannot make any appreciable difference in the Indians's diet.

Oranges are prized by the Tarahumaras of this area. In the Batopilas canyon there are many fine large trees, whose ancestors were introduced by the Spanish centuries ago. These orange trees bear large fruit in the spring. The *Gentiles* of Inápuchi and Quírare thus have much greater access to them than do the people of Aboreáchi and Samachíque. The Pagótome from these pueblos make long journeys to the *barrancas* to get oranges. Otherwise, they must secure them from itinerant traders. A few fig trees also grow in the canyons, as well as some sugar cane and a few sweet potatoes. Loads of cane are sometimes hauled by Mestizos up to the Sierra to sell at Tarahumara races, while the sweet potatoes, considered a great delicacy, are generally eaten as soon as they ripen.

The people of Inápuchi are also favored by another delicacy not available to their brethren of the higher elevations—the *nopal* cactus or prickly pear. In Inápuchi the climate is so perfect for this plant that most *ranchos* have gardens of them around the houses. Some individual plants are seven or eight feet in height. People from the uplands frequently make trips to trade for the fruit when it ripens, and on several occasions I met men from various *ranchos* of Aboreáchi who had come down to Inápuchi just to eat *tunas* (prickly pears) for a few days with relatives or friends. The Indians also have ways of cooking *nopal* leaves after removing the spines.

The simple diet I have described is quite different from that of the Mexicans, even though the same basic ingredients are used by both groups. The Tarahumara of this area have not picked up the Mestizo custom of frying with lard, nor do they include meat as a common feature of their meals. Meat is eaten only when an animal dies, or on ceremonial occasions, when a goat or cow is sacrificed. Pork is extremely rare in the Indian diet, as are chickens, which are prepared by boiling. The baked wheat bread, flour tortillas, and sweet pastries so relished by the Mexicans have not become a part of Tarahumara cuisine.

The Tarahumara diet consists chiefly of roasted and ground, and boiled food with very little meat or animal fat. In view of the remarkable endurance of the famous Tarahumara runners, which has been investigated by a team of physiologists (Balke and Snow, 1965), and the generally good health which prevails among those Indians who live beyond childhood, it is reasonable to conclude that their diet provides adequate nutrition.

Herding

Animal herding is an essential feature of the Tarahumara economy and it is intimately tied to agriculture throughout the region. The main subsistence use of goats is in their fertilizer-producing capacity. Cattle are used for plowing but they also are important fertilizer producers. Neither goat's milk nor cow's milk is used except on rare occasions, and as I mentioned above, livestock are rarely slaughtered for food. Dark *borrego* sheep, called *bowalá* by the Tarahumara, are kept for their wool as well as for their manure, but in proportion to the number of cattle and goats, they are relatively rare in the Sierra.

While agriculture provides more food than does herding, animals contribute significantly to crop production. Herding is also very important ecologically because it imposes rigorous requirements on Tarahumara life. Livestock are the economically significant symbols of wealth and prestige, and they constitute a form of savings, a hedge against starvation when corn is scarce. Agriculture and herding are so interdependent that the loss of either would threaten the Indians' precarious existence. Without their animal herds the Tarahumara could neither occupy their present ecological niche, nor could they maintain the relative independence from the Mestizos, which they value so much.

The present economic situation differs from that of early times. The Indians have been restricted in their territory by the encroachment of the Mestizos. Because most of the good land is occupied, they now cannot move their fields at will. In addition, goat herding has increased in importance as an element in the economy during the last two centuries. This development can be seen by comparing the figures given by some official visitors to the Tarahumara in 1725 and 1761. In eight of nine pueblos reported, there was less than one sheep or goat per family in both 1725 and 1761. On the other hand, there were from one to three head of cattle per family, a figure not far from what it is today in much of the region (Dunne, 1948:237).

By the time of Lumholtz's visit in the 1890s, the numbers of goats had apparently increased slightly, but still remained low. "The wealth of the Tarahumara consists in his cattle. He is well off when he has three or four head of cattle and a dozen sheep and goats" (Lumholtz, 1902:186). Since that time, the number of goats per capita has steadily increased. Bennett and Zingg do not give exact figures, but this statement is indicative: "...In the mind of the Tarahumara, the man with forty cattle is wealthy, while the man with one hundred goats is merely average" (1935:194). This may have been slightly exaggerated, but it suggests this far-reaching change. My observations in a number of pueblos indicate that residence groups now possess from 30 to 100 goats and sheep (predominantly goats), and from 2 to 50 cattle. (Only the very wealthy possess more than five or six.)

The important fact is that the shrinkage of potential land and consequent reduction in the uses of slash and burn techniques is correlated with an increase in fertilizer potential through increases in the herds. Slash and burn digging stick horticulture requires rotating one plot of land to another. Therefore, more land is necessary. The shift from a horticultural economy with subsidiary hunting and gathering to reliance on stock raising as an adjunct to plow agriculture, has thus had important consequences.

In addition to their loss of land through the encroachment of outsiders, the change from digging stick horticulture to plow agriculture by the Tarahumara has contributed to the further reduction of their agricultural potential. In situations where land must be plowed, farming is restricted to plots of ground of a certain minimum size on a certain maximum slope, whereas with digging stick horticulture even the most steep hillsides can be used. In most areas, the Tarahumara have so completely accepted the plow that digging stick horticulture on the more precipitous slopes was entirely dropped. Even small bean plots down in the subsidiaries of the Batopilas *barranca* are often plowed with cattle. This land-use pattern has thus had the effect of restricting the potential growing area, and the food supply has thereby been more limited. There is, perhaps, an unintended benefit here, in that the vegetation cover of the slopes is preserved in this process. Such natural limitation of food potential may have been relatively unimportant in times of land plenty, but with the growing population of Mestizos continuously imposing more pressure upon the resources of the area, it now is taking on significance.

At present, both the plains of Chihuahua and the best bottom lands and smaller plains of the Sierra are occupied by Mestizos. The Tarahumara have obviously been the losers in the process of political exploitation and land encroachment. Colonialism was everywhere a cruel and dreary process, but we cannot wish away history. From a carefully weighed point of view it is arguable that certain losses were balanced by gains in other spheres. Their loss of the better land and the reduction of wildlife was in some ways balanced by the acquisition of Spanish tools and domestic animals. With these new cultural accoutrements, the Indians were able to make a viable adjustment to the smaller, more scattered arable plots of the inaccessible Sierra. They lost much in many areas of life, but some of their economic conditions have been improved. With the oxen and plow to break the earth, with fertilizer to prevent the necessity of moving after depletion of soil, and with the axe to fell the large pines of the region, the Tarahumara have long been able to produce small surplusses of food. They were released from work and food pressure for a larger part of the year than they had been previously. By gaining new means for existing in more forbidding parts of the terrain, they have been enabled to maintain the physical separation from Mexicans which they have desired.

On the other hand, with the acquisition of domestic animals, herding has imposed new restrictions on their lives, while preoccupation with the plow limited the amount of potentially cultivable land. The Spaniards, and later the Mexicans, forced the Indians into more difficult circumstances, and for this there is no moral justification, but they provided a means to adjust to those circumstances. The adjustments made by the Tarahumara, in turn, have ultimately created a set of new difficulties.

AGRICULTURE

Preparation of the Land

Besides initial clearing of trees and brush (now rarely needed), the Tarahumara perform two operations on the land to prepare it for planting—fertilization and plowing. The main way of fertilizing is to herd 15-50 goats and sheep into a pen about 20 square feet each night. The pen, which is constructed of light interlocked logs, is dismantled and moved every four or five days. The effect is a line of 20-foot squares of fertilized soil. In 45 days an acre of land can be fertilized in this manner. This is a slow but fairly effective means of enriching the soil. A plot so fertilized is said to last from four to six years, though in each successive year the yield is less. Five to 15 cattle are penned in the same way in a corral about 25 feet square, which is moved after 15 days. This doubles the time to fertilize an area; the potency of cattle dung is less, and this process should be repeated every two or three years.

In the winter the stock are usually confined to one place rather than moved every four days. To protect the animals from the cold they are kept in a covered enclosure or cave in the hills (Aboreáchi), or in a cave or corral in the *barranca* (Inápuchi). The winter manure thus is concentrated in one place and in the spring it is transported to the fields by cooperative work parties using their blankets as sacks, or now sometimes burlap bags.

This system means that a family always has some fields which yield much less than others, and must leave at least a small area fallow each year. In Inápuchi about a fourth of each person's fields were left unplanted, but some *ranchos* are so limited in land that only that area can be left fallow which will actually be covered by fertilizing corrals. If a man owns few animals, he may plant his entire area by borrowing some for a month or two at a time in order to accumulate sufficient fertilizer.

In areas like Inápuchi, where population pressure on the land is not so great, crops may be rotated in the same field. For several years a field may be planted with maize, then planted with a crop of wheat followed by beans. Indicating the variation even within local areas, this is rarely done on the *rancho* of Uarárari, where there is much less arable land, and where its depth is very shallow.

Animal fertilizer is used almost exclusively for maize. Not all families possess enough animals to fertilize. Some have none at all, but even the poor can prepare some land by borrowing animals from wealthier relatives or neighbors, who may own several hundred goats and 20 or more cattle. When each of several families of a *rancho* have too few animals for effective fertilization, they often pool their animals and take turns with the herding tasks. Such a rotating division of labor is a great service to all parties, and makes most effective use of the fertilizer.

The stark countryside of the Sierra offers little pasture, and the daily pressure of animal care is very great. Only for a short period after the beginning of the rains can suitable pasturage be found near the *rancho*, and during this time herding is relatively easy. Even small children can care for the animals, leaving the adults free to pursue other tasks or to attend *tesgüinadas* without worry. After the rains cease, and as the dry season wears on, nearby pasturage becomes exhausted, and herding necessitates longer and physically more wearing foraging trips, sometimes lasting two or more days. Relief from this constant herding pressure is accepted with pleasure, and it is during such a break that less fortunate people may borrow animals for fertilization. The pay received for this loan is simply the relief from the responsibility for the care of the herd for a period. Dedication of an *olla* of corn beer at a *tesgüinada* is another way to express gratitude.

A wealthy man in Aboreáchi or Yehuachíque has 100-200 goats and up to 50 cattle. In Inápuchi, the richest *Gentile* had 156 goats, five sheep, and five cows. Such wealthy men are in a position of relative power since the have-nots need to borrow their animals. Wealthier individuals may be able to lend half of their goat herds,

Plowing

while retaining enough for their own use. Wealthy men also frequently lend their oxen for plowing. They are repaid by having an *olla* of beer dedicated to them, and an understanding that they will get support should they desire leadership.

At *ranchos* where a good deal of flat land is available, beans may be fertilized as described above, but another method is more commonly used. Beans require less land than maize, and they are secondary in the Tarahumara diet. They may be grown on narrow strips and on more of a slope, or along a stream, wherever a small plot is available. The usual method of fertilizing beans is with the ashes of burned leaves and branches which have been cut in the winter and allowed to dry for about a year. They are then dragged to the patch, burned, and the ashes plowed into the soil. Burning is done in late spring though the plowing is not accomplished until late July or August, after the rains have well softened the soil. Beans are planted much later than maize, yet both of these crops mature and are harvested at the same time, in September and October.

Repairing Plow

The Indians break and work the shallow stony soil of the Sierra with the ox-drawn wooden plow. The Tarahumara *arara* is a very efficient plow which appears to be as good or better under Sierra conditions than metal ones of urban manufacture. Derived from the sixteenth-century Spanish *arado*, it is a solid and heavy instrument hewn from a small green log of oak or other hardwood. The carefully selected log must have a projecting branch which can be fashioned into a handle. The share of stone, metal, or hardwood may be slipped into a notch cut near the point, but sometimes a point is carved from the end of the log itself, and serves to break the earth. The plow can be controlled with one hand by the operator who walks beside it (rather than behind it) wielding a long switchlike pole to keep the oxen in the proper line. The yoke also is carved from a long piece of hardwood, and if it has two curves which fit over the horns of each of the oxen, it is lashed on with leather thongs.

Plowing is done several times during the year. If the soil is especially intransigent, it may first be done in late fall after the harvest. The field is plowed again in spring before planting, and sometimes again during the planting process itself. The final furrows are made in a direction at right angles to the direction of the original plowing so that the soil is thoroughly broken. As mentioned, plowing the beans takes place after the rains have begun. The industrious man, or one with extra time, may also plow one of his fallow maize fields at this time so that in the following spring it will be easy to work.

The Agricultural Cycle

In addition to preparing the land, agriculture involves three main activities—planting, caring for the fields, and harvesting. This is a cycle approximately seven months in length. In Aboreáchi, the period from planting to harvest runs from the middle of April to the end of October, roughly from six and a half to seven months. In Inápuchi, because of the later appearance of the rains, the same cycle runs about three weeks to a month later.

After the spring plowing, planting of maize may begin. The exact time is determined by the moon, rumors of rain, availability of help, and personal tradition. Men driving one or two yokes of oxen plow the furrows while several others follow with heavy oak planting sticks. With rhythmical motions, the stick stabs the earth, making a hole about six inches deep; each time as it is withdrawn, four kernels are dropped into it and it is covered with the foot. The planter then carefully advances a couple of paces to repeat the process. Maize stalks thus grow about four feet apart.

The yearly rains are uncertain in this part of the Sierra Madre, and this creates anxiety among people dependent upon them. As the figures given show, in the summer months rainfall is relatively heavy and regular, and it can be relied upon to come almost every year. Uncertainty surrounds the planting of maize, however, because though rains nearly always come, their precise arrival time cannot be predicted. Timing is important. According to Tarahumara experience it is best to plant maize several weeks before the rains so that the plants will be about a foot in height when the first rains deluge the fields. If it rains too early the small plants are beaten down, the ground becomes packed too tightly, and most of the crop is lost. If the rains are late, the stalks may get up to a height of about two feet, but then, without water, they will wither, turn rust color and die. After a certain point they are not revivable, even though the full yearly quota of moisture may finally arrive. Selecting the best time for planting then is a precarious matter. In the Inápuchi area, tradition says that the rains arrive near June 14. If this day passes without rain, San Juan's day, June 24, is believed to be the destined day.

In the first part of May the men of Inápuchi plant maize, but there is considerable individual variation among them as they attempt to interpret the weather signs. Rumors pass through the region that a certain rich man is going to plant on a given day, and others then plan to follow suit. Some men watch the moon. The tiny clouds that begin to form in this season are all carefully observed and discussed. There are a few who plant strictly according to the tradition of their fathers. Rodrigo Uarárari *rancho*, *siríame* (governor) of the Inápuchi community, is one of these. He always plants about three weeks to a month later than anyone else. If an early rains comes his maize may be ruined, but if the rain comes late, he is then the only one in the community to harvest a good crop. When this occurs he is in a powerful position in the community. He justified his planting time,

Planting Maize

saying: "My grandfather did it that way because it is best for this *rancho*."

From the time of planting until the end of July is a period of unremitting anxiety. In addition to the unpredictability of the rain, they have knowledge from experience that occasionally years do occur in which almost no rain falls. The older members of the community of Inápuchi remember three great droughts. In the most recent bad year the Indians were able to get relief from the Instituto Nacional Indigenista. Maize was shipped in from other parts of Mexico, but it was not enough and still there was much hunger in the land that year.

Another danger to the crops for which no physical remedy is available is the great number of worms which in some years attack the roots and leaves of the corn and later demolish the ears. The Tarahumara of Inápuchi believe that one should not harm these worms or they will get angry and completely ruin the crop.

Added to all the other fears is the belief that *Onorúame* (God) will someday destroy the world. He will wreak vengeance when the people do not dance enough or make the proper sacrifices.

Furthermore, anxiety is high before the rains because by this time the food resources of many people are exhausted. During this annual period of drought, the animals, as well as people, are weak from hunger and thirst. Some of them are near death, and most people are physically exhausted from shepherding the animals greater and greater distances in search of forage. The higher frequency of animal sacrifices at this time of year probably has survival value through providing added protein to the diet when people most need it.

This is a time when everyone in the Sierra is looking forward to the wonderful rain which will make the corn grow, give green pasturage, make the hills green, and bring water to the streams again. Just at this point, when the peoples' fears are highest, powerful shamans throughout the Sierra have dreams in which they are commanded to begin the yearly "curing" ceremonies. The rituals may then be performed which protect the animals against sickness and accident for the coming year. The rain is "called," and the worms, which may not be molested physically, are ceremonially petitioned to cease destroying the maize. The people are given protection from lightning and from sickness, and the fields are "cured" with "medicines" in order that the crops will again yield. *Wirómera* (animal sacrifice) offerings are made to *Onorúame* so that the world may be spared from destruction once again, and people gratefully consume the meat of the sacrificed animals in their *tónari* feasts.

Caring for the fields

Dangers to the young maize must be countered by ritual means, but there are other dangers which can be circumvented by humans. These come largely from animals and weeds. When the stalks of maize are small and fragile they must be cared for tenderly and personally. Usually the small fields are fenced about with crude log fences or stone walls, but often these are not proof against wandering cattle, pigs, or horses. Nothing substitutes for personal surveillance, and the somewhat inefficient fences must be repaired frequently. There are always a great many domestic animals loose in the Sierra, and Mestizos and Indians are continually making journeys looking for stray cattle, horses, burros, and sheep. These searches are time consuming, but they provide diversions from the boredom of daily life.

Some Mestizo ranchers, and some Indians also, carelessly allow their animals to forage without restraint, and much Tarahumara litigation involves this kind of damage. All young crops are under considerable hazard; a cow or two can demolish a large patch of new corn in two or three hours. A dog can ruin several ears of corn in a few minutes and even small rodents such as chipmunks, squirrels, and gophers may completely destroy a field of seedlings.

Tarahumara life appears passive at this period, and people seem to be idle, but important tasks are being accomplished. Due to the necessity of watching fields in different areas, family members are separated more than usual. A man or woman may travel an hour or two to a field and stay there several days to care for it. During this time of quietude most people attend to whatever small handicraft or repair tasks which may have accumulated. Women weave baskets as they sit with a vigilant eye toward the field, perhaps from time to time telling a youngster to chase a threatening cow from the maize patch. Clothing is mended, and the never ending task of grinding corn on the *metate* must go on. Men cut and carry firewood, sharpen tools, prepare hoes for the coming weeding, or set small deadfall traps for the squirrels and chipmunks that each night damage some of the precious ears. They also may repair fences and perform other maintenance tasks. Often they sit in contemplative repose, strumming a homemade guitar or playing a violin, as they look out across their fields.

After the precarious first month, the maize usually has reached a good height and less attention is needed. However, since cattle, goats and dogs try to get at the tender ears of corn, and may strip the stalks and leaves as well, vigilance must be continuous until the harvest is in. Dogs are responsible for so much damage that they are sometimes poisoned with a paste made from deadly mushrooms of the area.

When the rains have well begun, weeds begin to gain on the young corn and would choke it out were not people to intervene again. In Aboreáchi the time for hoeing is the first two weeks of July; in Inápuchi it is the last two weeks of the same month. Weeding is usually a cooperative task and the men greatly enjoy it. The host makes *tesgüino* and invites people from the surrounding *ranchos* for the work and beer party to follow. Weeding time is a period of great euphoria. It rains nearly every afternoon and the men do not mind. They laugh drunkenly as they work. The period of famine and drought is coming to an end; the *elotes* (ears) are bulging from the stalks and all will be well for another year. Now the tasks of caring for the maize are diminishing, pasturage is springing up nearby, and children are often left to care for animals and fields while their elders join in a round of weeding parties.

The communal battle with the weeds is repeated again some six weeks later. For this work several men work abreast, each taking from one to four rows each as they may decide. The weeds are simply chopped on the first hoeing, but on the second round a small hill is made around each stalk, a process requiring from three to five strokes for each plant. The tediousness of the job is relieved by a joking group spirit, assisted by *tesgüino*.

The next major task in the agricultural cycle is the planting of beans and this is usually done between maize weedings

Watching the fields

(Aboreáchi—after the middle of July; Inápuchi—about the first of August). *Tesgüino* is also sometimes made for this, but much less labor is required, and usually the work is done by the members of each individual family in its own fields.

The method of sowing beans is similar to that of maize except that the plots are much smaller and the seeds are simply thrown at intervals into the furrows and covered, instead of being planted with a stick. They are planted much closer together, only about one foot apart. Hour after hour for a week, a husband and wife, two brothers, or a father and son may crouch in a small bean patch pulling the weeds by hand, placing them in neat piles and carrying them to the side of the field. If the family has several bean fields, it may take a month to complete the weeding process.

At the time of weeding the beans, the spinach-like green *maquásori* is also sown in some of the newly fertilized ground which is being prepared for the following year. Late in October and early November, the harvest of both maize and beans is the last major job of the agricultural cycle. However, prior to this, in late September or early October comes the task of cutting winter fodder for the animals, another activity involving communal labor. Men chop off the top section of the corn stalks and store them in the low branches of nearby trees or other safe places. With cooperative help the collection and storage of fodder takes no more than a day, and again a series of beer parties gather the necessary labor force at each *rancho* in turn.

Harvest usually finds the individual family picking until about half the crop is in. Meanwhile, they make beer and try to time its readiness to correspond with the amount of work left to be done. A cooperative *tesgüinada* is then held to finish it, since in the final picking process it would be too strenuous a job for a man to carry all the heavy sacks of ripe ears to his corn crib, in addition to the large squashes and bundles of beans which need to be placed in storage at this time.

Activities of the Winter Months

The agricultural cycle varies in duration between two-thirds and three-fourths of the year. The cold months are agriculturally unproductive, and they pose a problem for the domestic animals.

The Tarahumara believe that cattle, goats and sheep will perish unless somehow protected from the cold. Zingg over-emphasized this point when he alleged the "spurious" quality of Tarahumara culture. He claimed that the culture "fails the individual" because it has not devised adequate shelters for protection in the cold months, making it necessary for people to move to the caves in the gorges until the cold passes. "Away from the influence of Spanish masonry, the Tarahumaras have no recourse but to migrate to distant cave dwellings" (Zingg, 1942:80). However, many of the Tarahumara do not migrate in winter. Many *Pagótome* stay at their *ranchos* near a pueblo center, where their winter rounds of ceremonies are performed. Most of these families have one of their fields in a more sheltered place than the others, perhaps at a slightly lower elevation, or a higher one near a wood supply, where the family may take the goats. Such a shelter is frequently at no great distance and it need not involve a long trip to the *barranca*.

Actually, only those people who live close to a *barranca* move to it. For example, most people of Aboreáchi, Samachíque, and Norogáchi, do not migrate in winter. However, those of Coloradas and Santa Anita, who live near the *barranca* of Huérachi do move. Since most *Gentiles* live in proximity to *barrancas*, they do follow the yearly movement pattern. The people of Inápuchi and Quírare, for example, take up winter residence in the more mild climate of the canyons.

Many highland communities use other means of protection for themselves and their domestic animals. For example, during the really cold spells, the Indians of Aboreáchi and Yehuachíque stay in their houses near their fires. Of course, they must venture out for firewood, and sometimes they wrap their sandaled feet in cloth for short dashes into the snow. During the winter period they occasionally gather in *tesgüinadas*, and they unite for the three winter fiestas of the Christmas season (December 12, 25 and January 6). Their animals are protected in old houses or caves.

In Inápuchi the weather becomes cold enough in late November that everyone moves below to the bottom of the gorge which is some 1,000 feet below their various plateaus and mountainside *ranchos*. Here in the greater protection of the canyons are the scattered caves and the stone and brush houses which are the *Gentiles'* winter quarters. For most families this means a move of no more than one or two miles. The *barranca* is very familiar to the people, since the goat herders often descend these gorges at other times of the year. People also go down to fish, to secure *mezcal* for beer, and to collect *agave* leaves to make baskets, string or other necessities, and to gather the "medicines" used in curing ceremonies. For their winter move they do not even need to take much corn with them. There are stone grain storage houses in the *barranca*, but since the *ranchos* above are so near, trips to get corn or other supplies can usually be made in an hour or two.

During this winter stay in the canyon there is not much work to do. Violins and guitars may be made, and sewing and weaving are done. The goats must be tended, and firewood must still be hauled, usually from greater distances, and some chiles and tobacco are tended in little terraced patches by the river or in the arroyos of small streams.

Further down to the west where the Barranca Batopilas is wider, the *Gentiles* of Quírare experience even milder winters. They have a number of orange trees, sugar cane, sweet potatoes and

Grain house in the *barranca*

even a few bananas. These orange trees in the *barranca* are very large and old and produce a surplus of wonderful fruit which the Quírare *Gentiles* sell in Mestizo settlements for a few *centavos* each. The Inápuchi people seldom descend that far down in the *barranca* and though they possess a few orange trees and grow some sweet potatoes, they are not as fortunate as their Quírare friends and relatives.

The winter period is a time of reduced physical activity because of lack of agricultural work, the absence of the racing and trips of the active season, and the lack of movement to *tesgüinadas*. Much more time is spent in resting, playing music, and leisure activities than is possible during the rest of the year. Despite the relative inactivity in winter, herding still creates some regular economic demands, as does other work required for minimal subsistence, such as caring for small gardens, collecting of wood for the fires, and handicrafts.

Daily Rhythm

The following few excerpts from my diary give some feeling for the quietude of the daily life of the *Gentiles*, and provide an

Tying the wheat

indication of how an average day went in the course of our field work. The content of the interviews is excluded.

April 27. We started for Inápuchi about 7:30 A.M. and arrived there about 9:00 A.M. It was a beautiful day—blue sky with a few wisps of cloud. Stopping by several houses, we found that at each one the adults was sleeping off the effects of drinking at a *tesgüinada* the night before. Most of them were outside under the peach trees or *nopal* cacti. Some children were sleeping too, but a group of three near the ages of six or seven were wandering around playing in the fields. At one house, Jesús woke up when we arrived and shook his wife, telling her to go in and get us some *esquiáte*. She came out with a gourd of *pinole*, some water, and a dish with baked *mezcal* roots. He was holding his infant son of about a year while we conversed with him, and was affectionately playing with him. Because of his evident hangover we kept this interview informal and brief. We returned in early afternoon when, after a complete round of Inápuchi houses, we found no one else awake.

April 28. We arrived at Inápuchi about 9:30 A.M. Rodrigo and his wife were plowing their fields. Each of them was driving a yoke of oxen and handling a wooden plough. We stopped and chatted with old Dionicio who was lying under a large *nopal* cactus in front of his house. I estimate Dionicio's age to be about seventy, but he still carries firewood great distances and attends races and *tesgüinadas* at other *ranchos*. He told us of a large race he had attended last week at Yoquívo. It had been won by the other side and he lost five meters of muslin cloth in the betting. Dionicio apparently didn't want to talk further so we passed on to Seledonio's house nearby. Seledonio was sitting in the shade of his corn storage house leisurely shelling dried corn into a basket and relaxing. His young wife was lying on the ground nearby, and their two children were playing. We talked awhile, but suddenly the richest Mestizo rancher in the area appeared on horseback looking for some of his cattle. He decided that he wanted to chat with us, but since he had disturbed our work we left after a few moments. We passed by the *rancho* of Pisáchi on the way home and picked up three *wáris* (baskets) which we had ordered the week before. The ten-year old boy of this family accompanied us home to receive two liters of salt in payment since they preferred this to the two pesos which I would have paid them.

Saturday, May 28. Arrived at Inápuchi about 9:30 A.M. Seledonio was the only person we could find. He was replanting his maize, that is, seeding the places in the field where no corn had come up. He seemed pleased to stop and chat for about an hour. Then Seledonio excused himself and continued to work. Finding no one else around we left for Pisáchi to see if we could interview Valencio. We found no one, and being exhausted, headed for home.

Thursday, June 23. Arrived at Inápuchi around 10:00 A.M. The sky was overcast and it looked like rain. No one was around except Seledonio, who was kneeling in his small wheat field cutting wheat with a knife. The wheat was very sparse and only about 10 inches tall, but it was ready to harvest. A boy about 13 was assisting him, and later we learned that he came from Chuvérachi to stay some time because there is "much hunger" at his home *rancho*. He is helping Seledonio in exchange for his keep. Soon Seledonio left him tying the small bundles and came over to chat with us. He opened his granary and brought out a very beautiful *yúmari* rattle he was carving (see Chapter 4) and continued to work on it as he talked. Pretty soon the clouds became very forbidding and we decided to start back. We met Patricio and his stepson Cruz, who is about 14. They were tending the goats and Patricio was playing his violin as we walked along. We talked with them for awhile and they told us where we might buy a chicken. We followed their advice and returned in the rain with a chicken to cook on my saint's day (San Juan's day, June 24). Several Mestizos in the area have told me they will visit us on that day.

Monday, June 27. We left about 6:30 A.M. for Pisáchi to continue interviewing Valencio. We found him ready to leave for his other field in Arroyo Durazno. His purpose was to care for this field which is in danger from cattle and rodents. We wanted to accompany him, but he seemed reluctant and suggested we come tomorrow, since he intended to sleep there overnight.

Since we could do nothing at Pisáchi we went over to Inápuchi. At Seledonio's house, his wife told us that he was down in the *barranca* caring for the goats. Arriving at Juan-Tasio's house we found his son (about eight) making a miniature dwelling exactly like a Tarahumara house. He said his father was away looking for cattle. At Jesús's house, we found that Jesús was gone on a journey to one of his fields, but a group of people were there.

They were his mother, his wife, his brother the *hombre-mujer* (man-woman—see later discussion) and a small boy of about five whom I had not seen before.

We sat and chatted a bit after they offered us *pinole* and *quelite*. The *hombre-mujer*, who was spinning yarn from wool, was trying to sell Venancio a young bull for four *etolitros* of maize. He spoke in his normal high falsetto voice. As we were talking, two bulls broke through a fence and got into a nearby corn field, but they were quickly chased with stones thrown by the young boy.

Pretty soon Jesús's wife came out but kept her face averted and almost completely covered with her dirty muslin shawl. Knowing she had a reputation for promiscuity at *tesgüinadas*, I found her extra-shy behavior somewhat surprising. When we tried to interview the *hombre-mujer* he insisted that he knew nothing at all about anything at all.

Finally we passed by the house of Rodrigo where we found only his wife threshing some tiny bunches of wheat by hand rolling them on a rock. Keeping her face averted, and continuing her work, she ordered her small boy of about five to bring us some *esquiáte*. We drank a little and left, since we did not want to offend Rodrigo by spending an inordinate amount of time with his wife. As we crossed the plateau we met Cruz who was carrying a piece of pine with a large glob of pitch on it, which he was going to use to mend some pots. He told us that both Patricio and Dionicio were also out herding the goats, and would not be back until evening, so we decided that, since only women and children were around on the Inápuchi plateau, it was prudent to leave. We felt frustrated, because it was a fine day, and we had come up empty once again. Back at the cave, I used the extra time to write some notes, while Venancio went in search of firewood.

CHAPTER 3

LABOR, LAND, WEALTH & SETTLEMENT PATTERN

Labor

Two types of social groups perform all the agricultural and herding tasks among the Tarahumara of Aboreáchi and Inápuchi: the *residence group*, which is small, relatively stable and unified by bonds kinship—and the *cooperative work group*, which is larger, shifting in composition, and united by ties of reciprocal obligation, friendship and mutual need. Most labor could be performed by the residence group alone, but some tasks and emergencies require more labor, and for social reasons additional help is enlisted at every opportunity. In general, the larger the residence group, the more work tends to be a family affair. However, social obligations and the sure knowledge that assistance will be needed at some future time create pressures upon even the most isolated and self-sufficient families to brew corn beer for cooperative work gatherings.

Property is owned individually, but the effective stable economic unit is the residence group, a unit which varies in composition from the nuclear family to matri-or patrilocal extended groups, as circumstances dictate. But whatever its composition, the group of people residing together make joint use of land and animals and form a labor unit. Even if the family can handle the usual labor tasks, cooperation is felt to be necessary for certain tasks, and the cooperative labor pattern developed by the Tarahumara has been called the working *tesgüinada*. When a person needs to accomplish a major task such as weeding, harvesting, cutting fodder, spreading fertilizer, cutting *canoas* for roofs, fence-making, or house-building, the way to get the job done is to make an appropriate amount of beer. When it is properly fermented people are invited from surrounding *ranchos*. *Tesgüino* is the "pay" for the work and an adequate amount is regarded as a mandatory obligation of the host. People enjoy getting together to drink and work, but the more basic motivations for attending stem from underlying sets of reciprocal obligations and privileges among the men in the vicinity. Because of their shifting, voluntary, and overlapping nature, the cooperative labor units coming together in this fashion are not constant, as are the familial residence groups. Their memberships change with the vicissitudes of shifting alliances and animosities.

A man may choose to perform any economic task alone, or he may elect to make a *tesgüinada*. Most men prefer the latter when they can afford it, because much time and effort is saved in performance of larger scale tasks, and because group participation and heavy drinking create a euphoria and social spirit in complete contrast to the relative solitude of everyday Tarahumara life.

For several days a man and his family may work alone on some job such as weeding or harvesting, while in the meantime they are preparing *tesgüino* (a six-to-seven day process). A group of neighbors will then be invited to finish the job quickly. Often the individual family or residence group completes the small amount of work remaining after the cooperative group has done most of it.

On occasion some men make *tesgüino* two or three times within a few days, in order to complete a single task, such as weeding a number of fields. Some men rarely host *tesgüinadas*, preferring to work alone and shunning contact with their neighbors. Others make it more frequently than is necessary for their economic needs. I want to emphasize here the freedom and flexibility of the labor pattern. These qualities are created by the necessity to coordinate the efforts of widely dispersed men for jobs which vary in temporal requirements and in difficulty. Obviously it is self-defeating when several men make *tesgüino* at the same time.

Division of Labor and Other Features of Technology

Though the allocations of most particular tasks follow lines of sex in Tarahumara culture, the division of labor by sex is not rigid among either the *Pagótome* of Aboreáchi or the *Gentiles* of Inápuchi. Much of the sex-role differentiation which does occur reflects simple differences of relative strength, physical ability, and convenience, rather than strict cultural prescription. No stigma accrues from performing roles ordinarily allotted to the opposite sex unless the person attempts a change of gender, and even when this happens people are tolerant.

Agricultural tasks fall largely to men, while herding is generally a chore for women and youths. Men also do the axe work, house-building, collection of firewood, butchering animals, tool-making, and the manufacture of musical instruments. In addition to animal care, the women's work sphere involves such household tasks as preparation of food, cooking, weaving, pot-making, child care, carrying water, and washing and mending clothes. Convenience and practical necessity rather than strict sex norms dictate the allocation of particular tasks in most situations.

A good illustration of this is the correlation we find between the relative difficulty of the environment and the amount of time spent by either sex in herding activity. In the Aboreáchi area Indian farmland is largely found in small valleys and along streams, while in the Inápuchi region it lies on plateaus and shelves overlooking steep *barrancas*. Caring for goats is much more strenuous and hazardous in the rougher Inápuchi terrain and, reflecting the greater physical difficulties, we observe men in Inápuchi caring for the goats two to three times a week. Teenage boys also frequently perform this task. In Aboreáchi, on the other hand, women often spend weeks at a time in daily treks with the goats before being relieved for a day or two by men. Smaller children are also much more often entrusted with herding in this less demanding part of the Sierra environment. In the Inápuchi area, herding is not only more dangerous, but it is more physically demanding. Women get more tired, and this leads to a series of consequences, such as their not being as able to devote as much effort to household tasks and child care, which in turn produces more stress in the family, etc.

Agricultural labor is primarily a male sphere, but women do participate in the less strenuous tasks. Older widows or single women sometimes must do all types of work. Under ordinary circumstances, women's agricultural work is restricted to situations where the family is working alone. When a cooperative labor *tesgüinada* is called they participate in the drinking but not in the outside work. They cluster at the house where they gossip over domestic tasks and prepare the food and drink. Women usually join the men for weeding of beans (performed by hand) harvesting of all crops, and planting, as these are jobs which can be carried out even with a small infant on the back. It is not usually their job to sow with the heavy planting stick, plow with oxen, or hoe corn, but in emergencies, which frequently arise, they perform these tasks too.

Other activities considered men's work are those performed with the axe, the basic tool of the culture. I noted earlier how all men are proficient in its use, and how log houses, finely fitted grain storage structures of hewn boards, doors, and plows are made exclusively by fine axe work. Trees must be felled, fences constructed, *canoas* made and firewood cut. Firewood is extremely important because it is necessary for heating and cooking. At least an hour nearly every day must be devoted to gathering it. Strength is needed for most axe chores. Heavy loads of logs must be dragged or carried over the rugged terrain. Women lack such strength and are not trained from youth to do the dexterous axe work which is such a remarkable skill of all Tarahumara men. Still, I have frequently seen women quite competently splitting firewood when men of the *rancho* were absent.

The greatest overlapping of work-related sex roles comes in the performance of household chores, which are ordinarily regarded as primarily the women's sphere. For instance, women usually remove the hard dry maize kernels from the cobs, but men and children are also frequently seen performing this never-ending chore. Women usually grind the corn daily on a *metate*, but men occasionally do this, and they also prepare meals when necessary. Once we arrived at a *rancho* where the wife was out herding and no food had been prepared. The host, embarrassed to have nothing to present visitors, went into the house and quickly ground some *pinole* for us. All male informants freely described their performance of such "female" tasks and did not hesitate to discuss their capability of doing them.

Men often sew and wash clothes, and many in Inápuchi know how to weave blankets. Clay pots and baskets are rarely fashioned by men, but male informants stated that they could make them if necessary. It is in such daily maintenance tasks that most sex-role overlapping occurs. The low emotional valence surrounding the sexual division of labor seems clearly related to the practical necessities arising from the frequent relatively long absences of the members of Tarahumara households. Basic maintenance and productive tasks must nevertheless be done.

Several activities are exclusively male. No woman makes violins, guitars, or ceremonial rattles, and only men kill animals and skin and butcher them. Women's nonparticipation in these activities seems to be connected with their sacred character, though no explicit sacred taboos against women doing them were recorded. Killing of domestic animals is always done ritually. Tarahumara musical instruments are used in all ceremonies and have a symbolic significance, while women's participation in rituals is very limited.

One would not expect to find much in the way of occupational specialization in the subsistence agricultural economy of these Tarahumara communities. Only in the ritual sphere do we find some tendency toward occupational specialization. Some Tarahumara shamans (*owerúames*) gain high reputations as "curers," protectors of the people and crops. Several of them are so widely sought that they have little or no time for mundane farming activities, and are fully supported by contributions from the members of the community. These rare full-time ritualists have great prestige. They are in constant demand for curing illness, and are considered necessary at all Tarahumara ceremonials outside the domain of the church.

In the whole of Aboreáchi pueblo, there was only one full-time *owerúame* at the time of the study. Quite naturally he finds it impossible to be present at each of the dispersed *ranchos* throughout the area when his services are desired. At the same time, the territories of various curers are not defined by pueblo boundaries, but by reputational spheres. These somewhat hazy territories overlap, and families may prefer a curer from quite a distance to one close at hand. For example, Martín Mamórachi is favored in Aboreáchi, but at least two families there prefer another shaman from Tatawíchi, who comes all the way from that pueblo to treat them. Many minor rituals are performed for these families by part-time specialists.

Aside from the *owerúames* there are no genuine occupational specialists among the Tarahumara of the region, but to state this without discussion is to oversimplify. While all necessary tool and utensil manufacture and construction theoretically can be done by members of each family group, certain people are more sought out for such activities according to their skill, ability and available time.

The problem of procuring clothing, for example, is solved partially through hand sewing of purchased manufactured cloth, and partially through the weaving of semi-specialists. The Tarahumara in Inápuchi wear a distinctive dress which serves as a symbol of cultural identity, and it is largely hand-sewn or woven by females of the family. For men, a collared, long puffed-sleeved shirt (*napácha*) is worn over the loincloth (*sitabácha*), and an added triangular piece of muslin (*huisibúra*) is tied over the hips with a woven sash (*púraka*). A headband (*coyéra*), blanket (*kimá*), and sandals (*acá*), now universally cut from automobile tires and lashed with thongs, complete the traditional male attire.

Women wear a blouse resembling a man's shirt over multiple long full skirts (*sipucháka*). In addition they wear several strands of glass beads around their necks, a headband or kerchief and sandals similar to those of the men. The whiteness of Tarahumara muslin clothing stands out in the Sierra, where it has symbolized Indian ethnicity. However, industrially manufactured colored prints (sometimes flannel) are becoming popular in the *Gentile* region, after having been adopted earlier in *Pagótome* communities. Though it appears that there is a trend for Indians in the Sierra to adopt Mestizo dress, Tarahumara from the more conservative areas can distinguish the pueblo from which a person comes by the cut of his loincloth and the manner in which his headband is wrapped.

Among the *Pagótome* of Aboreáchi, boys who have been to school and assimilation conscious adults wear denim trousers and jackets, and some have the cheap cotton shirts and blankets sold at Mestizo stores. Most blankets and belts, however, are still hand-woven, and the majority of people still wear native clothing of hand-sewn muslin for some occasions. The general difference between the *Gentiles* of Inápuchi and the more acculturated *Pagótome* of Aboreáchi is quite striking. Only one man in Inápuchi wears factory-made denim jeans but he wears a *huisibúra* over them to show that he is still Tarahumara, not Mestizo.

The art of making the *púraka*, or woven sash, apparently takes years to master. Seledonio Inápuchi was teaching his young wife to weave blankets during our entire stay, but he said it would be several years before she would be proficient, and a very long time before she would learn the complicated art of sash-weaving. Aside from the difficulty of learning the craft, young girls spend much time taking care of children and herding animals, and therefore contribute little in the way of weaving.

For most crafts the same pattern prevails. Ceramics of this region are crude, unpainted and not greatly varying, yet considerable skill is necessary for their manufacture. Several sizes of rounded pots with flared rims called *sekorí* range from small ones only three or four inches high used for cooking greens, to the giant beer pots, which may stand as high as two to three feet. Between these are several vessels of varying sizes.

The most unique of these is the *sakíriga*, an elongated pouch-shaped vessel from about 10 to 15 inches long with an elliptical mouth. This is designed to lean over the fire for toasting *pinole* or beans for grinding. Another specialized ceramic form is the clay griddle or *comal* from 15 to 20 inches in diameter and several inches thick, upon which tortillas are baked. The common dish used for reheating beans, serving greens, etc., is simply a small clay bowl about five to eight inches across, three to four inches deep and one-quarter inch thick.

The method of pottery manufacture is coiling and hand-shaping of local clays which are sometimes mixed with old crushed potsherds. After completion it may be smoothed with a stone or gourd. The pieces are dried in the sun and then fired by placing dry branches, pine, manzanilla, and cedar around and over them. Sometimes a coating of crushed red ochre is painted on, either covering the surface, or in simple designs of lines or crosses. The more elaborate decorations of the past which Lumholtz recorded when he passed through the area before the turn of the century are not now found in the Aboreáchi region.

People in the 18-household *Pagótome rancho* of Yehuachíque procure most of their pottery from one of several expert women. This is especially true for the large *tesgüino* jars which are difficult to make with the simple technique of open firing. One old man in Yehuachíque also whittles most of the flat wooden bowels (*bateas*) and wooden spoons, though he has neither the time nor the incentive to keep everyone supplied.

Of the few other items upon which some degree of craftsmanship is exercised, musical instruments such as violins, guitars, and rattles for the Yúmari dance are most important. The Tarahumara are literally a society of violinists. A violin can be found somewhere in the possession of most families, and virtually all men play passably by cultural standards. Guitars are also made but are less common. These wooden stringed instruments are entirely handcarved and constructed, a task requiring considerable ingenuity. Despite the relative complexities of construction, an amazing proportion of the men make violins. Though somewhat crude when judged by Western standards, these instruments are quite remarkable.

Many people make their own instruments, but if a man wants a really fine violin or guitar, he obtains it from one of the few reputed craftsmen in the area. Very fine rattles made of wood shavings or from small gourds are also made by the curers of the area. By watching their elders, people learn the basis of these crafts as children, but they rarely activate their learning until well into adulthood.

The task flexibility I have described is general, and there is a tendency for what incipient specialization there is to follow sex and age lines, but day-to-day life chores are guided by an attitude of convenience and practicality. Most economic roles do become anyone's duties under *some* circumstances. Variabilities of strength, endurance, individual ability, and free time available influence the timing and selection of personnel for the performance of most tasks.

Work Routine

Work routines in the Aboreáchi-Inápuchi area are also indeterminate and flexible; the timing for most tasks fluctuates within fairly wide limits. Tasks for any given day are usually decided by members of the family on the day prior, except on those occasions when cooperative labor is planned. When a large job is necessary, work activities for a particular day must be planned at least a week in advance, since corn beer generally takes between six and seven days to prepare. The first part of the *tesgüino* making process is the dampening of the corn, so that it may sprout. Making beer takes about four days, but if something should occur to make the *tesgüinada* impractical at the planned time (e.g., if a curer necessary for scheduled rituals cannot attend) the second stage of the process (grinding and boiling) can be delayed a couple of days.

Even though a minimal degree of activity scheduling is required, considerable latitude exists, which allows adjustment of plans to unforeseen needs. Often schedules for a particular day must be changed. A man may plan to weed his beans, or cut his wheat, etc., while his wife will care for the goats. He may hope to have his teenage son make a trip to a Mestizo village to buy cloth, and expect the son's wife to stay home to make *pinole* and mend clothing. But when a visitor appears that evening to invite the family to drink *tesgüino* at a neighboring *rancho*, a quick change of plans may be made. Such occurrences are not unusual because invitations to drink *tesgüino* are always made only when the beer is ready.

Many other conditions conspire to create unpredictability in daily activities. For example, customary work patterns do not impose rigid time limitations. Within the loose limits of the seasonal agricultural requirements a great deal of freedom is possible, and I would say even necessary to this type of economy. None of the important economic tasks of the Tarahumara require strict scheduling. Neither plowing, planting, weeding, hilling, cutting fodder, harvesting or cutting *canoas* imposes a necessity for precise timing for beginning or completion.

Herding, on the other hand, places a grinding daily demand on family time and effort. The constant pressure of this demand works in the same direction as the agricultural tasks in accentuating the flexibility of role behavior and activity scheduling. For instance, I have seen a woman who has been exhausted by several days herding insist that a man of the household take the goats out on a particular day. The elder son relieved her for two days.

A passing traveler may tell a man that one of his cattle which has been missing was seen in a particular area, a bit of news requiring urgent action to recover valuable property. Prolonged sickness of a child eventually provokes such a sense of urgency that a trip to bring an *owerúame* is imperative. Regardless of other demands, the requirements of the animal herds continue without abatement. A relative or neighbor must be persuaded to take over their care or, if a journey is necessary, the goats, sheep, and cattle must be taken along.

Since normal conditions call for such flexibility and freedom, it is not strange that Tarahumaras should find wage work confining and boring. When an important or large-scale task is contemplated in the Indian community, *tesgüino* can be made, provided that maize is available. Some planning is done to avoid overlap of working *tesgüinadas*, but I recorded instances when several *ranchos* in the vicinity simultaneously put on drinking parties, each without knowledge of the other's intentions. This resulted in loss of manpower for each, and in some cases a great deal of ripe *tesgüino* had to be kept a couple of days beyond when it was best. The characteristic flexibility of Tarahumara work routines reflects the implications of the isolated living patterns imposed by the rugged Sierra environment.

Land Tenure and Inheritance

The rule of land holding in the Aboreáchi-Inápuchi area is that a person has the right to work a piece of land as long as he has obtained it in one of the traditional ways and kept it continuously in use. Six years is the generally accepted length of time a piece of land may be left idle, with others being prohibited from claiming it. Thus, the rule specifying continuity of land use as the important criterion is flexible enough to allow for rotation, fertilization, or other reasons a person might have for not using a plot for several years. In spite of this, however, variables such as regional differences in population densities, available land, quality of land, aggressiveness of personality, and lack of the means to fix time limits in writing, lead to a fairly high frequency of land disputes. Because of the criterion of keeping the land in production, a concept of land use or land rights, rather than "ownership" in the modern Euro-American sense, is a preferable term to describe this kind of a system.

By a related unwritten rule of land use in these Tarahumara communities it is understood that an individual is at liberty to clear and fence any unused parcel of land, after which he may cultivate it as his own. This custom seems derived from the earlier period of shifting agriculture, but today it is of negligible importance as a means of securing land because potentially productive pieces of uncleared land are now scarce.

Three other means of acquiring land are by sale, trade, and inheritance; of these inheritance is by far the most important. There is strong attitude against selling land, reflecting the fact that subsistence is directly and heavily dependent upon it. Also migration out of a community into another pueblo is rare, though there is some movement to such larger towns as Guachóchic and Creel. Land almost never changes hands in exchange for money or other goods, and I found no cases of men trading extra land for animals in order to build up their herds.

The inheritance rules are simple and well known to all. In theory all children inherit equally from both mother and father, and throughout life each person maintains individual rights to the land bequeathed him by his parents. These rules apply to other property as well. The occurrence of land disputes is not the result of ambiguity of the rules as much as the other variable factors mentioned. Most disputes arise from the condition that offspring vary in age and number in proportion to fixed amounts of property, and while all children have equal rights to the property of a deceased parent, amounts of family land and other goods vary in amount, desirability, and value.

That nearly all transfers of land are made by the method of equal inheritance is an extremely important feature of the Tarahumara economy. It militates against the disproportionate accumulation of land by a few members of the community. The Tarahumara system of land division is supported by the value principle of equality; it is strongly felt that each person of adult age should possess enough land to provide for his needs.

As it works in practice, the situation is complicated by the tradition of advance inheritance. In principle, legal transfer of the land is not made until death of the parent, but often a child at marriage is allowed to take over a part or all of his inheritance. Here the principle that all adults should have a means of self-support is evident, since it is felt that at marriage the new couple should have subsistence independence. One way such situations actually work out is the case where a family has several children, each of whom receives his plot of land when reaching marriage age. Parental land thus becomes diminished and there may be none for a later child. In such a case the deprived one must seek a spouse with land rights (either through advance inheritance or in actual possession) so that he or she can be married.

Much importance is attached to individual possession of property, yet a major method of acquiring access to land is through marriage. Bilateral incest rules operating within the dispersed *rancho* settlement pattern, along with a general tendency for relatives to live close to one another, often create a necessity for traveling some distance to find a wife. Since the woman usually has her fields near her parent's residence (or at least nearer to them) such a circumstance may bring about a separation of family fields in the next generation. An even greater dispersal of land plots is created when a person inherits from both mother and father, one of which has originally come from some distance.

This system provides that the wife retains ultimate control over her land as a guarantee and indication of her independence. In practice the husband generally works his wife's land, the family uses the products jointly, and all land of both parents is passed on to the children. However, in case of divorce the wife retains her land, unless it has been given to the children by advance inheritance. It is clear then, that the overall effects of the inheritance rules are pressures toward equalization of land distribution, and toward the spatial dispersal of plots possessed by any one family.

The priority of inheritance is fixed as follows: 1) children, 2) siblings, and 3) grandchildren. In the rules there is no provision for spouses, but in practice if a wife will be destitute she may be granted a small parcel for her support from the deceased husband's land.

Grazing land is not inherited. It is open or free land, which anyone may use, including people from other pueblos. It is not considered communal land except as belonging vaguely to the pueblo as a whole. All people have equal grazing rights in the mountains and canyons.

It can be seen that with this mode of inheritance, and under such conditions of land dispersal, various kinds of combinations of land possession can potentially occur for any one person. For example, it sometimes happens through accidents of survival that a man has rights to two pieces of land from each of both of his pairs of grandparents, and his wife has rights to two or three pieces also. A perfect case of this would be extreme and rare, but it illustrates the general type of situation which does arise. Such occurrences inevitably mean the eventual relinquishing of several of the pieces because of inability to take continuous care of them all, given the traveling distances involved. Because of the norm stressing equality of ownership and provision for all, there is additional pressure toward redistribution by the other people of the area.

Thus, it happens that over the generations family members are gradually but inevitably distributed throughout the Sierra Tarahumara in a random manner, which is rarely apparent to the people themselves. This results in the condition that there is no real tie to land by perpetual occupancy by a family over many generations. Land is not revered by the Tarahumara in the sacred way that is among true peasants, and this ecological process, very likely, is a major reason. Along with the effects of bilateral inheritance, this process may also be related to the characteristic lack of family names among the Tarahumara *Gentiles*.

Other factors working in the same direction are seasonal mobility, as well as the history of semi-pastoralism which was adapted to the pre-Colombian economy of hunting and gathering and slash and burn horticulture. Seen from a historic view and considering the inevitable pressures of the ecological conditions, the picture of land tenancy in this region is one of a slow moving but perpetual flux. By dispersing individuals in a random fashion throughout the area, after several generations, such conditions inevitably produce a homogenization of genes and culture. This partially accounts for the truth of Bennett's observation. "Considering the size of the area, the Tarahumara present a remarkably uniform culture" (1935:181).

Wealth

When I asked about status differences in the community, the people of Inápuchi and Aboreáchi always replied, "All are equal." It is true that most Tarahumara families live in the same type of house, and that clothing does not effectively mark off the wealthy man from his fellows, but socially important differences in wealth certainly do exist between different members of these communities.

Though the *Gentiles* of Inápuchi have access to small amounts of Mexican money and do some evaluating in terms of money values, they could not be said to be integrated into the money economy. Mexican pesos are in use, but they are used sparingly because they are difficult to acquire and because most local transactions can easily be accomplished through barter of goods and animals. People acquire small amounts of money through the occasional sale of an animal to Mestizos and by the sale of baskets or fruit or *nopal*, but pesos had not entered the community through wage labor during the ten years prior to my study. Most money which they get is channeled back to the Mestizo stores and traders for the purchase of the white muslin cloth for the traditional Tarahumara clothing or used to acquire such small items as dishes, soap, needles, knives, beads, salt and sugar. The traders do not require money for these items and they are more usually bartered for with corn, beans, and fruit. Between community members of both Aboreáchi and Inápuchi monetary transactions are even more rare. Barter is generally sufficient, or debts are engendered which must be repaid in kind.

Land and Maize

Wealth can be built up by acquisition of animals, but even such a stable asset as land does not remain entirely constant. Accidents of inheritance may result in a man's acquiring more than an average amount of land, or for reasons of personal acquisitiveness a person may invoke the rules of inheritance to the letter; he may choose not to relinquish control of his land to his children when they marry, thus countering the equalizing tendencies of the distribution system.

One can gain control of more land than other people despite equal inheritance by being more aggressive than one's siblings, by simply being more competent, or a combination of these. In the Inápuchi community, for instance, there were two sets of brothers on the *rancho* of Uarárari. In each case, the brother with the stronger personality controlled virtually all the land bequeathed by the parents. In one household the younger brother planted all of the family land except for one small rocky patch which did not yield nearly enough food for the needs of his older brother's family. About 50 years of age at the time, Felipe, the elder brother, was as close to an incompetent as I have seen among the Tarahumara. He was small, weak, and of limited intelligence, but not totally incapable of functioning. However, according to other members of the community he did no work. Since laziness is regarded as a very negative trait, the younger brother, a man in his mid-thirties, was believed justified in using his land. Seledonio Uarárari gave his brother Felipe enough food and minimal clothing, but Felipe's family was emaciated, poorly clothed, and his wife had recently died from pneumonia.

Another man with his wife and child resided at the same *rancho* with his younger brother, who also had a young wife and child. The elder (about 45) permitted the younger (about 30) to work one small patch, but he himself worked most of the land left by their parents. Even though the two men worked together, made *tesgüino* together, and were married to sisters, the elder completely dominated the relationship. The younger man privately expressed resentment about this situation, but he submitted to the stronger personality of his brother. Thus, the theoretical inflexibility of the inheritance rules is modified in actual experience by personal and chance factors.

Having more land may put a person in a better economic position if he works it, but in terms of local concepts of wealth, the consequent effect of having a surplus of maize is not nearly so important as is having a large herd of animals. Maize does not preserve well beyond two years, so it cannot be accumulated indefinitely, but must be used. Furthermore, the quantities of maize expended in making *tesgüino* usually are significant enough to prevent the accumulation of saleable surpluses.

An estimate of the amount of maize so expended may be calculated by using a minimum figure of one and a half *ollas* of *tesgüino* each time it is made; one large *olla* requires two *decalitros* of corn (one *decalitro* is approximately twelve pounds of maize), and one smaller *olla* requires one *declalitro* of corn. This is probably a minimum. One may make more *tesgüino* but not less than this. Combining this figure with our estimate of six times per year per family for beer making, around eighteen *decalitros* or 216 pounds of corn would be consumed annually per family in the form of beer. This estimate is on the low side, because, while very few families fall below the minimum figure, a considerable number of wealthier men make more *tesgüino*. The total expenditure of corn is slightly reduced, however, by the use of green corn stalks (*caña*) for beer at least once a year by most families. In some areas the seasonal availability of *maguey* juice also provides another substitute for some of the corn. The total corn expenditure is slightly offset too, by the pattern of cooperative donation to the host for some of the larger religious ceremonies (about a half *decalitro* per family).

Tarahumara families in both Aboreáchi and Inápuchi expend at least 200 pounds of maize annually in the production of *tesgüino*. Certainly, the beer has some nutritional value, but it must be realized that such an amount would last a family of four or five members more than a month. For people so close to the subsistence level, it is clear that a significant amount of basic food is used for this purpose.

Opportunities for distributing any surplus maize are not generally exploited by the Indians in spite of the fact that at certain times of the year people in the wider region may be almost starving. Relatives have first call on a family that is better off, and they do not use credit. In comparison to animals, maize is so low in the hierarchy of local exchange values that even though an animal or two might in rare cases be acquired through trade, one cannot build up a herd by producing a surplus of corn.

Mestizos in the area are much more eager than other Tarahumaras to sell corn to needy Indians. They transport it great distances to areas of shortage and they have few scruples about charging triple the regular price for maize during the famine season. The Tarahumara, on the other hand, are not entrepreneurial. They usually wait for a needy person to come to them rather than taking the initiative in selling.

In spite of all this, a surplus of corn is important for wealth and prestige because it allows an individual to make *tesgüino* more often for cooperative work, allowing larger areas to be kept under cultivation. One who does this is regarded as living up to his obligations and benefitting the whole community. Everyone enjoys *tesgüinadas* and considers them important. Just as significant, the *tesgüinada* host remains a giver rather than a taker and thus merits prestige and leadership. He is one to whom others must come for help (*kórima*). Beer and beer parties are basic to the social life of the community, and the ability to make *tesgüino* in the season when some people are wondering where their next meal is coming from is a critical indicator of wealth and power. The drinking parties are highly valued as one of the few means of communal gathering, recreation, and social intercourse. Further, the man with a surplus of corn can afford to have hired help, to maintain more destitute relatives, and to have his son or daughter stay with him in a joint household, or at least nearby, after marriage.

Animals

The cumulative effect of having access to more land and or producing more corn than other members of the community certainly has important socio-economic implications but the acquisition of animals is the most important means for building up one's economic position. With care and luck, herds increase over the years.

The total number of animals possessed is the important indicator of wealth, but cattle are of highest value, followed by sheep, goats, pigs, horses (in Aboreáchi), burros, and chickens. Among cattle, oxen rank first, cows second, and bulls third, with the last two being almost equal. Horses and pigs were not owned by any of the *Gentiles* of Inápuchi, and they were of little importance in Aboreáchi. The relative values of these animals appear to bear a direct relationship to the number of uses to which they are put. Oxen rank highest in value because of their economic worth. They make no more contribution to fertilization than other cattle, but they have been gelded and trained to pull the plow. The added strength, docility, usefulness, and investment in training time are reflected in their value. Among Aboreáchi Mestizos, a good ox was worth 1,000 pesos at the time of this study. For the Indians their value is difficult to assess in monetary terms, but in the *Pagótome* community an ox was priced about the same as among the Mestizos. In Inápuchi, their value was slightly less; there a healthy young ox was worth either two bulls, two cows, or fifteen goats. Though oxen serve as an upper limit of value, they seldom change hands in comparison to other animals.

The worth of cattle is increased by their scarcity, and their scarcity is increased by ceremonial use. The Sierra environment makes cattle raising precarious. This becomes evident when we see how geographical conditions between the *Gentile* and *Pagótome* communities differentially influence the values of cattle. The terrain is particularly treacherous for these animals in the Inápuchi area, and the search for forage in the dry season frequently results in one of them wandering too far. Cows frequently fall and expire before being rescued. Thus, the search for cattle is a very anxious activity of the *Gentiles* during this season. Men often save fallen animals by helping them to their feet and driving them to water, and thus a great expenditure of energy is added to the ordinary routines at a time when the year's work is most demanding. In the period when food is most scarce the hardships are compounded by heat and drought, which affect humans as well as animals. In the less rugged region of Aboreáchi, the problem of lost, injured, and thirsty cattle seldom arises.

In addition to the relative difficulties of terrain which affect the numbers of cattle held in the *Pagótome* and *Gentile* subareas of this region, a number of other variables result in differences between these communities. For instance, horses are an important aspect of wealth and prestige in Aboreáchi, while no one in *Gentile* Inápuchi owns one. In the *Pagótome* community, some officials and important men demonstrate their prestige by riding into a community gathering on horseback. A saddle is an added criterion of status. Like Mestizos, Indian youths of Aboreáchi take great delight in riding anywhere on horseback. The richest Indian of Aboreáchi pueblo owns five horses, the most possessed by any Tarahumara in the area. Some of the rich Mestizo ranchers, on the other hand, own as many as 15 or 20. Mestizos value mules highly for their great endurance, but Tarahumaras generally do not like them because of their intractability, and none of the *Gentiles* owns one.

Despite the evidence that numbers of horses have been in the area for at least two and a half centuries (Dunne, 1948: 237), they are still not well integrated into Tarahumara culture. Relatively few Indians own them and there is a general lack of knowledge concerning their value and of methods of training them. Horses are actually of little economic use under present conditions of Tarahumara ecological adjustment. Individuals in Aboreáchi who possess a horse occasionally use it to carry burdens, but for the most part they are ridden by the few who own them for purely prestige reasons. Ability to walk and run great distances by foot is a valued personal attribute in the traditional Tarahumara culture, and many persons who do not own a horse express the opinion that horse owners are not good on the trail and are lazy.

Another important difference between the *Pagótome* and *Gentile* areas is in the degree of animal reduction brought about through customary ceremonial requirements. In the Aboreáchi area, people of the community sacrifice at least eight bulls a year. Responsibilities for these ceremonial feasts fall upon eight community officials (*fiesteros*) who must, among other duties, provide meat and tortillas for two of the four important community-wide or ,"church" fiestas. Two bulls must be provided on October 12th and six must be provided on December 12.

The obligation (*cargo*) for providing a sacrificial bull rotates among the men of the Aboreáchi community, so that several years usually pass before one's turn comes up again. Since some men do not have cattle, poor *Pagótome* may become even more impoverished by having to borrow from a richer relative to make good on this *cargo*. In *Gentile* Inápuchi, there are no observances of the Catholic holidays, and even though they occasionally sacrifice a cow, they have no regular responsibilities for offering cattle.

The situation for goats and sheep is different. Since these animals are more resourceful than cattle, the micro-environmental differences between Inápuchi and Aboreáchi do not seem to be large enough to cause differences in their accumulation in the two communities. In both areas some goat herds exceed one hundred, and the average size of herds is the same.

The *borrego* sheep of the Sierra is dark brown in color and very hardy. They are rarely sacrificed and are only eaten when they die a natural death, yet I never saw a large herd of sheep in the Sierra. Actually, a family does not need more than four or five sheep to provide the wool necessary for their blanket and sash needs, and most herds contain about that amount. Wool is accumulated gradually, and often several months are necessary to collect enough yarn for a blanket. Contributing to the much smaller proportion of sheep in comparison with goats is their greater vulnerability to the hazards of the terrain, their lesser propensity to procreate and their need for more care during infancy.

Despite the higher value of cattle and the greater economic potential of sheep, goats are the most important stock animal of the Tarahumara. Because of their greater adaptability to the environment, a much greater percentage of the people have goats, and thus, they constitute the principal means of fertilization. Goats make it possible for the people to maintain themselves in their particular ecological niche. However, the demands of goat herding determine some of the major patterns of life activity.

However, are these means by which the sizes of the goat herds are limited? Since the Indians do not use their animals as a *regular* source of meat it might be assumed that due to the high reproductive rate of the animals, the herds would increase much too rapidly. Though the sizes of their herds *have* increased steadily for the last century at least, the rate of increment has been quite gradual for the area as a whole. Rapid increase is limited by at least four conditions: 1) Animals are slaughtered on ceremonial occasions several times a year, and the meat eaten in *tónari* feasts. 2) The difficulty of the terrain and the severity of the climate take a certain toll, which works toward the maintenance of a natural balance of herd size. The Indians claim that animals sometimes die because of the cold if they are not taken quickly enough to the *barranca* or other warm quarters. Animals also occasionally fall, are lost, succumb to disease, and so forth; these particular dangers are much more acute for cattle than for goats. 3) Animals are exchanged with Mestizos for maize or beans when the food situation becomes difficult. This means that nearly every year a few of the goats or sheep are subtracted from each herd, and these are often some of the best animals. 4) Goats may be traded for wanted items at Mestizo stores. For example, bolts of cloth, metal buckets, or Hohner accordions are occasionally secured in this manner.

The steadily increasing numbers of Mestizos settling in the Sierra have created more of a market for meat than the Indians want to fill. At the same time the accompanying increase in access to the material goods of Mexican culture has increased the wants of many of the Tarahumara, even though their dependence on the Mexican economy remains negligible.

In combination, the four conditions mentioned seem to be sufficient deterrents to the build-up of inordinately large herds. Nevertheless, despite these limiting factors overgrazing is occurring. This is not only because the Indian herds are increasing, but also because the growing Mestizo population with its own herds shares much of the same open mountain "pasture" area.

Even though there are limiting conditions upon their growth, animal herds serve as reservoirs and symbols of wealth for the Tarahumara. Some consequences of this form of wealth are that goats serve as a medium of exchange and that they constitute insurance against bad times. It has already been noted how the natural multiplication of animals can result in a steady increase in a family's wealth over the years, and one result of such slow capital accumulation is that wealthy individuals tend to be in the older generation.

On the other hand, herds do not always automatically increase. They sometimes diminish over the years, and when this happens an individual moves downward on the scale of prestige and wealth. One way of losing goats is through improper care; with lackadaisical attention they may get lost or be caught by coyotes.

After its fertilizing capacity, the insurance characteristic of the goat herd is its most important economic feature. In a bad year what does a man do when he runs out of food? He trades his goats one by one to Mestizos or rich Tarahumaras for maize and beans. One man in the Inápuchi area inherited more than 150 goats from his father when he was fairly young, but some 15 years later at the time of the study only 30 remained. His "wealth" had slowly diminished year by year. The main reason for his decline, according to others in the community, is that he had very little land to farm, and a very large family to support (seven children). Consistently, his production ran behind his consumption. Gradually, he had to reduce his reservoir of livestock at a faster rate than its natural increase, while during the same period the size of his family steadily increased.

Kórima

Another insurance feature of the economy is the custom of *kórima*, a word connoting a gift of food to one who asks for it. There is a strong Tarahumara custom requiring the better-off people to share with the less fortunate in times of hardship. A person or family whose food supply has been exhausted visits the *ranchos* of relatives and the households of wealthier neighbors, picking up a kilo or two of *pinole* at one, a few beans at another, until enough has been gathered for a week or two. Sometimes this must be done two or three times before the harvest. If the need is great, a person or small family may stay at the house of a wealthy family and work as temporary *peones* (which in this case means sharing the work of the household). No lasting debt is engendered by *kórima*. The custom serves its purpose of redistributing food under famine conditions and of protecting members of the group from starvation.

Settlement Pattern

Wealth differences exist among the Tarahumara of Aboreáchi and Inápuchi but they are not great. The society is essentially egalitarian; nobody limits associations on the criteria of wealth, and there are no true distinctions in life-style. However, my study revealed more differentials in wealth than had previously been reported for the Tarahumara, and some socially important differences in power and status which are correlated with them.

The Tarahumara low-power subsistence economy in an area of such limited resources provides no opportunity for economic expansion in the modern sense. A significant tendency of the inheritance rules is to equalize the economic status of members of the community. The chances of inheritance largely decide who will have more land. Corn is perishable and there is a lack of markets to facilitate the amassing of money. Although it does bestow significant economic and political advantage, greater production from the land generally does not result in significant status mobility for members of the community.

The greatest source of wealth lies in the accumulation of animals, a process which usually takes many years, and the importance of herds as sources of wealth lies in the fact that animals are the only economic good which is cumulable in an almost moneyless economy. Livestock utilize the non-arable parts of the terrain, which is available to all who work hard enough to utilize it. This is another condition which makes it possible for wealth differentiation and limited mobility to take place through accumulation of animals.

Besides this, however, more animals permit more productive crops through greater fertilization, and they also provide insurance against starvation. Thus, a large herd places a man in a relatively powerful position in relation to the poorer members of the community. The people depend upon the wealthy men to hold the highly valued *tesgüinada* gatherings, to lend oxen for plowing, to provide wool to make blankets, and finally, to provide means of fertilizing their land.

From a spatial point of view, the settlement pattern of Inápuchi is characterized by relatively small and varying groups of people living at considerable distances from one another. Some *ranchos* are physically within several hundred yards of one another but this proximity is deceiving since they are separated by canyons requiring one or two hours of exhausting hiking to cross. In the rainy season the swollen rivers and streams usually make these gorges impassable. Effective communication may be cut off for days or even weeks at a time. In general, the extreme dispersion of community members has a profound importance for Tarahumara social activity.

An important question for cultural ecology is the degree to which the sizes of aggregates of people may be related to environmental adjustment, and thus to spatial distribution. It was impossible to secure precise information on the amount of land cultivated per capita, but a different kind of data permit reasonable inferences relating to ecological adaptation. Given the Tarahumara mode of adjustment with plow agriculture, the ratio of population to the entire area, or by square mile, is not as economically important as the population ratio to *arable* land. That is to say, most of the Sierra region is agriculturally irrelevant, except for the indirect connection through animal fertilizer, but it is impossible at this time to estimate how many animals could be supported by an area which is so topographically and botanically diverse.

A number of facts indicate that in the Inápuchi area the person-to-land ratio is relatively close and that the condition is one of relative population balance. The most obvious basis for this inference is the correlation of numbers of people with land available. The following materials support the contention that population and land vary together in this region.

Let us take, for example, the *rancho* of Inápuchi, lying on a plateau varying in width from one quarter to one-half mile with a length of approximately one and one-half miles. It is a high relatively flat peninsula of land jutting out between two deep converging canyons, upon which 39 people reside. They cultivate about ten acres of land. In considering the problem of population equilibrium these questions seem pertinent: "Is there more land to cultivate?" and "Does the land under cultivation properly support the individuals living there?"

In attempting to answer the first question I concluded that virtually all of the land on Inápuchi plateau which can be efficiently cultivated by means of the plow is being used. This was not immediately apparent, for at first glance it appears that there are relatively large expanses of untilled land on Inápuchi. However, informants stated that most of this land is too rocky or the soil is too shallow to permit plowing. Much of it too, is eroded by wide gullies draining off to the canyons on both sides, and some seems to be heavily limed, making it unfit. Another area of about ten acres is covered with a small stand of forest. Informants state that, besides the rockiness of this plot, the trees have not been cleared because if they were gone, the distance to firewood would be too far. This is an important consideration when the only source of heat and light is wood, and when several times a week people must carry loads of oak, cedar, and pine.

One of the most persuasive pieces of evidence supporting informants' statements concerning the lack of more tillable land on the *rancho* is the existence of long-standing land disputes (see Chapter 6). If there were an abundance of extra land which could be brought under cultivation, the deprived disputants could easily clear it and lay out more fields. Another fact suggesting this is in the informants' agreement that the reason Rodrigo's brother took his family back to Quírare some years ago was because he was unable to grow enough corn to support them; there was only enough for Rodrigo's family.

On the other hand, there is some evidence to show that the people of Inápuchi *rancho* are well off land-wise in comparison with many other Tarahumaras. All available land is tilled, but it usually produces more than enough to satisfy subsistence needs. Only two families here now work land in more than one *rancho*. For the most part, enough maize is produced from the fields in Inápuchi alone to support the people of the *rancho*, and the *rancho* population is a comparatively large one. Two men of the *rancho* usually produce a considerable surplus above their needs in good or fair years. This is evident because they make *tesgüino* much more often than other members of the community and *tesgüino* requires considerably extra corn. These two households also give *kórima* to many more people than do the other members of the *rancho*, or indeed any other people in the area. In one instance, Seledonio was asked to support a girl from Chuvérachi for six months of the previous year because there was not enough food at her home *rancho*. She, in turn, was a great help to Seledonio's household because she removed much of the pressure upon the adult family members' time. For example, Seledonio was freed to make a blanket. Another example of Seledonio's ability to give *kórima*, is that during the season of hunger several people came to his house from as far away as Quírare to petition for small gifts of corn. Some people from Charérachi traded him some pottery bowls and horsehair ropes which they had made for some of his corn and beans.

Dionicio Inápuchi was also sought for *kórima*, but the amounts he could give were much smaller than those given by Seledonio. His household contains two more members than does that of Seledonio and five of them are adults. Such differential ability to dispense and sell food is a good indicator of the relatively greater wealth of these two Inápuchi families. Still we must remember that such surpluses are dependent upon a good season and other conditions. Even though the previous year had been a relatively good one for Seledonio, the other inhabitants of Inápuchi *rancho* barely held their own. One man who ran out of food late in the season had to petition *kórima* from Julio Rynárachi. These customs of sharing and trading serve to redistribute resources and thus temporarily level economic differences. This should not obscure the fact that they actually reinforce existing prestige and status differences.

It is also clear that under existing conditions of technology, population and land are in close balance on this *rancho*. As indicated, when there was a surplus in the atypically good year of our study, several more people might be supported there if other circumstances were constant. However, in bad years the present population size is probably the maximum.

Another way an increment of population might be supported would be the condition in which marrying-in outsiders possessed land in other *ranchos*, but this would be simply a typical redistribution of people and resources in the area and would add no new productive potential. It is also possible to cultivate a few more tiny plots of beans in the *barranca* below, and if conditions became more grim, people could respond with an increase in the expenditure of energy in labor. When all is considered, however, the potentially small amounts of added production by these expedients would make little appreciable difference. Such measures might allow the population to maintain its size under conditions of scarcity, but they are hardly means which would permit expansion.

The evidence for these inferences is not as complete as we would like, but there is also some indication that as people on

Inápuchi *rancho* die and others grow up, the population fluctuates rather constantly around the present figure. Our informants told us that there were a few more people three years ago when Juan-Tasio's father, Seledonio's father, and Pablo and Ignacio's mother and father were alive. At about the same time Rodrigo Inápuchi had also brought his brother and wife from Quírare to live with him in a joint household. However, at that time three infants now living on the *rancho* were not yet born. The average age was therefore slightly older than at present. Since then, Juan-Tasio's father has been murdered, Seledonio's father has died, and his mother has married Rodrigo Uarárari and moved away to Uarárari. Ignacio and Pablo's father also died, and Rodrigo's brother's family moved back to Quírare. This is the kind of shifting which seems to be the typical pattern. Personnel changes slightly from year to year and from generation to generation, but the *rancho* population maintains a rough equilibrium.

The other *Gentile ranchos* show a similar fluctuating balance around a mean number. Rynárachi, for instance, is in a phase of relative land abundance because one family of three died out completely leaving no close heirs. Since three of the nine people now on the *rancho* of Rynárachi are older than 50, it is probable that the population of this *rancho* will decrease even more in the near future. However, it can be predicted that it will balance out again quickly when both Pablo Inápuchi, who even now cultivates one of his wife's fields on Rynárachi, and Manuel Inápuchi, who recently ran off with a Rynárachi girl, transfer there permanently. These moves will again reduce the population of Inápuchi by five, even though both men may cultivate fields on both *ranchos* until their own children grow up.

In contrast to Rynárachi, both Pisáchi and Chuvérachi show signs of population pressure. On Pisáchi there are three brothers of marriageable age who cannot marry until they find girls with land, and there are two younger children who must also marry out when they are old enough. Informants report that Awírachi, Rejóvachi, Dieciocho, and Sopilíchi are remaining constant in population.

On the four *ranchos* of Inápuchi, Rynárachi, Uarárari and Pisáchi, I calculated the average amount of cultivated land per person to be a little less than one-quarter acre. This figure must be fairly close to subsistence requirements under the conditions of an agricultural-herding economy in the western Sierra Madre.

CHAPTER 4

THE TESGÜINO COMPLEX

The most important pattern of interpersonal relationships in Tarahumara society, with the exception of those governing household interactions, occurs almost exclusively in the context of beer parties. To appreciate the significance of the *tesgüinada* institution in the social life of the Tarahumara, we must first understand its form and quality. I quote from my field notes to provide a sense and feel of these important gatherings.

What happens at a tesgüinada?

Sunday, July 16. We set out for Uarárari about 6:00 A.M., having been informed that the people there would be doing cooperative work on this day. We arrived tired about 7:45 A.M. (The trail involves crossing a deep arroyo and climbing a small mountain.)

As we approached the *rancho* we encountered Seledonio's son, who told us that everyone else had gone to Inápuchi to drink *suguíki*. We were tired but decided that rather than returning, we would go to Inápuchi. After we rested a few minutes the boy agreed to show us the shortest trail across the *barranca* between Uarárari and Inápuchi, since he also wanted to go and drink.

We arrived exhausted at Inápuchi about 9:00 A.M., and encountered Seledonio Inápuchi lying drunk on the ground half-way between his house and the house of Rodrigo. Sitting beside him patiently waiting was his young wife with a baby slung on her back with a piece of cloth, and a young girl of about four. He sat up and stared at us glassy-eyed before falling onto his back in a deep sleep. As we were standing there, Seledonio's wife and the girl arose and began walking toward Rodrigo's house, a couple of hundred yards farther on. As she passed us averting her head, she told us to hurry on to the *tesgüino* at Rodrigo's. We looked up to see Rodrigo's wife coming down the trail from his house shouting "We *sepúka!*" (*Hurry up!*) to us.

The three of us walked over and stopped about 50 feet from Rodrigo's house, as required by Tarahumara etiquette. After a couple of minutes Rodrigo came out and beckoned us inside to drink.

Inside the house it was apparent that they had been already drinking all night. A group of men and women were sitting, leaning and lying near the *tesgüino olla*. We recognized two of the men as Martín and the *hombre-mujer*. His brother, a man of about 24 or 25, was serving and he handed me a large full *hueja* (drinking gourd) which I drank before he gestured for me to sit behind the *olla*.

I looked around the room, my eyes becoming accustomed to the darkness of the interior. In one corner sat Cruz, a boy of 14, who, a short time before, had run off from his parents' *rancho* to live with an older woman. He was playing an accordion, three notes again and again. Nearby sat two men in earnest conversation, while a little farther away three others were laughing loudly. Rodrigo Uarárari, a man of about 55, and the elected leader of the *Gentiles*, sat quietly near the *tesgüino olla* with his wife, who was of about the same age. They soberly surveyed the drunken scene around them. Rodrigo broke up the Mexican cigarette that I gave him and used the tobacco and a shuck from an ear of corn to roll himself a long Tarahumara style cigarette.

After about 15 minutes, the *hombre-mujer* staggered to his feet and began a stumbling lurching dance in the small space in the center of the room. He could not keep time to the repetitive accordion tune. His filthy white clothing flapped raggedly. Dried *tesgüino* and mucous marked a white stripe on his face below one nostril. His hands swung wildly. Finally he stumbled and fell into a heap next to his brother. Two of his brothers, Ignacio and Jesús began talking rapidly to me in Tarahumara, as Martín pressed more gourds of the brew upon me. At first I refused, but he became so insistent that finally I gave in and drank a small one. The *tesgüino* was extra sweet, having been mixed with *maguey* juice. It was at an exceptionally agreeable stage of

108

fermentation, but much previous experience with this brew made me wary. I resolved to keep my consumption down, and if possible avoid stomach upset and diarrhea. I got up and walked outside the hut while the gourd was being passed to others.

Outside by the grain house about ten women were sitting together laughing and talking. Two others lay on the ground near the corn field completely passed out. Cruz brought two gourds of *tesgüino* out to the women and there was much laughter as they passed them around.

Shortly after I sat down I was accosted by an Indian I had not seen before who said his name was Román. I noticed that he had some kind of deformation of the lips. His upper lip seemed double, and it hung down over his upper teeth. He seemed to know only two words of Spanish, one of which was *cuñado* (brother-in-law). In Tarahumara the equivalent (*chiéri*) is a term used in an institutionalized joking pattern (described in Chapter 6). Román kept repeating *"cuñado! cuñado!"* and laughing. Finally, he asked for a cigarette and staggered away toward the youth with the accordion, who by now had come out of the house. Román came back to me and grasping me by the arm, led me over to a lean-to out by the corn field. He called me *cuñado* again and sat back, closed his eyes and then looked at me quizzically. My response was *"We gará húku!"* (Very good!). This seemed to satisfy him and he sank back into a rocking kind of trance. (I later found out that Román had killed a man at a drinking party about a year earlier. He had bashed his head in with a rock). This time there was no sign of aggressiveness, and the people did not treat him any differently than anyone else.

By this time it was afternoon, and I saw that Seledonio Inápuchi had aroused himself and was staggering out of the corn field into the cleared area by the house where the most action was taking place. Seledonio was holding an accordion in one hand. Almost losing his balance, he seized the one Román was playing and carried it off as well. He moved somewhat uncertainly across the clearing to where several women were sitting by the corn house with the *hombre-mujer* and his brother. Seledonio handed one of the accordions to a woman, who I then noticed was his wife. He was begged by the women to play the other accordion, but it had taken such a beating that only wheezes came from it. Meanwhile, Román had gone to Seledonio's wife and was trying to persuade her to give him the better accordion, but she refused.

After a few minutes, Seledonio gave up trying to play the beat-up accordion and said something insulting to the *hombre-mujer*. The latter did not respond, so Seledonio turned around and bent over, revealing a large split in the back of his pants (he is the only man in the community who wears Mexican denim pants). He parted the split even wider and pointed to his rectum, inviting the *hombre-mujer* to try it, but the latter only smiled. He then guffawed drunkenly and went back to trying to play the damaged accordion. After several minutes of this, Seledonio grabbed the other accordion from his wife, and with an instrument dangling from each hand he strode across the clearing. His proud gait made it very apparent to the watching group that he was wealthy enough to afford two accordions. Just before he stumbled through the doorway of the house, he handed the good accordion to the young boy who had previously been playing.

I continued to sit under the corner of the lean-to trying to remain as inconspicuous as possible. This was not only in order to observe the scene better, but I very much wanted to avoid having to drink any more *tesgüino*. I had not been allowed to refuse a *hueja* of beer since I had come outside, and was feeling slightly sick and tipsy.

I hadn't been sitting alone very long when a group of shouting, laughing women raced by me and out onto a grassy space behind the corn house. There they began an extraordinary game, which I had not observed before. First one of them tackled another and threw her to the ground, then they rolled over and over in the grass. One woman finally succeeded in getting astride the other and she began to pump up and down in simulation of coitus. The other, laughing, tried to push her off, and her breasts became exposed. There were two other female couples wrestling, but with a little less vigor. Pretty soon I saw that the main instigator of this game was a woman of about 55.

Then an old man of about 65 joined the group. He brandished an old corn cob and chased several of the younger women, threatening to run it up under their skirts. One of them engaged in a kind of mock combat with him. He put the cob between his legs like a penis and tried to grab her, while she pulled away laughing. Then another more aggressive woman took her place. She picked up a cob too, and tried to thrust it toward the old man's rectum. During all this I heard the term *"aparóche!"* being shouted by all of them, and I realized that I was witnessing an example of the joking relationship between grandfather and

110

granddaughter (see Chapter 6). The spectators were enjoying this suggestive play very much. The play continued on for more than half an hour before people tired of it.

A little later I noticed more patterned joking behavior; the 14-year-old boy who had been playing the accordion was beating Clemente, who by then was very drunk again. The boy teased Clemente, called him "*chiéri*" (older brother-in-law) and threw him down. Clemente could not defend himself, but he kept coming back for more.

Finally, about the middle of the afternoon, Seledonio Inápuchi came over and sat down beside me with his good accordion. I could see that one of his eyelids had been cut, and a streak of blood was dried on his cheek from eye to chin. He began talking loudly to me. Fortunately, Venancio, who had been off socializing, returned at this point and interpreted Seledonio's broken speech. It turned out that he had been in a fight with Juan-Tasio. He told me that Juan-Tasio is "very fierce" and not to give him any more cigarettes. He also threatened to "get him" later. He said no one likes Juan-Tasio (something which he denied

Weeding the corn field

when he was sober). Seledonio then began to play his accordion. The tune was simple but rhythmical, and a great relief after Román's tuneless noise. He was pleased when I told him it was good and gave him a cigarette.

A few minutes later Seledonio's sister (the wife of Juan-Tasio) appeared with a full gourd of *tesgüino* for him. Apparently, it was from the bottom of the *olla*, since people began to straggle off through the three-foot-high corn to Dionicio's house about 500 yards away, where another *olla* of beer was waiting. Ignacio Inápuchi insisted that I help him finish the *tesgüino*.

Nearby, Jesús, another of the *hombre-mujer's* brothers was gathering up the hoes which earlier had been dropped between the rows of corn. He called me and asked me to come with him and help him. I picked up three hoes which I saw lying nearby and followed him. He talked enthusiastically to me as we walked through the corn. However, Venancio had by then left, and I understood less than half of what he was saying. When we arrived at one of Dionicio's fields, fairly distant from the house, we found most of the men sitting down waiting for hoes to arrive before beginning to chop the weeds.

Rodrigo, Patricio, Juan Uarárari, and Venancio who was with them, all began working immediately, as Jesús and I did. After working up two rows, I realized that I would get no pictures of this if I didn't take them immediately, so I stopped and took some. There were gray rain clouds above, but a storm did not look imminent.

After about 45 minutes of work, Ignacio ran over to Seledonio's house, which is nearer the field we were working in than Dionicio's, and brought out the drunken Seledonio by the arm. In the other hand he carried a bucket of *tesgüino* with a *hueja* floating in it. Seledonio Inápuchi hoed for about ten minutes before Juan-Tasio emerged from somewhere in the corn field, playing his violin as he walked. He too began hoeing, and the group continued for another five minutes or so, before everyone quit and came over to drink from the bucket.

Jesús and Patricio started joking with each other, calling each other *chiéri* and *muchímari* and began pushing each other around. Jesús pushed Patricio saying: "You are not so strong, I will screw you." Patricio pushed him back laughing and they started to wrestle in the potato field nearby. Patricio threw Jesús to the ground repeatedly, making him very angry. Patricio just laughed uproariously, pounded his chest, and challenged Jesús again and again. They sat down together and drank more *tesgüino*. Then even though less than one-third of the field had been hoed, most of the group went off in the direction of Dionicio's house to drink the rest of the *tesgüino*. As we left I saw Jesús frustratedly taking out his still pent-up anger on the smaller Juan-Tasio. He threatened to rape him, then threw him to the ground face down, jumped on top of him, and moved his buttocks up and down as he laughed wildly.

At Dionicio's house there were several other men and the whole group of women. Most of them were inside drinking. Clemente was lurching around the yard angrily looking for someone to fight. Patricio had just thrown him out of the house. Inside, Seledonio and Juan took the accordions and began playing while a man and a woman danced a kind of clog step, something like a *pascól*. Clemente charged belligerently into the house, again and again, but each time Patricio threw him out. Patricio followed Clemente outside and kept throwing him down each time he got up until he was completely out of the yard. Patricio laughed and went back into the house. I had followed the two

Drinking in the field

out to see the upshot of it, and I saw Clemente pick up some rocks and broken pieces of pottery. He drew back his arm to hurl them at Patricio, but thought better of it and threw them angrily out into the corn field.

Clemente stumbled around in the field for a few minutes, and then came back into the yard. Seeing Venancio sitting by the house, he called him a thief. Venancio became angry and ran over and punched Clemente, who fell in a heap by the side of the house. He stayed there for several minutes before rousing himself to look for more *tesgüino.*

Meanwhile, Román came up to me and began hanging on me. His wife (who is about 15 years his senior) was meanwhile hanging onto *him*, trying to prevent him from getting into trouble. I sat down with these two still clutching me, and Rodrigo's wife went to bring me another large *hueja* of *tesgüino*. I refused, saying *"man bosári* (I'm full) so she finally took it elsewhere, noticing that Román and his wife were obviously in no condition to drink more. I looked over in another part of the clearing where Juan-

Wrestling

Tasio was angrily beating his young wife, who was sitting on the ground with a baby at her breast. He loudly accused her of unfaithfulness and she was crying.

Pretty soon Clemente and Román both wobbled into the hut again and I followed since the sky had darkened and it seemed about to rain. Thunder crashed overhead and lightning illuminated the scene. The hut was dark and smoky inside and I sat down on a small piece of wood next to Venancio. Three women were dancing a shuffling dance in the middle of the floor. Two of them, Seledonio's wife and Clemente's wife had babies on their backs. The other was an unmarried girl of about 16. Over at one side I saw a man I did not know hunched against the wall. His loincloth was half off exposing his genitals. A woman whom I took to be his wife went over and unsuccessfully tried to cover him. Venancio told me that he was Martín Yipó.

Over in a corner lay Dionicio, the owner of the hut, who must be about 70 years old. He seemed to be taking in the scene through

Victory

half-closed eyes. He didn't seem drunk, but just tired and bored with it all. Clemente's wife was now crying, as was Juan-Tasio's wife, who had now come in and was sitting in the corner with her baby. Juan-Tasio was now leaning over her trying to console her, and she took his head and pressed it to her breast in a motherly gesture of affection and forgiveness.

Meanwhile Seledonio had given his accordion to Venancio and as he tried to leave he stumbled over a *metate,* landing backwards on top of Román and his wife. Over in another corner by the *tesgüino olla,* old Rodrigo Uarárari sat with his wife next to him, chatting quietly with Patricio's father who was visiting from Arwírachi. I noticed that these older people station themselves by the *olla* in each house. After a while, I began to understand that this maneuver is not so they can drink more, but on the contrary, official dispensers can arrange to drink very little.

The tempo of activity picked up again as Venancio and the boy Cruz started alternately playing the only accordion which was still intact, while Jesús's wife and the 16-year-old girl were dancing in front of them asking for tunes. Clemente's wife told Venancio she liked him but that he looked like a *Chavóchi.* She is a large fat woman who was galloping around clumsily with a huge three-year-old child on her back. The child kept staring at me with its huge black unblinking eyes.

Suddenly the music stopped as someone shot out of the crowd, jumped on top of Venancio and lurched with him into the corner. I recognized Román, the murderer, who seemed berserk again. I quickly grabbed the accordion so that Venancio could defend himself. He being much soberer than Román easily pitched the latter onto his back on a *metate* which was against the wall. As I looked around the group I saw Juan Uarárari nodding approval of Venancio's actions. However, Román, with his wife again hanging onto his shirt, got up and made another dive toward Venancio. His wife was trying to calm him down. Venancio threw him on the floor again and several people held Román in a prone position while they urged Venancio to play the accordion. Nobody seemed upset by the incident and things went on as before. I counted about 30 people at this point, but I knew there were several more out in the fields.

I went outside and soon saw Patricio again pitching Román out of the house. He followed him into the side yard near the large *nopal* cactus garden, where they wrestled on the ground in the sprinkling rain. Román is very slight, but he gave strong Patricio a tussle before being pinned to the ground. Soon, Clemente came up to Venancio and called him a thief again. I had to hold Venancio to restrain him from assaulting Clemente. It was now dark and rain had begun to fall. Rodrigo Uarárari came outside and asked me for a cigarette. He invited me in to drink more *tesgüino*, but I had decided to go back to our cave. I put on my rain slicker and called Venancio to tell him. He followed me a short distance down the trail, but I saw him looking back wistfully, and when I looked again he had disappeared. I proceeded through the rain, arriving back at Agua Caliente about 9:00 P.M. I did not see Venancio until the next morning.

Sunday, August 28. I arrived at Inápuchi at 9:00 A.M. with Venancio and learned that the people were all at Juan-Tasio's house drinking *tesgüino*. The evident purpose was weeding his bean field, since about five men were working at this while another 13 were drinking in the yard. About six women were sitting in a group over by the corn house and others appeared to be inside the house. We sat down, were offered beer, and within about 15 minutes the group who had been weeding also joined us. It seemed to me that very little work had been done and that little needed to be done. Venancio confirmed that most of the weeding was done previously and that the main purpose of this gathering was to drink. I noted that all the people from Inápuchi were here with the exception of Clemente and his wife. In addition, there were two men from Uarárari and their wives, two from Yipó with their wives, one from Rynárachi (the 15-year-old son of Polinario), a man I did not know from Aboreáchi, and a husband and wife with their two teenage boys from Rejohuáchi, near Batopilas. This last family just happened to pass by and were invited to drink.

The *tesgüino* was passed around again and again but there was no sign of drunkenness. Rodrigo said that it was not strong because green *basiáhuari* was used to ferment it. Men and women sat around in the yard conversing quietly. Though one man was playing a violin, there were no dancing, fighting, or joking. Actually, there was not much *tesgüino*, only two small *ollas*, and it was finished by about 1:00 P.M.

About this time, Rodrigo suggested that a race be run, and everyone jumped at the idea. People became visibly more animated and excited as they divided into two teams. Everyone was a little high from the beer, but no one was drunk. Rodrigo

Uarárari and Dionicio Inápuchi acted as the *chokéames* (race organizers—see Appendix), to handle the betting. While the betting was going on, with their knives they carved two kicking balls from hard oak roots. It began to rain lightly but this did not dampen the group's enthusiasm. Everyone streamed up through the high corn of Juan-Tasio's field to the wide shallow arroyo which was to be the center of the race course.

The people divided into two groups according to their relationship or living proximity to the runners. Those chosen to be *chokéames* passed among the crowd asking for bets, which were quite small in comparison with what I had seen at large interpueblo races. Bets of one peso, one bar of soap, a string of beads, or a small ball of yarn were the extent of it—just token bets to give some incentive to the runners.

It was decided that the race was to be six *vueltas*, or circuits, across the plateau of Inápuchi. I estimated this to be a total distance of about 21 miles at three and one-half miles per circuit. Seven runners started for each side. The oldest was Rodrigo Uarárari (about 55), and the youngest was Cruz Inápuchi (14). Seledonio Inápuchi (about 45) also ran as did Pablo (about 40). The others were all in their twenties and thirties.

The object of any race is to get your team's ball across the finish line first. A number of runners begin for each team, but it is only necessary to have one runner take the ball across the finish. The hard wooden ball is not actually kicked, but is lifted swiftly into the air with the toe in a motion so rapid that it looks like kicking. The runners are not supposed to touch the ball with their hands. Most Tarahumara boys gain great proficiency in hurling the ball with their feet, practicing it from a very young age while out herding.

In this race most of the runners lasted for several *vueltas*, but old Rodrigo Uarárari dropped out of his group after only one lap, or about three and one-half miles. It was not until after the third circuit (or about 10 miles) that the two young boys, along with Clemente and Seledonio Inápuchi all quit. After four laps, or 14 miles, Patricio and Rodrigo Inápuchi and the man from Aboreáchi dropped out. After 16 miles everyone was out except for Román Inápuchi for one team, and Valencio and Martín for the other. Valencio stopped after about five and one-quarter laps, or about 18 miles, and Martín was able to keep going for only another mile or so. Román was already ahead when Martín stopped, so he did not have to finish the entire course. He simply quit when he reached the betting area again. I estimated that Román had run about 20 miles.

During the race it was interesting to watch how those not actually running participated. After the first half-lap, as the runners passed the beginning point, most of the spectators, both men and women, started running along with those they were supporting. They helped their teams by finding the ball in the deep grass. Sometimes they picked up a ball and set it in a clear spot so the runners could kick it. At one point I saw the wife of Rodrigo Uarárari, a woman of about 50, excitedly grab the ball and run about 50 yards with it before setting it in a favorable spot for kicking. This is a definite foul, but no one betting on the other team saw her. She and some of the other women had run about five or six miles in all alongside the teams by the time the race was finished. At least three of these women ran with small babies on their backs. The supporters never ran a whole *vuelta* but accompanied the runners about one-half or three-quarters of a mile from the starting point, then waited and accompanied them back to it again as they returned. They worked hard not to lose the beads they had bet!

While the race was in progress, some people from Rodrigo's side were complaining that their opponents cut short one of the *vueltas*, but since the cheating side lost anyway it did not matter. While the runners were out of sight, much joking went on among the waiting spectators. Some women aroused laughter by saying they were going to take the opponent's ball and throw it backwards. Then Rodrigo's wife said she would throw peyote (an act of sorcery). This again evoked peels of laughter. Dionicio said he was going to bet his wife, and this was followed by a number of sexual jokes. When Clemente and his wife and boy passed some distance away on their way home (they had not been at the race), Rodrigo Uarárari commented that Clemente must have been screwing good since his boy is big now. This brought shouts of laughter from the group.

When the race was over a controversy arose because it seemed that some of the bets had disappeared. Some accusations of stealing were made by the winners. Before it would become too serious, Seledonio Inápuchi stepped in and agreed to replace the missing items. This calmed the situation and, since there was no more *tesgüino*, everyone started for home around 6:00 P.M.

Wednesday, September 20. Venancio and I arrived at Uarárari about 10:00 A.M. and found several men drinking a small *olla* of *tesgüino* prior to beginning some cooperative work. We were first offered a gourd of *esquiáte*, and then some thick unpalatable *tesgüino* made from corn stalks (*caña*). We all then set off to drag some dry oak branches down from the hillside onto a small bean field of about 30 feet by 100 feet. They will be left there until late spring, at which time they will be burned, and the ashes used as fertilizer. I estimated that Seledonio Uarárari (the donor of *tesgüino*) and his 16-year-old son could have performed this job in a little more than half a day, but with the help of six of us it was completed in about an hour and a half. Venancio commented that this is the kind of thing people do when there is little work. They *make* work so that there will be a legitimate reason to brew *tesgüino*.

When we returned, the *olla* was dedicated to Clemente Rejohuáchi, and I noticed that five other people had arrived, conveniently too late to work. Seledonio handed a large empty *hueja* with a small one in it to Rodrigo. Rodrigo then dipped the large one full of beer and filled the smaller one from it which he passed to the next man. Each person was handed the two *huejas* in turn so that he might then serve whomever else he wished. The person who was selected to be served, in turn, reciprocated by serving the one who had served him. This is a different system from that in other places in the Sierra.

At one point a contest began between Venancio and Seledonio. Instead of offering the gourds to someone else, Seledonio, with a big grin on his face, handed them back to Venancio, who had to drink. Venancio then dipped one for Seledonio, and the two kept this up until each had drunk four large *huejas*.

After about an hour we went into the house where Rodrigo Uarárari was being asked to give a "sermon." He stood up and gave a brief moral lecture in a high pitched monotone. As usual, he said not to fight, lie, or steal, and that if really bad things happen, the culprits will be taken to Aboreáchi or Batopilas to jail. He then gestured to Venancio, asking him to speak, since he was a visitor. Venancio rose and spoke in a more conversational and vehement way about how the *Chavóchis* had been taking advantage of the Indians lately and that it should not be tolerated.

The drinking then continued and things became much wilder. Seledonio Uarárari, who is about 35, became very drunk and began taunting Rodrigo Uarárari (about 55), who is his *chiéri* (older brother-in-law). Rodrigo was sitting by the *tesgüino olla* when Seledonio rushed up to him and began making hip thrusting gestures toward his face while laughing loudly. He took off his loincloth and placed his flaccid organ close to Rodrigo's face. Then he turned around and pointed to his bared rectum which he pushed up close to Rodrigo, laughing gleefully all the while and asking him to try it. Finally he grabbed the older man and thrust him outside the house, where, to the amusement of some, he forced him down on all fours and simulated copulation with him.

Rodrigo appeared to be playing a disliked role; his behavior was much more restrained than that of Seledonio. He was enduring the indignities without resistance. His occasional laughs seemed very forced, while Seledonio was enjoying himself hugely. Soon after, Venancio went outside and fell into a drunken sleep, although it was still quite light. When I went to check on him, I noticed several people behind the corn house. I made out a woman seated with four men, and I later learned that, in a kind of very private trial, they were giving her a "sermon" about unseemly sexual behavior.

I looked around and noticed that there were less women than men present, though Clemente Rejohuáchi had both of his wives with him. His first and oldest wife appeared to be a semi-moron. She was dishevelled, very dirty, and very pitiful. The second wife was much younger, clean, and very attractive. She had two small children of about five and seven with her. (Later I found out that the older wife does little besides goat herding, which is about the only useful task she can perform.)

When I went back inside the house it was almost dark and I saw Seledonio Uarárari and Rodrigo Uarárari still engaged with one another. Seledonio had replaced his loincloth and they were now seated together on a bench. This time Seledonio was forcing his three-month-old baby on Rodrigo, who did not seem to know exactly what to do. Knowing that Rodrigo has no living children, but that the ten he had sired have all died, I wondered what he was thinking. Sometime later I noticed him playing with the baby and seemingly enjoying it. Then Rodrigo's wife took the baby away from him and carried it outside to its mother. I followed and saw that the mother was so drunk she could hardly sit up. She tried to nurse the child, but being on a hillside, she rolled over and almost crushed it before another woman took it from her.

Back inside, Venancio had awakened and returned to the beer. He helped me understand the animated conversation between Juan Uarárari, Martín and Feliz. Old Feliz was complaining of a fear of dying, and the others were trying to cheer him up. They were saying *"Onorúame* will tell you when it is time to go."

We decided to leave since we had to get back to camp, but before we could exit, Valencio Inápuchi accosted Venancio and accused him of having intercourse with all the women in Inápuchi. Venancio flew into a rage and I had to restrain him. Eventually Valencio apologized and his wife brought Venancio a *hueja* of *tesgüino* as a peace offering. Finally we left but only reached Inápuchi before the moon had set, so we built a fire and lay down to sleep there. In the morning, I found that I had lost my hat in the *barranca*. Venancio insisted on getting it before we left for Agua Caliente.

Significance of the Tesgüinada

Lumholtz, the pioneer ethnologist in northwest Mexico, said that it was chiefly through *tesgüino* that the Tarahumara tribe was able to perpetuate itself, since it was only while drinking that the bashful Indian men had enough courage to have intercourse with their wives (1902:342). My friends among them always laughed when I quoted this opinion to them, but their shyness and taciturnity have been mentioned by all writers on this group, who have felt that the *tesgüinada* helps to free them from these painfully inhibiting traits. My observations corroborate that they tend to share a shy quietness, and a stoic dignity as basic traits which are related to their isolation. This isolation, in turn, derives from their mode of subsistence in the rugged mountains. I agree too, that *tesgüino* serves as a lubricant of social interaction, enabling the Tarahumaras to temporarily overcome their fears of others in order to engage in needed sociality.

The people of Inápuchi and Aboreáchi say that to make *tesgüino* there must be a purpose, such as a need for cooperative work or a curing ceremony. Actually, all but one of the *tesgüinadas* I recorded was ostensibly held for these reasons, and the great proportion of party givers used cooperative labor as their reason. Occasionally a man makes *tesgüino* with no practical rationalization, but this is rare. As indicated previously, an important part of the economic system is the cooperative tradition where members of a group of households have reciprocal obligations to supply their labor to one another at times when the task would be difficult or tedious to complete alone. *Tesgüino* is considered to be sufficient pay for the labor and for what are often long trips of considerable difficulty. When the party giver makes his rounds to the various households he says, "Would you like to drink a little *tesgüino* with me?" or "We will have a little *tesgüino* tomorrow." It is unnecessary to first mention that work will be a part of the program; the verbal stress is upon the social aspect of the *tesgüinada* to follow.

The *tesgüinada* is the fundamental social gathering of the *Gentile* Tarahumaras of Inápuchi, and of the *Pagótome* of Aboreáchi and Yehuachíque as well. The above excerpts from my notes clearly illustrate the operation of the psychosocial dynamics of the beer party. The behavior I described is quite typical. Though I selected incidents to illustrate the full range of *tesgüinada* behavior, the general tone I described was observed in all of the 49 *tesgüinadas* I attended in the Aboreáchi-Inápuchi region.

Even though I had read about the Tarahumaras' extreme fondness for their beer, when I went into the field I was not fully prepared to understand the truly pre-eminent role of the *tesgüinada* in their social life. However, early in my stay among them, I learned that *tesgüino* drinking is extremely important to the Tarahumara, and in fact, is their basic social activity. In my daily visits to various *ranchos*, I often found the people absent. The children left guarding animals and fields would tell me their parents were away drinking. I began to note how *tesgüino* was a prerequisite to all important activities. Conversations frequently concerned *tesgüinadas,* and they also formed one of the dominant subjects of the dreams the Tarahumara told me about.

I observed that the Tarahumara etiquette of *tesgüino* drinking requires that all adults present drink as much beer as possible. When a drinking gourd (capacity usually between a pint and a quart) is passed to a person, he is expected to drink it without hesitation. Rarely is a person allowed to refuse the obligation to drink.

There are, of course, devices to escape these pressures. If a man has been seen to drink a great deal, he may feel that he has

Drinking in the house

sufficiently fulfilled his obligation and may push the gourd away, though he must argue firmly (sometimes almost to the point of blows) to persuade the giver to accept his refusal. It is not unusual that a person quickly exits when he sees that his turn is coming. Since people are always moving about, his departure is often unnoticed. Sometimes one may push the proffered gourd back to the giver saying, "You drink." The giver is then obliged to drink it himself. The reprieve may be brief, since another gourd is usually brought to the "generous" person immediately. In the darkness of a windowless, smoke-filled hut I have seen women secretly pour out beer they could not drink. More typically, the official server watches carefully to see that every drop is drunk. It should be emphasized that these avoidance methods are simply to control intake; most people like the beer and have an amazing capacity for it. It is clear that the missionaries have failed to eradicate drinking among the Tarahumara because the meaning and importance of *tesgüino* interpenetrate all major sectors of the culture and social organization.

How Tesgüino Is Made

The alcohol consumed by the Tarahumara of Aboreáchi and Inápuchi is entirely in the form of *tesgüino*, or corn beer and its variations. In the vicinities of the larger Mestizo towns, stronger distilled beverages such as *mezcal*, *sotol*, and *lechugilla*, provide the principal basis of entertainment for the Mestizos of the Sierra, but the Indians of the isolated areas still drink their traditional brews.

The Tarahumara of our area have two native names for the corn beer: *suguí* and *batári* (or *suguíki* and *batáriki*). It is a thick, milky, nutritious brew made from maize fermented with a local grass seed called *basiáhuari* which is ground on the *metate*. About three days are needed to grind, boil, and ferment the corn after it has been dampened and allowed to sprout (a seven day process in all). The beverage must be drunk within a short space of time to prevent spoilage. Because of this narrow interval when it is best (about 12 to 24 hours), a man holding a *tesgüinada* waits until almost the last minute before making his long journey of invitation to the surrounding *ranchos*. It would be unthinkable to allow the *tesgüino* to spoil, even though as much as 50 gallons is often made. The rule requiring complete consumption of the beer is undoubtedly related to the high value of corn to the people, since it takes from two to three *decalitros* of the precious food for each *olla* of *tesgüino*. Therefore, if the people present cannot finish the *tesgüino* during the night, they sleep awhile and begin again. Meanwhile, if they become too sick or too full to go on, they drink *esquiáte* as an antidote so that they can continue until the beer is finished. It is also etiquette (not always observed) for the donor of *tesgüino* to provide an *olla* of *esquiáte* for the guests before starting to drink *tesgüino* so that they will not become drunk too quickly. This satisfies any hunger they might have from traveling a great distance to the *tesgüinada*, or from the cooperative work for which the *tesgüinada* was given.

Two important variations of the beer are made in the region of Inápuchi and Aboreáchi; one using green corn as the basic ingredient and one utilizing the heart of the *maguey* plant. When the yearly supply of dried corn is reaching the end, and the new corn is nearly ready for harvest, the people make *pachíki* or *caña*. There are two main variations on this theme; new fresh corn may

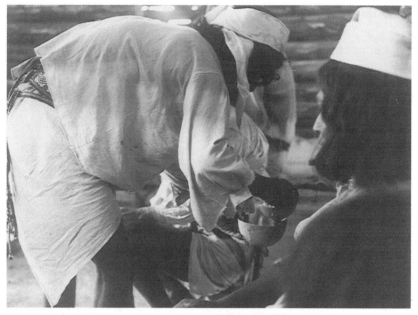

Hospitality

be mashed, cooked, and strained and made into beer, or corn stalks may be crushed in water and allowed to ferment after boiling. More commonly, either or both of these may be added to ordinary *tesgüino* during the brewing process. Also, there are an infinite series of gradations of proportions, as well as numerous possibilities created by using several types of fermenting catalyst; the result is a great range of tastes. (See Pennington, 1963, for an excellent discussion of Tarahumara beverage making, with botanical names.)

The brew made from the hearts of several types of *maguey* plants is very popular in Inápuchi, where it is called *meki*. Highland communities, such as Aboreáchi are too high above the canyon country to have *maguey*, and thus are deprived of this delicious beverage. For *meki* the *maguey* is baked in a pit oven, then pounded in water in a natural rock basin with a mallet fashioned from a limb of oak. The juice is then extracted by squeezing this pulp through a sieve made of thin agave leaves stretched between two sticks. This juice is put aside to ferment and then added to the regular *tesgüino* brew after it has been cooked.

If drunk at the right stage, *meki* is a most pleasant drink. However, both *caña* and *meki* have a tendency to produce diarrhea, and this danger increases in proportion to the use of materials other than corn. The Indians generally prefer their pure *suguíki*, and make the other two drinks only during the two or three months when maize is in limited supply.

There are no "alcoholics" as we would define the term, among the Tarahumara of the region studied. This is probably because *tesgüino* cannot be stored, it is expensive in terms of corn used, and the alcoholic content is relatively low. More important, drinking is a social rather than an individual activity. I was met with incredulous laughter when I suggested to informants that it might be possible for some wealthier men to make a continuous supply of *tesgüino* for their own private use. For these reasons, despite the consumption of large amounts of alcohol, Tarahumara traditional drinking does not produce the bizarre pathology of Western alcoholism.

Squeezing juice for *meki*

Religious Role of Tesgüino

To the Tarahumara corn beer has a sacred character. In Inápuchi it is said that this drink was given to the Indians by *Onorúame* so that they could get their work done and that they might enjoy themselves. Whenever an *olla* of *tesgüino* is drunk, it must first be dedicated to *Onorúame*. A little beer is dipped three times from a larger gourd and tossed in each of the four directions. This is done in front of a wooden cross in order to give God first access to the beer so that He will not be angry.

The host presents each full *olla* of *tesgüino* in turn to an influential man in the community. The one to whom it is presented then usually takes an honored place next to the *olla* and serves the *tesgüino* to others in order of their rank in the community. The ritual dedication of *tesgüino* is performed by the recipient of the *olla*, or, if there is a large group, by one of the younger men whom he has delegated to help him serve.

The ritual significance of *tesgüino* is further shown by its inclusion as an integral part of almost all ceremonies. An *olla* of *tesgüino* is placed at the foot of the cross and remains there throughout curing ceremonies held to assure good crops or healthy animals, rituals for killing worms, petitioning for rain, and protection from lightning. It is drunk by the *owerúame* and other important men as part of these ceremonies, and later is used as one of the "medicines" which are sprinkled on the new corn and the animals. In the curing ritual for the prevention of disease in children the *owerúame* dips a small cross in *tesgüino* and touches it to the lips of the baby, whom he then makes drink a little of the sacred beverage. If a person is sick, the *owerúame* marks crosses on wrists and the top of the head of the head of the patient with a crucifix dipped in *tesgüino*. At various points both patient and doctor imbibe small amounts of the beer.

When a boy about the age of 14 is allowed to drink *tesgüino* for the first time, he is given a short "sermon" about his manly responsibilities and may thenceforth drink with his elders. Before this age children are customarily excluded from the *tesgüinadas*. Besides the important role of the *tesgüino* as an integral part of these and other rituals, each religious fiesta of the *Pagótome* is followed by a large *tesgüinada* which may last as long as 48 hours.

Unlike Aboreáchi and most *Pagótome* communities, which have a number of ceremonies taking place in the church, all of the ritual activities of the Inápuchi community take place at *tesgüinadas* which rotate from *rancho* to *rancho*. *Gentile* religious ceremonies are all called for the purpose of "curing" the crops, animals, or people. Beer also must be made in order to bring a curer to a sick person, or to counteract sorcerers. All rituals for such personal anxiety-provoking events, as well as those for the larger collective ceremonies require *tesgüino* and are accompanied by a *tesgüinada*. (See Chapter 5 for details.)

The Quality of Social Life

An alternation of extremes in the frequency and intensity of social interaction is a striking social consequence of the dispersed settlement pattern with its individualized daily economic tasks, in conjunction with the *tesgüinada* institution. One side of this dichotomy is social isolation. A man's daily activities, such as caring for his herd of goats, hoeing his fields, checking the whereabouts of his ranging cattle, or watching one of his widely separated stands of corn, are such that they can be performed alone. A woman, alternatively performs the lonely role of goat herding while the remainder of her tasks are carried out in the semi-isolation of the household, often only in the company of her one or two small children. Distances between *ranchos*, seasonal mobility, the typical wide spacing of houses within the *rancho*, and the time consuming nature of daily activities, all work to prevent frequent social visiting. At night the elementary family is usually together, but exhaustion, custom, and lack of light make for an early bedtime. There is little opportunity or inclination for conviviality or social intercourse. At this extreme, both the frequency and the intensity of interaction are low for days and sometimes weeks at a time.

At the other extreme is the *tesgüinada*, a relatively short period into which is compressed a great proportion of Tarahumara social intercourse. When one approaches a household where a *tesgüinada* is going on, he is immediately impressed by the din. The loud hum, punctuated by shouts and singing, mixed with noise of drunkenly operated violins, guitars, accordions, and harmonicas, is a striking contrast to the usual peaceful silence of the *rancho*, broken only by the raucous barks of hungry mongrels.

To the *Gentiles*, the *tesgüinada* serves all the functions of social life outside of those served by the household groups. The *tesgüinada* is the religious group, the economic group, the entertainment group, and the group in which disputes are settled, marriages arranged, and deals completed. At the *tesgüinada*, with his neighbors, and under the influence of alcohol, the individual can play the roles in his repertoire which are dormant during his isolation. The aspiring leader gets to his feet and gives a "sermon." Deals are made for animals or maize. A marriage may be arranged, the unmarried may find a mate, or the married can vary his or her sexual experience. Kinship roles, other than those of the nuclear family, rarely find a chance or mood for expression except at one of these parties. Here, the clown makes his reputation, and much laughing follows sexual jokes and horseplay. The ritual role of the native religious practitioner is largely played out in this atmosphere. The *tesgüinada* provides practically the only opportunity for the release of aggressive impulses, and frequently a fight occurs for one reason or another. The motive is often sexual jealousy, and not infrequently the result is serious injury. This is in contrast to the virtual absence of fighting outside of *tesgüinadas*.

The social status system, too, is intimately connected with the *tesgüino* complex. Social ranking is minimal, in comparison with most societies, but what there is, is based almost entirely upon wealth, as demonstrated through the possession of cattle, goats and horses, and the ability to harvest surpluses of maize and beans. A loincloth of new white muslin and many strands of beads around the neck of his wife, are nearly the only marks which, in daily life, symbolize the wealth of a man who outranks his fellows. The *tesgüinada* serves the important function of publicizing rank and power in the community. All men feel the need to make *tesgüino* occasionally to maintain their positions, but the wealthier man can make it oftener and make more of it. He especially demonstrates his wealth by being one of the few who can afford to sacrifice the amount of corn necessary to make *tesgüino* during the few months before harvest, when there is much hunger in the land.

At the time of the study, a recently introduced symbol of wealth in this region was the cheap button model of the Hohner accordion. The music-loving Indians listen enviously as the wealthy man sits in the corner playing his repertoire of one or two melodies again and again. The accordion symbolizes wealth because few people can afford the three-year-old bull which is the usual price for one charged by Mestizo traders. The time and place the accordion may be displayed, of course, is the *tesgüinada*.

The size of the *tesgüinada*, reckoned by the number of people attending, is another indication of the giver's status. A man who is known to drink "very far" and who reciprocally invites people from far away to his own beer parties is envied and respected. The degree of drunkenness attained is a third measure, and a man who does not usually provide enough beer for all to get completely intoxicated drops in ranking. Conversely, a man who is consistently not invited to the *tesgüinadas* of his neighbors is disgraced. Regardless of how physically or socially close the individuals involved may be, participation is by specific invitation. Not inviting someone is an effective form of social control. If it is consistently practiced by community members against an individual his low social ranking is clearly indicated.

The entertainment function of the *tesgüinada* is obvious, but should not be overlooked here. Such parties are times for relaxation, the playing of music, joking, and so on, but more important, they constitute practically the *only* group entertainment of the *Gentiles*. The nonchristians lack the drama of the winter season *matachines* and the Easter pageantry of processions and *pascolas* which, though, performed only a few times a year, are important entertainment in the *Pagótome* church centers. These *Gentiles* also hold fewer races than do the *Pagótome*. Most of the races they hold are not of the larger intercommunity variety, but are simply between all the men present at a *tesgüinada*, who divide up into two fairly equal sides. The betting is small compared to the heavy wagering done at the large interpueblo races of the *Pagótome*.

Entertainment, of course, is not restricted to the *tesgüinada*, alone. In the privacy of the household a man may play his violin at night before sleep, and shepherd boys may carry a violin, or amuse themselves kicking a ball while out watching goats. A few weeks before Easter the sound of drums and flutes can be heard throughout the mountains, as the herdsmen of the Aboreáchi area advance and recede on their daily foraging treks. The point of emphasis here, though, is that by far the principal mode of adult entertainment in *Pagótome* as well as in *Gentile* areas is the *tesgüinada*.

A similar situation holds in the more serious domains of life. Unlike the more formalized method of handling legal matters in such *Pagótome* communities as Aboreáchi, in Inápuchi most formal affairs of social control are taken care of within the context of the *tesgüinada*. In Aboreáchi, a large meeting is called to settle questions of crime or dispute. The *gobernador* and his officials sit gravely in special positions in the patio outside the church. Their attitudes are formal and their special canes lend sanctity to their offices.

In Inápuchi, on the other hand, there is no special place for trials, and the much smaller group of officials do not have canes symbolizing their authority. For the most part, a trial is conducted by the influential men at any *tesgüinada* being held in the vicinity. Though a serious attitude is maintained, the atmosphere is nevertheless affected significantly by a relative lack of formality, the shifting of locale, and the fact that there is nothing to symbolically mark off the sanctity of political or legal office. *Tesgüino* drinking, however, is what qualitatively most affects the character of such events. It creates an extemporaneous informal atmosphere, which contrasts greatly with the courtroom gravity typical in Western society.

The unusual feature of *Gentile* society which I want to emphasize here is that all important affairs, much economic work, community business, entertainment, and sacred rites, i.e., all significant social activities outside the household, are carried out in the context of the *tesgüinada*. This cannot but have profound influence upon the way in which the important social functions are carried out.

The Tesgüino Network

The most significant social group for any *Gentile* individual, aside from his household, is the set of people with whom he drinks *tesgüino*. Therefore, it is appropriate to call the overlapping structural entities defined by *tesgüino* drinking, networks, rather than groups. The interlocking nature of this netlike system has centrifugal effects which work in opposition to the formation of close knit bounded entities which are properly called "groups" in sociological usage.

As I have pointed out, the great proportion of social functions required by the *Gentiles* of Inápuchi are performed during the meetings of the shifting and varying personnel of *tesgüino* networks. As a social form, the *tesgüinada* thus bears an extremely heavy institutional load in Inápuchi society. Kin groups are absent here, as are sacred societies, a church, separate legal institutions, recreation groups, or other ascribed or voluntary associations and groups.

If we can draw away and see the system from a macroscopic point of view, a definite structural form may be observed in *Gentile* social life. The sets of people defined by reciprocal *tesgüino* invitation are the individuals who form the real and meaningful "community" for each person or household unit. The most significant characteristic of this type of structure is its centrifugal character, resulting from the condition that the socially meaningful groupings shift their locus of meeting from household to household, with the consequence that personnel at each gathering vary by proximity, for the most part. From a broad perspective we can see that a netlike system of household-centered, overlapping interaction systems stretches across the region.

To indicate this concretely, let us take the household of Seledonio on the *rancho* of Inápuchi as an example. Seledonio invites all the other people of Inápuchi *rancho* (six households), those of Rynárachi (two households), Uarárari (three households), one household from Chuvérachi, one from Yipó, one from Rejóvachi, and occasionally one from Awírachi. He and his family are invited to these *ranchos* as well. Outside of Inápuchi *rancho* itself his closest and most frequent invitations go to Uarárari, Rynárachi, Yipó, and Chuvérachi, in that order.

However, Julio Rynárachi, across the gorge to the northwest of Inápuchi, invites the other household of Rynárachi, five of seven households from Inápuchi, three from Charérachi, one from Rabó, and occasionally one from Churichíque, one from Yipó and one from Pisáchi.

On the south of the gorge from Inápuchi, Rodrigo Uarárari invites the other households from Uarárari, five from Inápuchi, three from Sumárachi, two from Awírachi, one from Rejóvachi, and two from Yipó (one *Pagótome*).

In each of these examples, the *tesgüino* network is composed of most of the surrounding *ranchos* (though not every household in them), and it can be seen that the groups overlap. For example, Julio Rynárchi does not ordinarily invite people from Uarárari, or vice versa, except on occasions of a large curing fiesta, though households from both Rynárchi and Uarárari invite those of Inápuchi. If Inápuchi is taken as the center, people from both Rynárachi and Uarárari may be seen there at *tesgüinadas*. If Uarárari is the center, one rarely sees a person from Rynárachi (two deep canyons away), but encounters people from Inápuchi and Sumárachi interacting with each other as well as with people of Uarárari *rancho*. Figure 2 schematically illustrates the overall character of the system. Each dot represents a household. All the dots touched by lines surrounding any one point represent the members of the *tesgüino* network for the household in the center of the circle.

The overlapping interwoven net of household centered interaction systems defined by the criterion of *tesgüino* drinking takes no account of pueblo lines as recognized by the government of Chihuahua. Even though the people living near the borders know to which pueblo they officially belong, and sometimes go to their pueblo center for various purposes, they are more meaningfully related to members of the neighboring *ranchos* across the pueblo line than to distant *ranchos* which may technically lie within their own pueblo. It is this overlapping character of the system that is responsible for the vagueness which has been noted for Tarahumara groupings in general (Bennett and Zingg, 1935:333).

In the rare situations where large *ranchos* exist, the *tesgüino* network may be almost restricted to one *rancho* alone. One such instance is the *Pagótome rancho* of Yehuachíque, a valley only about a mile in length and a quarter mile in width, where eighty-seven people live in eighteen households. At this *rancho* near the pueblo center of Aboreáchi the concentration of people in one place seemingly makes it unnecessary to extend the lines of *tesgüino* invitation outside of the *rancho*. Exceptions are nearby in-laws or other relatives, and curers.

It is interesting that the average number of households with which all men in the Inápuchi sample are connected by *tesgüino* invitation is about 17, which is close to the total number of households at Yehuachíque. This suggests that there may be an optimum number of households of the supporting "community" needed by any one Tarahumara residence group. If such is the case, it would explain what appears to be a tendency toward equalization of the number of people with whom a household interacts.

A final point here is that the stability of *tesgüino* networks in many parts of the Tarahumara area is broken by the winter pattern of moving, and in many cases, by the necessity of working fields in a spouse's *rancho*, which often is quite distant. In both of these circumstances a family finds itself temporarily in a partially different circle of neighbors, and at the center of another *tesgüino* network. This mobility feature of the settlement pattern further reduces consistent associations with the same people. It adds a further quality of irregularity and looseness to the Tarahumara social system, perhaps helping to explain why the underlying network structure of social organization and its dynamics has remained obscure to previous students of the group.

The structural significance of the *tesgüinada* institution and the form of the *tesgüino* network became apparent as a result of work among the *Gentiles* of Inápuchi, where it is the *only* structure above the level of the family. However, as can be deduced from the discussion of Yehuachíque above, this institution and social form are critical to an understanding of the social organization of *Pagótome* Tarahumara communities as well. In these, many social tasks such as trials for offenses against group norms, and community-wide decisions, are handled in a much more institutionalized fashion at the pueblo centers. Nevertheless, the *tesgüinada* is nearly as fundamental an institution in these *Pagótome* communities as it is to the *Gentiles*, and its influence upon the history of the Tarahumara as a whole has been profound.

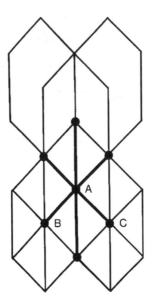

Figure 2. Abstraction of *Tesgüino* Network Form. Household "A" is the center of a network including "B" and "C." "B" includes "A" in its immediate network, but not "C," etc.

SUMMARY

Let us now summarize the forms of groupings in this society, in order to assess the role of the *tesgüinada* institution within the general social framework.

The smallest and most stable social group to which people of Aboreáchi and Inápuchi belong is the elementary family. Despite pressures exerted on it by a variety of factors inherent in the Tarahumara life-style, the family unit is stable in comparison with other groupings and associations in this society.

Elementary families often join with the parents of either spouse or with siblings into residence groups of varying composition. These compound households cooperate in agricultural, herding, and household tasks. They have a sense of unity, but their relative stability is reduced by a yearly and generational process of fission and fusion of their component elementary families, a process to be detailed further on.

The next wider unit is the *rancho* group. This is composed of a number of residence groups which occupy a given site where there is enough arable land to supply most of their support. The numbers of people composing *rancho* groups vary greatly according to land available, ranging from *ranchos* occupied by a single nuclear family up to those with twenty or more residence groups. In eleven *ranchos* of the Inápuchi area, the average number of households per *rancho* is between three and four with an average of 15 people. Households average about five persons each. For some 15 *Pagótome ranchos*, the average number of households was nearly four per *rancho*. This calculation does not count as *ranchos* those plots with a dwelling which are merely visited a few days at a time throughout the year, nor does it count people who have a field, house, and granary on the *rancho* of others.

Above the family and the residence and *rancho* groups are two more social entities of importance. These are what I have called the *tesgüino* network, and the pueblo. The intermediate and unstable grouping formed by *tesgüino* invitations which lies between the pueblo and the family is a significant unit in the area studied. It is really not a true group, but it is fundamental to *Gentile* social organization. This importance of the *tesgüino* network is not confined to Inápuchi and Aboreáchi; it constitutes the underlying community structure throughout the Tarahumara region.

Moving to a social level above the pueblo, there is recognition by these Tarahumara that there are other *Rarámuri*, or Tarahumara people, beyond their immediate localities. However, there is no feeling of unity with them and no formal ties. There is nearly as much suspicion of people from other pueblos as there is of *Chavóchis*. No Tarahumara that I met in Aboreáchi or Inápuchi had the faintest notion of the extent or boundaries of the Tarahumara people or the tribe as a whole. Even though I.N.I. has instituted a *Consejo Supremo* (Supreme Council), there is no formal Tarahumara organization of social significance at the tribal level, and relations of this ethnic enclave to the state of Chihuahua and to the Mexican nation are still minimal and of little importance.

Within the total Tarahumara social framework, the *tesgüino* network is the fundamental social form. In recent years there has been a great deal of use of the concept of "network" to analyze social relations. This emphasis has been partly a reaction to the limitations and rigidity of social structural theory. Network theorists have demonstrated the importance of individual strategies in building up sets of meaningful relationships outside of the rigid structures which constitute complex societies.

I mention this recent direction in social analysis only to point up that what I have described here differs radically from what the network theorists have proposed. Instead of showing how networks operate within the context of other institutions, I have delineated the *tesgüino network* as the *major structural form* of the Tarahumara social system above the family and residence group. The social structure which itself has a network form, is a distinct structural type. It is a social system quite different from that of segmentary lineage societies, with their typical feuds and aggressive expansionism, and it also contrasts strongly with partilineal bands, with peasant villages and with cities.

CHAPTER 5

THE REALM OF THE SUPERNATURAL

The Belief System

The Tarahumara have not elaborated a complex religious system. Compared with most North American Indian groups, they show little interest in mythology or theology, and the beliefs of the *Gentiles* are generally simpler than those of the *Pagótome*. This difference in complexity seems to derive mainly from the fact that, along with many technological innovations proffered by the Spanish, the *Pagótome*, with their acceptance of baptism, also unwittingly accepted a large body of Spanish religious beliefs and practices, which they then had to assimilate and integrate into their own system. For instance, they ostensibly accepted the baptism of children with water as a naming ceremony and as a sign of identification with the Catholic system. However, they already had a naming ritual, a "baptism" by fire bestowed by a shaman shortly after birth. They kept both of the naming rituals and thus the child is given two names, a Spanish water name and a Tarahumara fire name. This is a situation which works to create a tendency towards ambiguity of identity, or "cognitive dissonance" in the *Pagótome* basic personality. The tendency is emotionally reinforced by the fact that water and waterways are culturally given sources of fear and anxiety in Tarahumara culture. It now seems very likely that most of the early mass baptisms of the tribe reported by the early missionaries were motivated more by panic stemming from the devastating epidemics of smallpox and other European diseases that were ravaging the people, than they were being won over to the new belief system. It seems likely that they perceived the baptisms as "curing" ceremonies similar to their own, which they accepted in desperation, in spite of the inclusion of water in them (Slaney, 1991:126-141). (See Chapter 6 for more on names.)

The *Gentiles,* on the contrary, in rejecting baptism, were rejecting the political domination of the intruders as well as most of their beliefs and practices. This relieved them from the pressures to incorporate the corpus of new ideas and practices into their religious system, allowing them to avoid most of the contradictions and conceptual problems faced by their Christianizing counterparts.

Whether *Pagótome* or *Gentile,* however, the Tarahumara never have had a written means of preserving a consistent body of myth, nor have they had an emphasis upon an oral tradition. Many individuals in Inápuchi report rather hazy religious ideas. Some claim no knowledge at all about the origin of the earth or that of the Tarahumara, and many disclaim knowledge of any but a few details relating to the spiritual realm. However, in speaking of their religious ideas as "simple," I do not wish to convey the notion that the beliefs of the Tarahumara are in any way less effective or important than more complex ideas would be. One only has to compare the music of Mozart with that of Anton Bruckner to understand the advantages that simplicity often has over complexity. Neither do I wish to imply any negative evaluation, or any idea of secular life when I speak of the Tarahumara as being relatively uninterested in theology. Though they certainly are a pragmatic people, it needs to be emphasized that, like many other nonliterate societies, their entire existence is seen through the lenses of a magical world view. Every action and thought is underlain by the set of assumptions and understandings concerning the supernatural realm which I shall now delineate.

A striking feature of Tarahumara religious ideas in general is their basis in fear. There are two major deities—*Onorúame,* or "The one who is our Father" (also called *Tata Riósi*), who has been more or less assimilated with the Christian God, and his adversary *Diablo,* or *Reré Batéame,* the one who lives below. Each of these is conceived of as being assisted by many *sontársi* (soldiers) or angels. Of the two major deities, *Onorúame* is much more clearly visualized. He is usually described as an old man with a long white beard who with his wife, *Iyérame*—the one who is our Mother—lives in the sky. In many of the "Christian" communities *Iyérame* is vaguely associated with the Virgin Mary. Both Father God and Mother God are accompanied in the upper world by their sons, *Sucristo*, and their daughters, *Santi* (Merrill, 1988:71, 144). The system of the Gentiles is uncomplicated by these extra deities. However, in both systems God's arch enemy, *Diablo*, who sometimes appears as a serpent or a fox, lives under the ground in a place with a great fire, or, according to many informants, under the river.

Concepts of the cosmos are nebulous. Most people seem to believe that there are three, or sometimes five "worlds," or layers to the universe, supported by giant columns: one stationed at each of the four directions. The middle level is the one of present daily living, while the one above is governed by *Onorúame*, and the one below is the province of *Diablo*. The inhabitants of the worlds above and below (that is, the souls of the dead, the Ancient Ones—*Anayáwari*—along with God's family and his soldiers or angels) are engaged in activities similar to those occupying people of the middle or present world. In particular, they spend a great deal of time in drinking parties.

A difference between the middle and the upper and lower worlds is that every action is carried out in reverse, and life there is a mirror image of life in the middle world. This means that when we have summer here, they are having winter there. When it is day here, it is night there. When we sleep, they (as well as our souls) are awake. Our moon is their sun, while their moon is our sun, and so forth. An important consequence of these conceptions is in what they mean for ritual behaviors. Most Tarahumara rituals involve counterclockwise gestures and turns, but when the occasion relates to death or contact with ghosts of the dead they must be performed in a clockwise direction; the shaman performs his ritual gestures with the left hand instead of the right, and *ollas* of *tesgüino* are dedicated with the left hand, etc.

Many Tarahumara concepts bear an obvious resemblance and relationship to Biblical notions. However, there are many exceptions to this, such as the reversal ideas I have just mentioned, and the notion that both of the major spiritual beings are almost unremittingly threatening to people in the middle world. At death, *Diablo*, who is much less clearly delineated than *Onorúame*, is a being of much more power than his European Christian counterpart, the Devil. He is said to take murderers, persistent thieves and *Chavóchis* down to the underworld when they die i.e., under the earth (or the river). *Onorúame* takes the majority of Tarahumara people up to the sky. It is important to note, however, that there is no belief in Hell or everlasting punishment.

The really salient fears and concerns of the Tarahumara are not with what will occur after death, but are focussed on portentous happenings in *this* world. Notions about life in the other worlds are sketchy. They are much more interested in problems pertaining to their pressing immediate needs and to dangers in the present "middle world," than they are in philosophical speculations or theological musings about life after death.

Onorúame gets hungry from time to time and lets the Tarahumara know that he wants offerings (*wirómera*). He does this by sending one of his angels or *sontársi* with a message that he wants the people of a given area to offer him a white goat, a chicken, or a deer and that this must be accompanied by a long period of dancing. These messages are sent in one of two ways; either a shaman (*owerúame*) is contacted through a dream, or an angel speaks to someone through the mouth of an animal, such as a cow, horse, goat, or occasionally, a deer. *Onorúame* threatens great catastrophes if he is not fed through sacrifices. He will cause all the mountains to fall, bring showers of blood, cause gigantic floods in the canyons, cause the animals to die, make the rain cease, or bring a wasting sickness to all the people.

Valencio of Pisáchi told me that in the previous year the crops were bad because it rained too much early in the season. Travelers brought news that many were drowned in the floods. Two great serpents passed through the sky and warned the people to dance, or the whole earth would be covered with water. Also a *borrego* sheep gave the same warning in Sitanápuchi, and a cow spoke in Munérachi. Each warning stated that white bulls must be sacrificed, and that dancing should be performed. These white animals are hard to secure and according to Valencio, delays in finding them was one reason for the trouble. He concluded by saying that "*Chavóchis* don't offer *wirómera* at their fiestas. They are like coyotes."

Nothing *Diablo* can do compares to these dire consequences. The Evil Being, who is said by some to be *Onorúame's* estranged elder brother, is believed to incite aggressiveness in individuals and fighting at *tesgüinadas*. He is the patron and creator of the *Chavóchis*, and their souls go down with him to the lower world when they die. There is no reference to eternal punishment, but it is not a comfortable place because one is separated from friends and relatives. *Diablo* must be placated to some extent in Tarahumara rituals but he does not present nearly the danger to the people that *Onorúame* does.

None of the attributes of kindness, helpfulness or love, which are associated with European concepts of God, were attributed to *Onorúame* by informants. He is much more in the mold of the Hebrew Yaweh. In Lumholtz' time *Onorúame* was identified with the Sun while Mother Moon and the Morning Star were also important deities, but everyone in Inápuchi disclaims knowledge of these ideas.

However, even though *Onorúame* constitutes the major supernatural threat in the lives of the Tarahumaras, in addition to fears of *Diablo*, their earthly affairs are haunted by a number of lesser spirits as well. These inhabit whirlpools and whirlwinds, waiting to cause such deformities as dwarfism, as well as other maladies, to the unsuspecting. Magical serpents live in rivers and bodies of water, and the ghosts of the dead, who occasionally return to their communities, are also feared. Finally there are the *Anayáwari*, or Ancient Ones. These seem to be the souls of the peoples who occupied the Sierra before the creation of the Tarahumara. These Ancient Ones apparently are still wandering the earth and on occasion encounter and endanger the souls of Tarahumara who have left the bodies of their hosts during night dreams. (See Slaney, 1991, for a good discussion of this neglected topic.)

Sorcery by malevolent human beings who possess mystical "power" is a constant danger, as are certain animals and plants which are also believed to possess supernormal qualities. For example, toads and horned toads may cause sickness if touched.

The plants *híkuli* (peyote) and *bakánoa* are believed to be powerful spirits which also may cause illness if they are somehow offended. Only a few powerful *owerúames* who have special relationships with these dangerous spirit plants can treat the illnesses they cause. (See Merrill, 1988:121-127 for a fine description of a *bacánoa* shaman at work.)

The Indians have a great fear of sickness, and they believe the main cause of it, and of death, are the loss of some or all of one's souls (*iwígara*). This word is derived from *iwí*, the word for breath, with which souls are associated. Most Tarahumara believe that a person has several souls. In Inápuchi it is believed that women have four souls while men have three. I could find no explanation for this, except that it follows the normal pattern of male-female symbolism. In many areas they believe that one or two of the souls (those of the head and chest) are larger than the others, and these are more critical for one's life and health.

The souls are very volatile and can escape the body easily. The large ones, such as those centered in the head or the heart, leave the body when a person is drinking corn beer, and this is the cause of drunkenness. Souls also have a tendency to escape at night when the person is sleeping. Dreams are a record of sorts, of a soul's activities in one of the other worlds. When they stray too far from the bodies to which they belong they are in peril from dangerous spirits which can frighten or capture them, causing weakness and sickness. Also one way a sorcerer strikes down an enemy is by "eating his souls." Therefore, one of the main skills of the *owerúame* is the tracking and retrieving of lost or endangered souls. (See Merrill, (1988:85-120) for an informative discussion of soul concepts in Tarahumara cosmology.)

Before describing Tarahumara rituals in more detail, a bit more should be said about the religious universe of these people. Informants gave somewhat varying accounts when asked to explain their ideas of the origins or the explanation of the world. Valencio Pisáchi commented that:

> *Onorúame* made people and all animals in the world as well as the maize fields. He molded the first people from wet earth in the same way a pot is molded by a potter. Dogs were created as the "soldiers" of men, but coyotes, rattlesnakes, and toads were

created by *Diablo* as enemies of men. *Onorúame* first made the corn and planted and harvested it. Then he left it for men. *Onorúame* and *Diablo* are jealous of each other and fight, but *Onorúame* usually does not let *Diablo* take his people. When people are fighting it is because *Diablo* is making them do it, and when they wound one another *Onorúame* is bleeding and in great pain.

Onorúame sends sickness so that Tarahumara will die because he needs people up in the sky. *Diablo* gets some more people too, those who kill others. When *Onorúame* is sick, we are all sick too. The only thing to do is to dance and to give food so that He can gain strength.

Seledonio Inápuchi said the following:

Onorúame made the Tarahumara and all wild animals from wet clay. He breathed life into all of them simultaneously when they were completed. The earth was beautiful in those times and the corn was abundant. They did not need domestic animals. There were many deer and other animals to eat. Then after a long time the soil became weak, and when the *Chavóchis* came the Tarahumara traded for cows and goats so that they could fertilize.

Some people differed from the accounts above by saying that *Onorúame* made the Tarahumara, while *Diablo* created the *Chavóchis*, but most of my informants simply said they did not know anything about these things. When I asked Rodrigo Uarárari about such matters he said that neither his parents nor grandparents told stories or explained anything of this kind to him.

The only thing I know is that before *Onorúame* made the Tarahumara there were only coyotes in the world, but who knows what happened? I have heard that the earliest people were very fierce. They fought a great deal. This changed when the *Chavóchis* came.

When asked what *Onorúame* looks like, he replied:

I don't know. I have never dreamed about him. I know he needs sacrifices from men because he is blind. He cannot see to catch animals himself. He sometimes shows himself to people in the shape of a man. He gets angry and threatens to destroy the world because people do not feed him enough. Once a long time ago, he made the sun go dark. He only relented and let it come out again when everyone danced and made *wirómera*. When a person dies he goes up to the sky, but killers go to a place below the river with *Diablo*.

The many discrepancies in the accounts I collected go along with the general lack of expressed interest in the whole question of origins, mythology, or of explanations in general. Burgess (1985), and Merrill (1988), have collected a number of folktales in other Tarahumara communities, indicating slightly more complex belief systems in some regions than we had thought. However, I believe that from a comparative viewpoint, these meager collections make it even more clear that the Tarahumara are ritualists, not theologians. They act out their religious conceptions through dance and ceremony, rather than concerning themselves very much with nuances of philosophic argumentation and distinctions of doctrine.

The Practitioners

The *Gentiles* have institutionalized only two religious roles: the *owerúame* (doctor or shaman) and the *sawéame* (chanter). Of these, the *owerúame* is by far the most important, since he is the ritual specialist and protector of the people against sorcery and disease. The role of *sawéame* is not insignificant, however, because dancing for *Onorúame* is serious and necessary business, but the role is more restricted than that of the *owerúame*, and most older men can perform it. As indicated earlier, if the *owerúame* is widely respected he may be fully supported by the community.

The term *sawéame* means "he who has the rattle" since a *sawára* is a ceremonial rattle. The *sawéame* performs an important role in all rituals requiring dancing, all the curing ceremonies held for protection of the fields from hail, worms, and drought. He also dances at funerals and before important races. His major dances are the *yúmari* and the *tutubúri*, which I will speak more about later. Here I only want to emphasize that the *sawéames'* dance is hard and serious ceremonial work. It requires an older man who, with his blanket draped across his left shoulder, and keeping measured time with his ceremonial rattle, must dance for hours back and forth across the special "dance patio" *(awírachi)* before one or three cloth-draped crosses over an altar.

The role of the *owerúame* is much more complex and important. His title is translated as shaman, or "great curer" but this latter term is somewhat misleading since the concept of "curing" is so much broader for the Tarahumara than it is for us. It includes almost all of the ritualism of the *Gentiles* and a great proportion of *Pagótome* ritual as well. For example, for both groups the annual ceremony for assuring rain and a good crop is called "curing," as are the rituals for protecting people and animals against lightning and disease. Additionally included as curing are all those acts embraced by our own medical meaning of the term. As the reader will remember, fertilization of the fields with animal dung is also called curing. Thus, from a Western point of view, the *owerúame* is a blend of priest and doctor. He rivals the priest as one of the major ritualists for Christian or *Pagótome* Tarahumara ceremonies, and is the only important religious leader of the *Gentiles*.

The *owerúame's* most important power is his ability to "see" what is happening to people's souls, and to do something about

Sawéames Inápuchi

it by projecting one of his own souls out. He usually does this in a dream. In some parts of the Tarahumara region, particularly around Narárachi, the *owerúames* use peyote to produce a curing trance. In the Aboreáchi-Inápuchi area I could find no trace of this (see also Bye, 1979). The peyote plant here is widely feared as a spiritual substance having an independent soul, which can "see." It is used by sorcerers to harm, or preferably to kill, other people.

The *owerúame* is a necessary ceremonial figure in both the *Pagótome* and *Gentile* communities, and each family has one to which it appeals for its curing needs. The status is basically an achieved status, even though according to Tarahumara theory, the power is born in one. It is evident that considerable training in "medicines" and ritual is necessary, and there are many differences in popularity and reputation among the various holders of curing powers. Many people claim to hold such power in one form or another, but only a few enjoy wide reputations and are sought from great distances. Female curers exist, but are rarely seen.

In the development of an *owerúame's* career and prestige three major stages may be discerned. The initial stage usually begins in youth for those who feel "called." Because a major part of curing and divining is done in dreams, requisite qualifications are imagination and a propensity for dreaming. Generally, the *owerúame* dreams that a person's souls are in some kind of danger and he rescues them, thereby effecting the cure. A boy who dreams a great deal and is very imaginative is likely to begin to think of himself as having curative powers and will be encouraged in this. Seledonio of Inápuchi began his career at about age 12 when he received a warning from an angel in a vision. It threatened disaster if the people did not dance and sacrifice a white bull and a white chicken.

In addition to a perception of being "called," the neophyte must learn the details of the various rituals. These are fairly simple, and the youth reporting such visionary experiences is often given a subordinate ritual role under the tutelage of an *owerúame*. He may act as leader and flag bearer of the troop of boys who parade through the young corn in the annual field curing ceremony, or he may assist in lightning prevention rituals.

In the second stage of his career the *owerúame* begins to perform some rituals alone, and sometimes receives invitations to cure the

Master shaman

sick at nearby *ranchos*. When his supernatural activities become known in the immediate vicinity, his career development then depends upon opportunity, his sense of drama, manipulative skill, and early successes in those rituals he is called upon to perform. His opportunity comes sooner or later, since not only do the older practitioners eventually die, but often they must make long journeys to distant *ranchos*, and may not be available for emergencies in their own territories. On some occasions a small curing ceremony may not require a great *owerúame*, and this allows the neophyte (*owéame*) a chance to practice his ritual skills.

Seledonio Inápuchi was in the middle stage of evolution as an *owerúame*. When he was visited by a Spirit in his youth he ran to tell his parents of the experience, but they were unable to see what he saw. He has since performed curing ceremonies at a gradually increasing rate and for years has treated sickness with moderate success. Some six years prior to the study the most famous *owerúame* of the region died, and Seledonio began to take the initiative for some of the larger curing fiestas at the *Gentile ranchos*. People gradually began to come from greater distances to request him to cure sickness, and now he occasionally cures at Uarárari and Sumárachi as well as Inápuchi.

However, Seledonio has not yet attained the highest rank, or third stage, as an *owerúame*. He still has little reputation outside of the circle of *Gentile ranchos*, and for large-scale field and child curing ceremonies he himself feels it necessary to bring Tomás of Rabó *rancho* in Samachíque pueblo to take charge, while he plays a subordinate role. He still cannot suck out worms, a skill of powerful full-time *owerúames*, but he occasionally uses a crucifix to suck small stones out of people's arms or legs which have been in their blood, causing pain.

The role of the *owerúame* is exactly the same in both *Pagótome* and *Gentile* areas, and one of them from either area may be called to a *rancho* of the other. This is because curing ceremonies in all Tarahumara communities are basically pre-Christian, even though small crosses and some priest-like gestures are evident in the curers' rituals. In other words, the *Pagótome* have two separate sets of religious functionaries—the aboriginal *owerúames*, who are the same as those of the *Gentiles*, and the Priests and their assistants, along with *matachínes*, *pascolas*, and so forth, who all arrived with the Spanish missionaries.

A final point regarding *owerúames'* prestige is that a man may have ambition to play this important role, but yet grow old without obtaining much success and fame. Such is Manuel of Yehuachíque, who regards himself as an *owerúame*. He wears three large crucifixes under his shirt, is a respected man in the community, and may be called upon in emergencies for curing. However, Manuel is regarded by the majority as possessing very little power, and for a ceremony to be done properly, one of the more famous practitioners should be called. Some old would-be curers turn to sorcery as a means of gaining recognition, as much from frustration as from personal hates. One of these *sukurúames* in Aboreáchi is rumored to have "eaten the souls" of five people.

Reputation as an *owerúame* is one factor which, combined with other qualities, may contribute to any individual's overall prestige, but it alone also may serve as an avenue of status mobility. Because of the indefiniteness of the qualifications, many men claim some *owerúame* powers. Assertion of one's supernatural abilities is thus another of the few ways to achieve higher community status.

Some Examples of Dreams

These dreams and incidents illustrate beliefs about sickness and curing as well as about the souls. They also reveal the Tarahumara preoccupation with environmental dangers and with *tesgüinadas*. Seledonio Inápuchi told me the following:

> I dreamed about the animals. Why do they die? (It was the driest part of the season and several cattle had died.) Because there is no water I saw people from many *ranchos* and they asked me to help them. I went calling the water and a man with a beard told me it will come in one week. It was *Onorúame*.

> I dreamed I was walking down in the *barranca* when I saw Cruz hidden in the water of the river. (Cruz is a 14-year-old boy living in the next household on Inápuchi *rancho*.) I pulled him out and brought him up.

When asked what this meant, Seledonio replied that a major soul of Cruz was lost because of something bad he had done at the *tesgüinada* at Rynárachi the night before. Seledonio had not been there, but he said it must have happened, otherwise Cruz's soul would not have been in danger. Later, I learned that Cruz had tried to run off with the daughter of Polinario during the *tesgüinada*, and Polinario had threatened the boy with sorcery.

When I was visiting the house of Seledonio of Inápuchi, a man arrived from Chuvérachi. It was the rainy season and he had crossed the dangerous swollen river in the gorge below to reach Inápuchi. After some delay, he let it be known that this was his destination. He was seeking the help of Seledonio on behalf of a child who was extremely ill back at Chuvérachi. Seledonio promised to do what he could and the man left. Several days later I asked Seledonio about this and he said he had "gone to see" the boy in a dream, and had cured him by returning his soul from beneath the river. Later I verified that the boy had indeed recovered from his illness. Seledonio also related the following:

> Yesterday afternoon Martín of Roinápuchi came to secure help for his sick wife. She had great pain in her stomach. I went to visit her in my dream last night. She has *masíwari*, a sickness in which certain grains grow inside the stomach. If she does not recover, I will go to Roinápuchi in a month and make some medicine. Meanwhile, I will fight the evil in my dreams. Last

night I was wandering down in the *barranca* in my dream and I heard Martín calling for me, but I did not follow him. If his wife does not get well, I will give her *iyáni*. It is a plant which we completely crush up, from its roots to its leaves. It is then mixed with warm water and drunk by the sick one. It is good for diarrhea too.

In answer to my question as to why he could not show Martín how to make this medicine, he said: "No, that is impossible. It must be given by someone with power. If it is not given by an *owerúame*, nothing will happen." He also told me the following dreams:

I dreamed that hail came down two nights ago, but it passed on one side and did not harm the corn. That is a good sign.

Juan-Tasio came over this morning and said his boy (about 10) is still ill. He fell in the arroyo and was frightened. He was vomiting. I found him there crying yesterday, and I looked at him and took him to his mother. If a child in such condition of fright is not found quickly and treated by an *owerúame*, it will die. Now he will be all right.

Last night I dreamed that a blanket had been stolen from my grain house. I was following the thieves, who were drunk, but I did not catch them. I woke up. This was a warning.

I dreamed that Seledonio Uarárari's son Candelario is ill. His heart was hurting. I have not heard anything from there but I will protect him. Those of Uarárari are probably well now because I dreamed about them. People get very sick and may die if an *owerúame* does not dream about them quickly.

Rodrigo Uarárari (not an *owerúame*) recounted the following, which is a very commonly reported type of dream:

Last night I dreamed about the Ancient Ones (*Anayáwari*), the first people who were here. They looked like us and were drinking *tesgüino* like us. They invited me and talked "very pretty," but I did not go with them. I knew they wanted to take me to the Other World and that I would get sick and die.

Sorcery

Among the Tarahumara sorcerers are called *sukurúame* (he who rasps). In the past a main method of projecting evil magic was by use of a notched rasping stick (Lumholtz, 1902:323). Now it is primarily done by an evil "thought" of a person with power, or through use of some evil "medicine" such as peyote (*híkuli*), which can travel mystically and by "seeing," strike down the enemy. *Híkuli* also may kill if used as a poison in *tesgüino* or food. There seems to be at least two notions involved. Sometimes the sorcerer is believed to eat one or more of the souls of his victim, causing him to become ill or to die, but often he is thought to project objects such as worms, stones, or knives into the victim's body causing pain. For recovery these must be extracted by an *owerúame*.

In addition to their beliefs about peyote, another rather unique feature of Tarahumara sorcery is the notion that certain individuals possess invisible birds which in the night may be directed by their masters to attack the souls of enemies. Seledonio Inápuchi claims that as an *owerúame* he can see these birds and repel them. He said they are usually large and red, but sometimes they may be black. A person reputed to have such a powerful weapon must be handled carefully, even though he may never use it. One man in Yehuachíque is known to have inherited such a bird from his father, but he himself is said never to have used it against anyone. These birds are usually called *rosíwari* in the Aboreáchi-Inápuchi area. However, one man spoke of a blue bird with this power which he called *orimáka*.

Though the sorcerer is generally called *sukurúame*, he or she is also referred to as *cháti* (evil) and mothers often say to their children "*tí rijóy*" when they see a stranger approaching. This means that the man (*rijóy*), is a "*tí*" (from *cháti*). Thus, the association of outsiders with mystical threat is implanted very early in the Tarahumara consciousness.

The following excerpts from my notes will give some indications of the pervasiveness and importance of these sorcery beliefs in the *Gentile* community.

> According to Valencio Pisáchi, Josefa, the wife of the great *owerúame*, Tomás Rabó, is a *cháti* or *sukurúame*. She is very powerful and fierce and has harmed many people. She has had four other husbands and has killed them all by sorcery. (This belief was verified independently by Seledonio Inápuchi and Rodrigo Uarárari). The way she does it is by "thinking bad" of

the person. Her first husband was from Siparíchi. At a *tesgüinada* she got angry at him and hit him. Then she "sent a knife into him" (by her thoughts) in the night. He awoke with an unbearably sharp pain in his abdomen which lasted about two days, until he died. She killed all of her previous husbands this way. Tomás Rabó is not afraid of his wife because he himself is a powerful *owerúame*. She now even assists him in performing ceremonies.

Rodrigo Uarárai remembers that when he still did not drink *tesgüino* (when he was about 13 years old) his grandfather killed the father of Tomás Rabó. He did it by sending a small invisible blue bird (*orimáka*) to devour one of his souls. Tomás' father fell ill and died within two days. Rodrigo then lived with his grandfather and grandmother and he as was afraid of the grandfather. His own father was not *parú* (fierce), but he did not work and could not support Rodrigo, who remembers being constantly hungry as a child.

Rodrigo's first wife was also bewitched by Francisco of Chawichíque and died about three years before. Francisco is a powerful *sukurúame* and he killed the 10-year-old son of Seledonio Uarárari by sorcery only a few months before. People know he did these things because each time he had threatened to do it prior to the event.

Seledonio Uarárari said he stopped running the ball (racing) about two years before, in spite of the fact that he is still younger than many runners. In a big race one of his opponents with the help of a *sukurúame*, made a kind of dust called *chuíki*. They placed it so that it got into his eyes, and since then he has not been able to see the ball to kick it.

Valencio Pisáchi said that there is much *híkuli* (peyote) in Narárachi, but that is rare in this area. He knows that some people in Quírare have it and use it to perform sorcery on people at great distances. The person who has been attacked by peyote gets a terrible headache and sometimes big welts appear on his head. The peyote spirit forms worms inside the person which must be sucked out by an *owerúame*. There is no one in the Inápuchi area powerful enough to do this; you must go to Ramón Chawichíque or Martín Mamórachi. Sometimes people put a tiny piece of peyote into the food or *tesgüino* of a person and this causes him to die within a month.

The motive for using peyote or other forms of sorcery is usually jealousy. People from Quírare have tried to kill Valencio and his family with it but they failed. He knows this because once they were at Pisáchi drinking and they threatened him with it. The next day the whole family was unconscious. Valencio finally sent for his son Ramón, the *owerúame*, who came and cured them by the sucking method. In spite of this he was ill for six months, though the rest of the family recovered more quickly. He said that Seledonio Inápuchi ordered the man from Quírare to do it because he wanted to get Valencio's field. Ramón told Valencio who the culprits were, so he does not go to Inápuchi to drink anymore.

Seledonio Inápuchi spoke of a long standing animosity he had with Francisco Rynárachi, an older and wealthy man who was known as *wé parú*, (very fierce). He had killed two people, his wife and another man. According to Seledonio, it started when at *tesgüinadas* the *olla* would be dedicated to him instead of to Francisco, who was very proud. Francisco was jealous and on three occasions physically attacked Seledonio while drinking. The bad feelings persisted about six years and several times Seledonio had to take counter measures against sorcery. Finally, about a year ago Francisco attacked Seledonio again at a *tesgüinada* and said, "Now I am going to kill you." Seledonio did not go to drink at Rynárachi again, but within one month Francisco had died of a fever. Seledonio said this with some satisfaction.

All informants stated that there are no sorcerers in Inápuchi, but most people claimed to have been attacked by them in the past. Without exception, older men stated that what had stopped their racing careers was malevolent magic practiced by the opposing teams or their backers. Several men claimed to have lost children or wives by sorcery. Informants uniformly stated that only special people could be sorcerers; some are born that way, but unsuccessful curers are the usual candidates. Others can claim harmful magical ability or threaten to practice sorcery on people at *tesgüinadas*, but unless they have some proven power it is regarded as all so much talk, and invokes no fear. The number of those claiming supernatural expertise is disproportionately large, so that the situation is ambiguous. However, if someone who is not regarded to have magical ability makes a threat which is followed by disaster, his reputation can be rapidly made.

While sorcery is considered to be very evil, an offender is never legally prosecuted. Informants claimed that this is because there is no direct proof; since you cannot see the harm actually being done there is nothing you can do. Besides this, most people admit fear of the powers of a person capable of such action and do not want to risk further attacks. An additional force working against prosecution is that the *owerúame* who may be called to diagnose some illness or trouble frequently "sees" that the offender is some distance away, sometimes even outside the pueblo (see case of Valencio, Chapter 7). Accusations rarely are made against someone in the immediate vicinity unless the person is a rival of the *owerúame*, or a person well known to be an enemy of the victim. For these reasons, it is ordinarily impossible to secure any kind of punitive action against the accused.

Curing Rituals

Among the *Gentiles* all major rituals are carried out at the level of the *rancho;* there is no central location which serves as a community center for ceremonial or other group activities. This contrasts strikingly with the *Pagótome,* who gather in their pueblo centers, each of which is oriented around an old church. The *Pagótome* not only hold their political meetings in these community centers, but also have fairly elaborate ceremonial complexes centering around the Spanish introduced fiesta periods of Christmas and Easter. The *Gentiles* having overtly rejected Catholicism, lack the *matachíne* and *pascóla* dancers which are major features of *Pagótome* ceremonials. On the other hand, the *Pagótome* retain the same aboriginal rituals that make up the total *Gentile* ceremonial complex. Actually these aboriginal rites constitute a nearly compartmentalized system which is parallel to the set of colorful Catholic-derived practices which they accepted from the Jesuit missionaries. Of course the *Pagótome* do not see their religious beliefs as being divided into two parallel systems; they view both the ancient and newly introduced practices as one coherent whole.

As stated earlier, the rituals of the *Gentiles* center around the concept of "curing," in a very broad sense. Everything of importance, from crops to animals and people, must be cured annually to prevent harm from befalling it. Beyond this connotation of "preventative maintenance," curing carries the same meaning for the Tarahumara that it does for us. Just as people or animals who are sick must be cured, so must fields which are not yielding properly. This does not mean that practical means or agriculture and health are not also carried out to the extent they are known and believed in. It only means that ritual is an integral part of practical affairs. Just as a man plants seeds and hoes the corn, he also performs the appropriate rituals to protect his crops as part of the cultural repertoire of normal activities.

Curing rituals are usually performed on a specially cleared spot which is found nearby any Tarahumara dwelling. This place is called a dance patio in former studies of this group and *awírachi* by the Tarahumara. It may be round or squared off, and is generally between 15 or 20 feet to 30 or 40 feet across, depending upon the amount of space available. Actually, an *awírachi* is simply a cleared area which is fairly level. The *awírachi* is the place upon which the animal whose flesh is to be served later at the feast is sacrificed. On the *awírachi* ritual dancing is performed and ceremonies initiated. Thus, it is a sacred place during the time it is being used; at other times it is treated like any other part of the living area.

At the eastern edge of this dance patio a ceremonial table or wooden altar is set up. The altars or tables always face westward and vary somewhat in appearance. Usually they are from four to six feet long and about two feet across. Such altars are generally two and one half to three or four feet high, and may be fixed in one place by having their legs set into the ground. Affixed to the east side of the altar are three crosses rising another three feet or so above the table. During ceremonials the crosses are draped with white muslin cloth which is tied about eight inches from the top. Often these figures are decorated with strings of beads. When thus draped and blown by the wind, the crosses give the appearance of human figures. Lumholtz (1902:172-174) claimed that they represented the Father Sun, Mother Moon and the Morning Star, the three major aboriginal deities, but now in Inápuchi these concepts are unknown. My informants said that the crosses are erected because *Onorúame* ordered it that way for his dances.

The altar serves as a table of offerings to *Onorúame*. For all important ceremonies it is stocked with baskets and bowls of *pinole*, tortillas, and tamales, and flavored boiled meat from the sacrificed animal. Everything prepared for the occasion, and which is to be later eaten during the feast (the *tónari*), has to be put here for several hours so that *Onorúame* may partake of the essence or smell of it before it is consumed by the people. Behind the table, on the east side, are placed the several large jars of *tesgüino* which will be drunk.

Underneath the table to one side is placed a broken piece of pottery on which a few peach pits or other bits of refuse are put, and beside this, stuck into the ground, are one or more tiny crosses (from eight inches to one foot high). This apparently worthless offering is for *Diablo* or sometimes it is said, for the fox spirit, to keep him from getting up and interfering with the sacrificial food for *Onorúame*. Some informants said the tiny offering prevents sickness by providing something to satisfy some spirits called *nawirí*.

When the regular *tónari* food is removed from the large altar after the ceremony, a hole is quickly dug, and with a short incantation, this minimal offering is buried. This is enough to keep Diablo and the *nawirí* at bay. Under the sacrificial table are also placed the "medicines" which have been collected for various curing purposes, and which will be taken out and used during this ceremony.

When everything has been arranged for a curing ritual, the most important sacred activity which then must be enacted is the dancing. In the Inápuchi-Aboreáchi the most important sacred dance is called the *yúmari*, a serious form of ritual work performed by the *sawéames*. Later in the ceremony before the feasting begins the tempo becomes quicker, and young men and women participate in a dance called the *tutubúri*.

The *sawéames* are nearly always among the older men in the area, though I have seen a younger man dancing *yúmari* for a small field-curing ritual to which few people came. My informants described the requisites as upright character and lack of "shame" (which means one who is not afraid or ashamed to stand up and orate in the presence of a group).

Yúmari is usually danced for many hours by two or three *sawéames*. They begin by having a ceremonial rattle presented to them by an *owerúame* as they stand on one side of the dance patio. Each is dressed in clean muslin clothing and has a blanket draped over his left shoulder, leaving free the arm with the rattle. One of the *sawéames* makes a short speech and then they start chanting in rhythm with their rattles. After a few moments of this they solemnly cross the patio, their steps in time with the chant. On reaching a position in front of the ceremonial table the *sawéames* face west, humming, and again chant and dance in place for several minutes before again crossing to the other side of this patio. All of my informants claimed that the occasional words interspersed within the monotone humming have no meaning. They were given by *Onorúame* for this dance. The *sawéames* often dance alone for hours through the night, taking only brief rests. Occasionally they may only dance for two or three hours while the feast is being prepared.

In the *Pagótome* communities colorful *matachíne* dancers move to the music of violins and guitars on one side of the dance patio, while the *yúmari* or *tutubúri* dancers move on the other. In the *Gentile* area there are no *matachínes*. The rattle is the only instrument used during the *yúmari* here, though the violin is played for the parade of the young men trooping through the new corn during field curing ceremonies. The *yúmari* is an arduous and serious form of ceremonial labor, and it is believed that the dancers need help from time to time. Thus, all men have an obligation to line up and dance back and forth across the dance patio several times with the *sawéames* at some point during the proceedings.

The other dance, the *tutubúri* is similar in many ways to the *yúmari*, but it is much more animated and involves more people. This is danced for a half hour or so prior to concluding the dancing part of a fiesta. The joyful *tutubúri* is a dance in which the women participate. The men's part in it is much the same as in the *yúmari*. They simply line up beside the *sawéames* and follow them as they cross the dance patio.

The pace of the *tutubúri* is quicker and the mood is one of laughing and joking. For their part in it the women join hands and form a line on the opposite side of the patio from the men. They are generally barefoot and they take short quick hopping steps to the time of the *sawéame's* rattle. Instead of facing the men and dancing toward them, their line moves back and forth in front of them from north to south. Then when the men move to the opposite side of the *awírachi*, the line of women dances around the patio in a counterclockwise direction, so that it again can be in front of the line of men, who are now facing in the opposite direction. In Inápuchi, occasionally three or four women dance the *tutubúri* in a whirling circle in the center of the patio, laughing all the while, as the men look on smiling.

When appropriate chanting and dancing have been done, and everything is in readiness for eating and drinking, the *sawéame* signals a halt to the *tutubúri*. Food is distributed to him first and then to others. Raising his bowl he says "*Matéteravá*" (Thank you). He may then say a few words regarding the purpose of the fiesta (e.g., to drive away sickness, to call rain), before eating and drinking begins. The dancing is still not concluded at this time however, because after eating and drinking, other parts of the ceremony often take place, followed by more dancing and feasting. In many fiestas food is served three times—at midnight, dawn, and noon, or at sundown, midnight, and sunrise. Often the drinking becomes so heavy that only one solitary *sawéame* dances alone for long stretches, occasionally joined by someone to "help" him.

In addition to offering *wirómera* and dancing, another important aspect of Tarahumara curing ceremonies is the use of "medicines" (*owáami*). These are substances which the spirits, and particularly *Onorúame* require. *Tesgüino* is the most important substance used in such a ritual way. All ceremonies are dedicated by tossing small amounts of the beer in each of the four directions, just as each large *olla* of *tesgüino* must be so dedicated before it is drunk. The blood of animals sacrificed for *wirómera* is similarly dedicated.

Cedar smoke is another frequently used ritual element that cleanses animals and men of evil which may have accumulated in

Dancing *Tutubúri*

Tutubúri

their bodies, tending to produce sickness. The smoke of three or four corn cobs whose tips have been briefly exposed to fire is used in protective ritual gestures over people's heads in several ceremonies. By this ritual procedure small white fibers invisible to all but the *owerúame* are severed. These constantly growing fibers, called *remugá*, are believed to cause susceptibility to illness if not ritually trimmed at least once a year. The smoke of the native incense called *molewáka* also is used in many protective ritual acts.

Other "medicines" used in curing rituals are common substances in the environment which boys are sent out to collect before important ceremonial events. Sometimes they must take trips of a day or two down in the *barranca* to assure that all the required materials are present. Many of the "medicines" may be used individually by an *owerúame* in ministering to a sick person, but a whole series of them is collected in bowls for large scale ceremonies.

Among the medicines identified by informants are two varieties of *maguey* water, *chilipiquíns*, ashes, red clay, powdered stone containing a salty mineral, *esquiáte*, the bark of the ash tree, and a number of plants, including *chuchupáte*, which is otherwise used to stupefy fish, and sometimes *bakánoa*, a variety of cactus reputed to possess spirit powers almost equaling those of *híkuli*.

All of these "medicines" were said to work together for the prevention of sickness to people or harm to the crops, although they are not all used in every ceremony. They are all relatively ordinary substances, but several of them have stimulus qualities which create a physical effect, for example, the intoxicating power of *tesgüino*, the burning sensation of the *chilipiquín*, the saltiness of the *goyáka*, the numbing effect of the *chuchupáte*, the hallucinogenic properties of the *bakánoa*, and the redness of the clay. The reasons for the inclusion of ordinary foods such as *meki* and *esquiáte* are not so clear, especially since other common foods like *pinole* or beans are not included.

Curing ceremonies feature a general pattern of symbolic gestures. The principal movements are usually performed by an *owerúame* and then repeated by the others, are the gestures and offerings to the four directions (sometimes, as in *tesgüino* dedication, followed by a gesture upwards to the sky), the counterclockwise circles made by lines of men, and the counterclockwise turnings of the body in patterns of three or four. The other standardized ritual movement is the marking of crosses in the air with smoke, *tesgüino,* or "medicines."

Sympathetic magic is clearly a part of the religious thinking here. For rain-calling ceremonies, several minnows in half gourds of water are set on or near the ceremonial table, and several worms are put there for the rituals petitioning the worms not to eat the corn. Being struck by lightning is a real hazard in the Sierra and the *owerúame* annually defends against it with a dramatic ritual. Lining the people up, he takes long burning sticks of pitch pine to make flaming crosses in the air above the head of each, and then outlines each person with fire. The concept here is that as time unfolds people, as well as all living organisms, such as plants and animals, tend to become enmeshed in invisible webs, which mostly, like the *remugá* threads, are produced by their own bodies. These webs entangle the souls, and by restricting their movements, make the person, or other living thing, much more vulnerable to the many supernatural threats which fill the environment. The ritual gestures cut these encumbering webs, freeing the souls, for a time, to move around in their natural healthy manner.

The following description of part of a large combination curing ceremony at Inápuchi illustrates how some of the ceremonial elements fit together. The maize had already reached a height of about two feet.

> *July 3, 1960.* Venancio and I arrived at Inápuchi about 8:30 A.M. Preparations were being made for the main curing, though the *yúmari* had been going on all night. As we watched the two chanters move back and forth across the clearing in stately rhythm, we were offered a gourd of thick *esquiáte.* I presented two packs of cigarettes to Seledonio who was the donor of *tesgüino* for the fiesta. Many people were standing and sitting in clusters. Several of the medicines were being prepared; *chuchupáte* was being crushed up on a rock by Patricio Inápuchi and put into a bowl, and pieces of hard red earth were being crushed and mixed with water by Dionicio. Six other bowls of "medicine" were sitting beneath the ceremonial table, which was decked with three fully draped crosses and loaded with baskets of thick tortillas,

bowls of boiled meat of the sacrificed goat, and bowls of boiled beans.

The *yúmari* dancers, Seledonio Uarárari and old Julio Rynárachi, occasionally stopped chanting and dancing for periods of five or ten minutes but they always resolutely resumed. Tomás Rabó, who was the *owerúame* in charge for this event, was dressed in a shirt of pink cloth, and a loincloth of white muslin. He had a large silver crucifix hanging around his neck. Tomás came over and inspected the medicines, which were by now all placed beneath the altar. The old *owerúame* then signaled Seledonio Inápuchi to call the ceremony to order, and after some delay the latter was able to round up the eight boys who were to assist in the curing of the fields.

Tesgüino was dedicated and drunk, and the boys stood in a circle in front of the altar while the *owerúame* and Seledonio Inápuchi dedicated the medicines. They raised each bowl in the air in each of four directions and thanked *Onorúame* for protecting the people. Tomás then took the first bowl and dipping his pine brush into the medicine made four crosses in the air over the first boy, before handing the bowl and brush to him. Each of the medicines

Annual Curing Ceremony

was similarly presented and the bowls were then passed down around the circle of young men, who each took a small sip of each substance.

When this preliminary ritual had been completed the medicines were returned to their places, and all the people, including the boys, gathered from the house and fields and formed a large circle around the dance patio. The women arranged themselves along the south side with their children, while the men were around the other three sides. On the east, behind the ceremonial table, stood Seledonio Inápuchi with Tomás Rabó flanked by two other older men. They faced west while the two *yúmari* dancers faced them from the opposite side of the circle about 20 feet away. At this point about 45 people were present. Tomás, the principal *owerúame*, was then handed three corn cobs whose ends were smoking. Beginning on the right he took the three smoking cobs in his right hand and made ritual crossing gestures on three sides of each person, after which he blew on the top of the person's bowed head and made another cross over him with the smoking cobs.

The boys picked up their medicines and followed the *owerúame*. Each individual of the gathering was given a taste of the medicine, and the air around him was brushed with crossing gestures. Even small children were given this treatment. Babies had to be treated by each of the boys dipping a finger into his ritual substance and then into its mouth. This ritual took about an hour.

When every person present had been so cured against possible illness for the coming year, Tomás took a large knife and made a circuit of the offering table. At each of the four directions he cut crosses in the air, severing the "threads of sickness" which had encircled the community in the previous year. Again the boys followed him in his counterclockwise circuit, sprinkling their medicines at each point around the altar.

At this time some of the people began retiring to other areas, as the boys were now readied to make their ceremonial rounds of the fields. Each boy was given from two to four tiny pine crosses about six to eight inches tall, which he stuck into his headband. Seledonio Inápuchi then picked up a white flag of about two feet square, and began leading the troop with their medicines on a circuit of the fields. Juan-Tasio brought up the rear playing

Cutting the thread of sickness

his violin. The old *owerúame* Tomás did not accompany the group nor did the crowd of people.

Each separate field on Inápuchi *rancho* was cured by this procession. The ceremonial task was to place one or two of the small crosses between the rows of corn in the field. Seledonio Inápuchi indicated each place by stopping and waving his flag. He then began the ritual circuit around the small cross by waving his flag three times on each of its four sides, after which the group circled it three times in counterclockwise rotation, sprinkling their medicines in each of the four directions.

The animals and corrals of every household on Inápuchi plateau were also cured. If the corral was empty it was circled three times, while medicines were thrown on each side. Then a bundle of green cedar branches was placed over some pieces of burning pitch pine in the center to create the cleansing smoke. If the corral contained animals, the animals had four crosses painted on them with each medicine, and then they were individually driven into the heavy cedar smoke for a few seconds. The curing of the Inápuchi fields and corrals took only about an hour, as the boys moved quite rapidly in their circuit around the plateau.

During the time that Seledonio was leading the field curing, Tomás Rabó was performing a special curing of several children at the house of Rodrigo. These were the son and daughter of Rodrigo (about eight and eleven), and the two sons of Seledonio Inápuchi, one about five years old and the other only eight months.

The ritual was enacted in the lean-to room at one side of Rodrigo's house. The mothers, with their small ones on their laps, sat with their back against one side of the house. The other children sat beside them. Tomás Rabó sat facing them and was being assisted by his wife, who is also a powerful curer. At one side was a large *olla* of *tesgüino* (with a small wooden cross). Both the curers worked simultaneously, though not in synchrony. They dipped their own silver crucifixes into the *tesgüino* and made three crosses in the air—on the right side, above the head, and then on the left side of the child. This was repeated three times. Then the tip of the crucifix was again dipped in the beer and touched to the child's mouth three times. All of these ritual gestures were accompanied by invocations of *Onorúame*. The curers then removed the crucifixes worn by each child for this occasion and performed the same ritual. Finally, a gourd of *tesgüino* was dipped

Curing the animals

for each of the mothers to drink, and each child also had to take three small sips, which they did with considerable grimacing and complaining. During the time these rituals were being performed inside the lean-to, other children were playing nearby. Some of them clambered on to the lean-to and peered in.

The *sawéames*, meanwhile, had commenced their dance again back at Seledonio's house; they had been dancing the whole time at the field curing and child curing. Three girls joined hands and laughingly began their hopping part of the *tutubúri* in front of the *sawéames*. They danced over towards a group of spectator girls, laughing and joking all the while. The boys who had by now returned for the circuit of field curing also joined this dance and it became very animated. After about 15 minutes, it concluded and all dancing stopped. It was now time to offer *wirómera*.

The people all gathered in a great circle around the patio and Seledonio Inápuchi stood in front of the ceremonial table with Tomás Rabó and Rodrigo Uarárari. He took a bowl of cooked meat, and after raising it first to the father God, dedicated it in each of the four directions. He did this also with a basket of tortillas and a bowl of beans. Two young men then stepped forward and lifted the board which constituted the ceremonial table and placed it with its load of food on the ground in front of these leaders. They began putting meat and beans on each of the tortillas and handing them around to the hungry people. The food was finished in about 20 minutes, and everyone moved to where the *tesgüino ollas* were set up in the house. Rain began to fall. Several fires were lit and the accordions were taken out for the first time. The rest of the afternoon and evening was given over to a typical large *tesgüinada*.

The above description of a curing ceremony indicates the ways in which the belief system and ritual of the *Gentile* Tarahumaras of this area are put into practice. There is no need to detail all of the various rituals here. They are all variations on the theme depicted. However, to assist understanding of Tarahumara religion a few remarks should be made about the way death is handled.

Death Rituals

Fear dominates the rituals of death. Most of the typical ritual elements already mentioned are used, but in a reverse order to that in other ceremonies. The burial ceremony, which is enacted

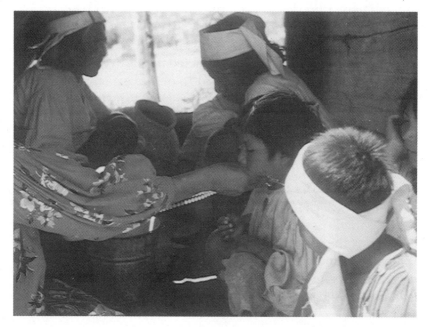

Child curing

Child curing

immediately after death is simple, but the later fiestas placating the spirit and commemorating the dead individual take the same elaborate form as other Tarahumara curing ceremonials.

Most of the ritual actions are enacted in sets of three for a man and four for a woman. This is said to be because the woman is weaker than the man and walks more slowly, just as she did in this life. However, it may be related to the belief expressed by a number of older informants that men have three souls while women have four.

When a person dies he or she is wrapped in their blanket and laid out inside the house, where they must remain until the following day. The hands are tied and folded across the breast with a crucifix or small wooden cross. A small fire is built beside the head of the corpse, and a foot-high cross is hung with a rosary of Job's tears and stuck into the dirt floor nearby. The dead person's important possessions are stacked near the cross. For a man this includes all of his clothing, his knife, his axe, his violin or guitar, his rattle if he was a *sawéame*, and so forth. A symbolic offering of food in a bowl or pouch is placed there too. This consists of three grains of maize for a man or four grains for a woman, three or four beans, some *pinole*, and perhaps three or four units of whatever other food is around. A bowl of *esquiáte* is also placed near the cross.

Members of the immediate family of the deceased sleep or remain outside, coming in only to maintain the fire during the night. They are genuinely frightened and when they enter they implore the spirit to leave the living in peace.

In the morning the family and any immediate neighbors on the *rancho* quickly gather in the house. No one else is summoned, and, according to informants, there have been times when even people living on adjacent ranchos did not discover that a death had occurred for several days. If no *owerúame* is present, the oldest men in the group makes a series of crossing gestures around the deceased with smoking incense. Each member of the family then kneels down and in a very subdued tone speaks to the spirit. He or she is asked not to molest the living and to accept being taken to the other world. He is promised food and *tesgüino* and the proper number of death fiestas. Finally, the spirit is implored to leave its possessions for the living without jealousy and is requested not to harm the fields or other people if and when it returns in animal form. (See Slaney, 1991, Chapters 4-5 for illuminating discussions of *najítame*, the return of the dead as animals, as well as many aspects of death beliefs and rituals.)

A violin is played three or four times, while the body, wrapped in its blanket, is being lashed in several places to a pole for bearing to the grave. Then, *esquíate* from the bowl near the cross is sprinkled on the corpse. In Inápuchi two men then carry the deceased to a burial cave in the barranca, usually one which already holds a number of skeletons. The pallbearers are accompanied only by a man carrying food and one carrying the rosary. Near the cave entrance, a fire is kindled at the head and feet while the food and rosary are placed at the head. Meanwhile, the stones which block the burial cave's entrance are loosened.

After being untied, the body is pushed inside and lying on its back is oriented with the head to the east. The food and rosary are put in beside it and the entrance is quickly walled up again with stones and mud. These burial caves are believed to be inhabited occasionally by spirits of the dead returning on some special occasions. Rodrigo Uarárari resolved some of the apparent contradictions which this belief has with ideas that the souls almost immediately launch off on a journey to other worlds, by saying that one of the man's souls (the oldest one) goes up to the sky with *Onorúame*, while one goes down below the river because it is bad, and one stays where the person is buried. He did not specify where the fourth soul of a woman goes after death. I do not know if these ideas are shared by others, or are idiosyncratic explanations. Rodrigo also claimed that he had heard the souls of the dead making a lot of noise in the burial caves when he passed by them. However, he said they are not dangerous unless used by a *sukurúame*, since they are all relatives.

When they return from the interment the four pallbearers are met by two men, each with a bowl of "medicine" made of *mezcal* and ashes mixed with water. These two curers, usually *owerúames*, make a clockwise circuit around them sprinkling the mixture in each of the four directions. Then each man in turn is handed the bowl from which he drinks a sip before he takes out a piece of the *mezcal* and makes a cross upon his forehead. The two curers then again take the medicines and make a clockwise circuit around the house and corral, sprinkling the substances as they go. The fire in the house, which has been kept burning is now smothered with cedar boughs, creating a purifying cloud of smoke. Everyone concerned saturates himself in this; the dead man's possessions are also passed through it, so that they may be used by the living. Some *pinole* and chili mixed with water are eaten in small amounts to protect the living from the sickness and death radiated by the ghost. The six men who perform these parts of the death ceremonies must not work until after the conclusion of the first death fiesta three days later.

Onorúame prescribed that three fiestas be given to commemorate the death of a man, and four to commemorate the death of a woman. The first death fiesta should be three (or four) days after the burial, followed by one three (or four) weeks later, and a final one three (or four) months after that; for women the fourth fiesta should come another four months later, in the eighth month. These schedules are not always adhered to. Some people do not make all the fiestas, and sometimes they are made at convenience rather than according to the ritual numbers, probably because of the expenses involved for sacrifices and *tesgüino*. It is said that for the last of the fiestas a cow must be sacrificed. In Inápuchi, due to lack of sacrificial animals, this often entails long delays. Thus, Rodrigo Uarárari reported that only a few months prior to being interviewed he had made one of these for a son who died more than three years earlier.

Regardless of what may happen later, the first death fiesta is given on the third (or fourth) day. Even though the amount of *tesgüino* available on short notice may be very small, the first fiesta is always given. This ritual very much follows the pattern already described for fiestas, though it is generally small in scale and focusses on the possessions of the deceased, which are placed on the dance patio near the sacrificial tables. Another difference from the normal fiesta is that a small fire of pitch pine is made near the small cross beneath the end of the table, where the belongings of the deceased are piled. This is an extra precaution to keep *Diablo* from interfering with the newly disembodied souls.

Informants said that a goat and a chicken must be killed for each death fiesta, and six *ollas* of *tesgüino* should be made for the later ones. Those who have been in joking relationships with the deceased are responsible for putting on these fiestas. These people are the siblings-in-law (*upíra* and *kunára*) and the grandparents (see Chapter 6). These categories of relatives have equal responsibility for collecting the maize for beer and for finding the sacrificial animals, but the siblings-in-law are more responsible for organizing the proceedings. The in-law joking partners place little bowls of beans and of meat and small bundles of tortillas in the rafters of the house of the deceased. The ghost eats these when he returns for his death fiestas. The "joking relatives" must dance and play violin music, and they are responsible for handling the possessions of the dead person. The immediate family is relieved of all obligations for these ceremonies because of the particular danger to them from the ghost.

The first death fiesta begins in the morning with its sacrifices of a goat and a chicken, and the sprinkling of their blood in the four directions. As in other ceremonies, the *yúmari* is danced until the afternoon, and the dancing is concluded with women joining to dance the *tutubúri*. *Tesgüino* is dedicated as always, but on the occasion of death it must be dedicated with the left hand. Food is served three times. Near noon, one of the man's "joking relatives" takes the small amount of food offered at the small cross, and after making three circuits around the dance patio goes to the burial cave, where he deposits it. When he returns he is cleansed with the medicine of ashes and *mezcal*. The remainder of the medicine is then sprinkled on the fields in the course of a clockwise circuit around them (the opposite of the usual counterclockwise circuits of regular fiestas).

One of the most interesting features of this, as of the later ceremonies for the spirit of the dead, is the dancing performed by the "joking relatives." In another instance of reversal, they dress in the clothing of the opposite sex and dance up to his belongings, kicking at them and making obscene jokes and remarks. They ask him if he wants a cigarette, a drink of *tesgüino* or something similar. After some minutes of this, they stop and offer the food to the guests. If the deceased has been a runner, a ceremonial race of only a few hundred yards is run. No betting is involved. If the deceased was a female runner, men dress as women for the ritual race and use the throwing stick and ring which are used in women's races. To end the death fiesta, the male and female joking relatives carry on a mock combat with machetes or knives. The clashing of the blades is said to discourage the ghost from returning.

Many of the customs having to do with ghosts and spirits, as with *Onorúame* himself, concern foods and materials used in day-to-day Tarahumara life. Even the age-old household implement the *metate*, reveals its supernatural character in certain situations. For example, if an individual is lingering near death for several days in a coma, it is believed that the *metate* of the house is keeping his body alive after his souls have departed. The *metate* must be turned over so that the body may be relieved of agony; dying then can be completed in peace.

Differences Between Gentile and Pagótome Religion

This description of *Gentile* Tarahumara ritual and belief should not conclude without being at least briefly contrasted with the set of Spanish-introduced ceremonial practices which constitute such a large component of the religious system for most of the Tarahumara. The Christianized Indians maintain the total set of customs and practices I have just depicted, but additionally, separate and parallel to them, they enact many rituals which are carryovers of seventeenth and eighteenth century Catholicism. An interesting feature of religion in the *Pagótome* communities is the degree to which the aboriginal set of customs, centering on the *owerúame*, has been kept compartmentalized from the Catholic set, despite almost three hundred years of acceptance of the latter.

The main cycles of these ceremonies are those of the Christmas season, which feature the dancing of the *matachínes*, and those of the Easter season, which feature the dancing of *pascólas* and the mock battles of sodalities called *fariséos* and *móros* (or *júdas, soldados,* etc.). The *Pagótome* ceremonials are oriented around Jesuit churches built in their pueblo centers. These ceremonial complexes have given rise to a whole set of roles which is lacking in the *Gentile* communities. For example, there are *maestros* who chant Tarahumara versions of the mass in the absence of regular priests and perform other ritual functions in the church. All large community ceremonies of the *Pagótome* are overseen by officials called *tenánches* in Aboreachi (or *fiestéros* in Samachíque), who for one year are responsible for providing sacrificial cattle.

The dancing of the *matachínes* is a feature of most ceremonials in these communities. These *Pagótome* dancing groups usually consist of a leader called the *monarco* who, carrying a *palma* and rattle, leads five or nine dancers through a stately dance in the churchyard and then inside the church. At one side of the dancing *matachínes* are "shouters," called *chapeónes* (or *chapeyókos*) who shout encouragement from time to time and sometimes don a wooden mask. The music for the *matachínes* is provided by a group of violinists at one side.

The *matachínes*, who wear bright costumes of colored cloth decorated with red bandannas, crowns made of mirrors, colored cardboard and cloth, along with Mexican manufactured shoes, have increased in popularity throughout the Tarahumara region. Judging by the little attention he gave them, they were apparently of little importance in Lumholtz's time, but now they are regarded as indispensable not only for the ceremonies of Guadalupe on December 12, Christmas, Pascua de Reyes (January 6) and Candelaria (February 2), but on Mexican Independence Day (September 17), and for *Pagótome* funerals as well.

The other important set of Spanish-introduced ritual roles are those of the Easter cycle. For several weeks before Holy Week until after Easter reed flutes are heard accompanying the pounding of large flat decorated drums. The men of most Tarahumara pueblos are divided into two groups who decorate themselves in distinct ways, and perform processions and rituals in competition with each other. Throughout the region one of the groups is always called *fariséos*, while the opposing one is variously named *moros*, *judas*, *soldados*, or *mulatos*.

Generally, the *fariséos* paint their faces with white clay and stripe their legs with the same substance. Those not carrying drums carry wooden lances or swords painted with red designs. They also have charge of one or two dummies (*judas*) constructed of grass, or in some pueblos, of wood. These are ceremoniously burned or destroyed at the end of Easter festivities. The group opposing the *fariséos* usually features headdresses of turkey plumes and the boys paint themselves with white clay to distinguish

Matachines Samachíque

Matachines Samachíque

themselves from their opponents. Instead of carrying grass dummies, these *moros* or *soldados* have other ritual duties, such as maintaining a vigil in the church for several nights, where, two by two, they guard a simulated body of Christ. Each group often has one *pascola* dancer who is painted and wears a rattling belt of deer hooves and ankle rattles.

Easter week for the *Pagótome* is a colorful and noisy time, dominated by loud drumming, clowning antics, competitive dancing, processions through special arches set up around the church to depict the stations of the cross, and various ceremonies within the church. The week is climaxed by the destruction of the judas figures and a series of *tesgüinadas* that last for several days. (See Bennett and Zingg, 1934; Kennedy and López, 1978; Merrill, 1978; and Kennedy, 1990 for full descriptions of these rituals.)

These Catholic-derived rituals of the *Pagótome* provide for them another dimension of drama, ritualism, a unifying communal activity, and a set of roles which the *Gentiles* lack. As mentioned, the *Pagótome* retain the same set of curing ceremonies, overseen by *owerúames*, which is the total ceremonial pattern of the *Gentiles*. However, overlaying it, creating another level of organization, and occupying many more days a year, much more expense, and so forth, is the set of European-derived ritual complexes sketched above. The *Gentiles* maintain their long-standing rejection of the more colorful pageantry and ritual of their *Pagótome* brothers, but no hostility is evident. Their attitude is rather one of positive value for their own ways, a self-sufficient indifference toward unnecessary novelties.

Religion is a domain of Tarahumara culture in which the influence of ecological factors is not as pronounced as in some other domains. Environment, for example, has little to do with creating such important differences as those between the rituals of *Pagótome* and *Gentiles*. Nevertheless, the postulation of some connections seems reasonable. The fear component of the Tarahumara religious system is outstanding. Much of it seems related to the uncertainties imposed upon life by their precarious adaptation to an unpredictable economic situation. The isolation from other people is certainly a component in the distrust of others revealed in the beliefs, accusations, and aggressive acts relating to sorcery. The fears of the dead appear related to the absence of fixed and permanent social ties. I do not want to overemphasize these things because many of the same kinds of beliefs and practices are found in societies with different environmental circumstances and different associated social structural features. Taken together, however, the pronounced and unrelieved fear aspects of Tarahumara religion certainly seem consistent with the ecological conditions.

There are attributes of flexibility in the religious practices of the Tarahumara, however, which are definitely tied to their kind of environmental adaptation. For example, the mode of attaining the role of *owerúame* through self-initiative is a part of the individualism created by the lack of formal institutions. This as well as the flexible timing and the variability of the place of ceremonies, is a direct function of the scattered settlement pattern, with its qualities of social fissiveness. This, in turn, has fostered the network type of social system.

CHAPTER 6

KINSHIP BEHAVIOR & FAMILY LIFE

In most non-literate societies the kinship system defines the social order. Among the Tarahumara kinship terms are elaborate and are fairly important in structuring domestic roles. However, in comparison with most other societies at this economic level, the importance of kinship in organizing social relations outside of the immediate family is very limited. How then, and to what degree are social interactions structured in this society, and what is the character of daily domestic life? Before I discuss the Tarahumara family in more detail, I will describe the process through which the infant child is given his place in the family and community—the bestowal of names.

As briefly discussed at the beginning of the last chapter, an infant of the *Gentiles* of *Inápuchi* is given a name in a ceremony in which a shaman ritually protects it with gestures of fire and cedar smoke, a "baptism by fire." The individual from then on is known by that name plus the name of his or her home *rancho*, e.g., Rijónsi *Inápuchi*. On the other hand, people in the Christian pueblos have two given names, a water name bestowed by the priest at baptism, and a fire name given soon after birth by a shaman or the parents. The fire name is given in a ritual in which the baby is passed through cedar smoke in a series of symbolic gestures. The baptismal or water name identifies the individual as a member of the Mexican Catholic world, while the fire name establishes his membership in the fundamentally Tarahumara community. My capable guide and assistant was baptized Venancio, but he was just as often called by his fire name—Petronilo. This led to some confusion on my part until I recognized that both of the names referred to the same person. The *Pagótome* of this area often change their water names. In Aboreáchi, for example, a man may decide to change his water name any time he feels like it. "It sounds better," as one informant from there explained his recent adoption of a new last name. The *Gentiles* are not faced with this initial ambiguity, and this may partly account for the more secure sense of selfhood that they present. A rigorous study of the two groups testing this hypothesis would be useful. (See Levi, 1993:1-3 for an interesting account of receiving a fire name as an initiation into another *Gentile* community.)

Kin Terminology

This system of terminology used by the Tarahumara is what is technically known as "bilateral." As in our own system, kin are reckoned through both parents, both grandparents on each side, and so on. The particular form of bilateral reckoning found here is the type which Murdock has classified as Neo-Hawaiian by criteria of female cousin terminology; female cousins on both sides are classified with sisters (1949:229). A marked characteristic of the Tarahumara system is a tendency to classify relatives by generation according to sex. The most numerous distinctions occur within ego's generation, where people are differentiated by relative age and often by sex of speaker. For example, a male calls his younger sister *wayé* and his older sister *kochí*. A female calls her younger sister *biní* and her older sister *kochí*. Distinction by sex of speaker is characteristic also of father-child relationships.

The relative lack of social importance of kinship in Tarahumara life, particularly outside the immediate family, is shown by the custom of using first names instead of kinship categories in most situations. That is, instead of addressing one's male parent as "father" the first name is used, etc. The kinship term is ordinarily only used when it is necessary to clarify the situation, or in special contexts such as joking relationships.

Kinship Behavior

The situations in which kinship exercises an influence upon social activities conveniently fall into two major types. The first of these comprises the day-to-day behavior toward kinsmen of the residence and *rancho* groups. It is marked by general attitudes of respect, affection, and responsibility. The second kind of kinship behavior is expressed almost exclusively at *tesgüinadas* and fiestas. It is an activity of the kind called "joking relationships" in the anthropological literature.

Day-to-Day Behavior among Kinsmen

Among the Tarahumara there is a tendency for some kinsmen, in addition to members of the nuclear family, to live near one another. Not only does a person generally live at least part of his life in the context of an augmented family, but usually some of his relatives live at the same *rancho*. Others reside at nearby *ranchos*.

Behavior toward kin outside of the elementary family generally follows the model of behavior within the elementary family. This is reflected in kinship terminology by the classification of all those within a generation with a few terms. For example, a number of men (father's brothers and mother's brothers) are called *father*, and a number of women (mother's sisters and father's sisters) are called *mother*. However, the extension of similar behavior to the others called by the same term is much weaker with regard to these "classificatory" relatives, unless they have spent long periods in direct day-to-day living contact with them.

Parent-Child Relationships

Up to the age of two and a half or three years, children spend a great deal of time in close body contact with their mothers. The baby is carried in a piece of muslin cloth which the mother slings on her back, or carries in front or on one side. This allows her to do daily chores without setting it down. It is usually given the breast on demand or if upset in any way. As the baby grows past a year of age it is left on the ground more often, wrapped in layers of cloth, so that the mother can easily work at the *metate* or the weaving loom.

Despite the care and the amount of time which the baby spends against the comforting body of its mother, the harsh demands of Tarahumara life and the nature of the frequent *tesgüinadas* profoundly influence its early years. The child's older siblings are pressed into child-care roles at very early ages, and a frequent sight throughout the Tarahumara region is the child of

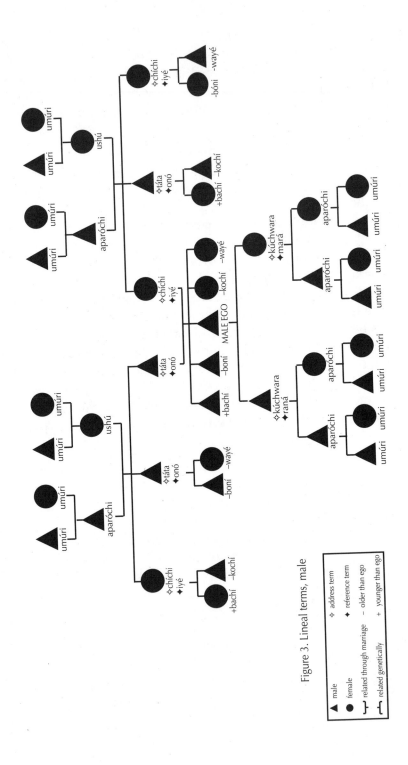

Figure 3. Lineal terms, male

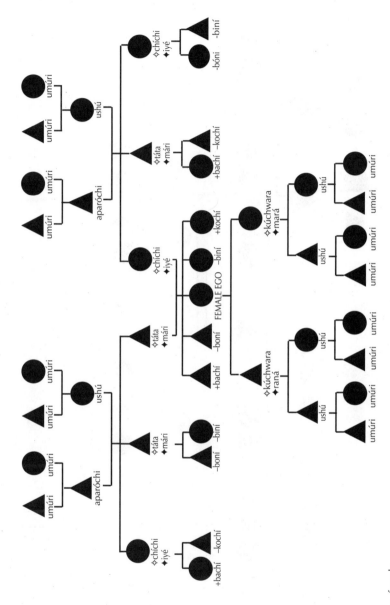

Figure 4. Lineal terms, female

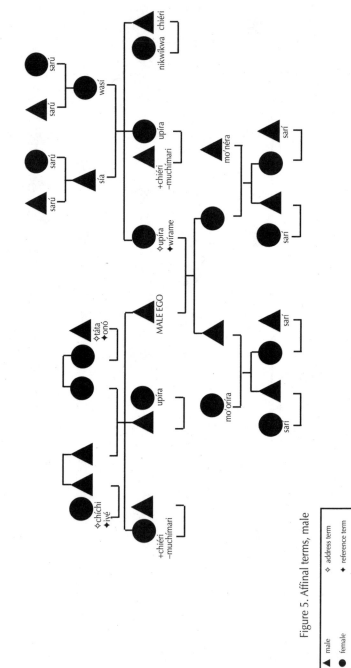

Figure 5. Affinal terms, male

male   ◇ address term

● female   ✦ reference term

} related through marriage   − older than ego

{ related genetically   + younger than ego

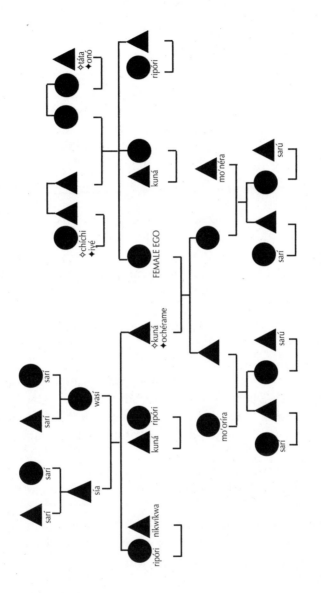

Figure 6. Affinal terms, female

seven or eight bending forward to balance a large infant on their back. Often the child is performing an important chore, such as herding goats. On some occasions too, an infant may be left unattended for some minutes while the parents or an older child performs some urgent task. On rare occasions I have observed babies lying on the ground in a pool of urine and under a swarm of flies for five or ten minutes before being rescued. Weaning is usually done by a gradual introduction of the ordinary Tarahumara semi-liquid foods, such as *pinole, esquiáte* and *atole*. If another baby arrives during the first year, weaning may be accelerated by application of some chili pepper to the nipple, but this is avoided if possible.

While parents are at *tesgüinadas* they do not like to leave small infants under the care of other children because they need to be breastfed during the long drinking bout. However, these parties are very hazardous. During the past several years three cases of inebriated mothers fatally rolling over on children were reported to me. There was also the case of a four-year-old boy who was fatally burned when he got too close to a fire which ignited his clothes. There are many dangers to small children in the beautiful mountainous environment of the Tarahumara. Many children are hurt or killed by falling from the steep trails, or from being bitten by rattlesnakes. The high infant mortality rate is partially a result of such accidents, but it is even more a result of measles, smallpox, and tuberculosis, along with malnutrition and even starvation in some years.

The Tarahumara are extremely affectionate and careful with infants during the early years, yet the demands of life often defeat their efforts to give adequate care. The baby is given a comparatively great amount of love and body contact, but this is interspersed with short periods of unavoidable neglect, occurring in the context of real and fearsome threats.

At the ages of three and four a child may spend long periods of time with other siblings or alone, if he has no brothers or sisters. At five and six children of both sexes may tend goats nearby the house, or they may accompany a parent, uncle, or older sibling.

While the father is responsible for disciplining his son, Tarahumara customs call for mildness and reasoning as methods

Father grooming son

of child rearing. I previously mentioned the belief that if a parent strikes a child, it may become "frightened" and perhaps die. Childhood mortality (which according to my genealogies runs more than 50%), and general sicknesses are prevalent enough to make most people watch anxiously for illness and accidents.

Gentleness and affection are manifested toward children by most adults, especially by their relatives. Toilet training is permissive. The baby is simply taken outside the living area if he is caught quickly enough. By the age of two or three most children have learned permitted and unpermitted locations of excretion through positive reinforcement and verbal explanation.

For disobedience or transgression of rules and commands the punishment is normally a lecture by the parent which follows the sermon-giving pattern typical of adult social control methods. If an offense is serious or repeated, the parents may request the *siríame* or an older man from another *rancho* to call the child aside to lecture him. Rarely is a child physically struck, though a few "very fierce" men have reputations for beating their wives and children. When this occurs, the individual is likely to be under the influence of alcohol, and community response is usually consistent with the attitudes of individual independence. That is, the victims have little recourse beyond escape and avoidance. However, such behavior is rare in the area studied.

From ages seven or eight, children may run away from home and stay with a relative at another *rancho* if they are beaten or if they become disgruntled with their parents. This expedient depends, of course, on the availability of such a refuge, but such escapes are not uncommon. The general acceptance of this sort of behavior by both the parents and the relatives is another indication of the value placed upon individual choice and independence in this culture; it extends even to young children. In areas where there are boarding schools, Tarahumara children, if reprimanded, often simply leave the school and return home.

Boys and girls are taught the cultural essentials mainly by the parent of their sex. The boy's father is his principal teacher, and at an early age the youngster begins to help with various economically important tasks. Here also the Tarahumara approach is gradual and permissive. Children are considered rational beings, capable of, and responsible for, making most of the decisions they will face in life. Since a boy does not take on the simultaneous responsibilities and privileges of cooperative work and *tesgüino* drinking until about the age of 14 there is little social pressure to perform tasks other than goat herding before that time.

However, in the spirit of play and motivated by what seems to be a natural desire to be like adults, the young boy usually begins early to emulate his father in planting, cutting fodder, hoeing, carving *canoas*, and performing similar tasks. There is no thought of coercion. The boy is progressively rewarded with the privilege of more mature tasks, so that by the age of *tesgüino* drinking he has achieved pride in his ability to perform the inventory of Tarahumara adult tasks.

During this period children of both sexes are permitted a high degree of freedom and independence. This is necessitated by the great amounts of time they spend in the mountains and forests alone or with only one or two siblings. There is a definite survival value in early learning of self reliance and in the ability to plan and make decisions. In a previous chapter I mentioned how from age five children wander great distances alone. From the ages of seven and eight until they form their own households (roughly between ages 14 and 20) they spend more and more time out with the goats. During these years children are generally excluded from the house at night. They are frequently responsible for the care of the family's animals and often they sleep near the corrals in small lean-tos. In this long period of relative freedom, a boy has ample time to watch his mother or grandmother weave sashes or blankets and to learn other ordinarily female tasks. Later when the need may arise, he too can perform them adequately.

While the Tarahumara pattern seems idyllic in some respects, some boys do not learn well under such circumstances of permissiveness, and so do not choose to learn adult skills until very late. One of these was Cruz of Inápuchi *rancho*, a boy of about fourteen who had only learned to plow the year before our study. Several men mentioned this personal choice as accounting for his slowness at this task. His recalcitrance to learn this important role in Tarahumara economics was cause for laughter rather than indignation by the people. It was even more amusing to them that

Cruz was thinking of marriage and, under this stimulus was rapidly learning how to plant. They joked about his trying to keep pace with the older men.

A similar example is Manuel Inápuchi, a youth of about fourteen years of age, who after a recent *tesgüinada* began to cohabit with a woman about six years his senior from Rynárachi. He was sent back to Inápuchi in a few months by his new father-in-law, who was disgruntled because he did not know how to work adequately. The attitude of fathers toward sons is one of *laissez-faire*. Indulgence, affection, freedom, and learning by imitation with reward are the characteristics of Tarahumara teaching, rather than techniques of punishment.

Girls have less freedom than boys, especially as they approach puberty. They spend more time in the vicinity of their mothers, learning their roles through imitation and careful repetitive teaching. Unlike the boys I spoke of, they always learn their adult roles early and well. Small girls of five or six are often seen removing the kernels from dried cobs or caring for goats. They also spend more time than boys in child care tasks. In two families where the mother had died, girls of eight and ten were performing all the female work for household groups of four and six members. In one family this included most of the care of a two-year-old sister. These girls did such tasks as grinding on the *metate*, washing clothing in the stream, herding, cooking, and collecting greens. They did this for periods of one and two years respectively, before their fathers were able to find permanent mates again. Girls ideally are married for the first time shortly after puberty to boys three or four years older than themselves, but they do not usually begin to drink *tesgüino* regularly until a year or two later.

After attaining adulthood a Tarahumara tends to treat his parents as equals with continuing affection and responsibility for them as they grow older. Age carries some right to deference, a fact evidenced by the age distinctions carried in the sibling-cousin kinship terminology, but this value is more often negated by considerations of prestige, personality traits, economic factors, and the general equalitarian value. In the context of the *tesgüinada* age deference is waived in the *aparóchi* (grandfather) relationship, but affection and respect are day-to-day reciprocal obligations of members of alternate generations.

Learning to spin from grandmother

Most sons continue to consult their fathers on matters of importance as long as they live, but fathers also consult their adult sons. This relationship is regarded as one of mutual help and trust, and behavior generally follows this expectation. For example, in their terms, sons often "order" their fathers to make journeys for various purposes, or "order" their parents to make *tesgüino* for them. A man may "order" his mother to make a blanket, or a father may "order" his son to participate in a race, to act as a messenger, or perform some task. However, "ordering" here refers to a reciprocal or democratic type of obligation between the two generations, with little implication of authority. In cases where a man lives near or with his wife's relatives, the same kind of relationship generally holds between him and his in-laws.

Father-daughter and mother-son relations in adulthood are marked by affection and respect, with the younger generation having obligations to care for the older when they can no longer care for themselves. There is no concept of retirement from productive work in this society. The aged work until death or until they are physically unable.

As mentioned before, the behavior pattern between children and their parents' brothers and sisters resembles that of parent-child relationships, but on a more limited scale. Prolonged contact with most of the people falling into these categories often is minimal. There were no special privileges or patterns of behavior observed or reported by informants for these relationships, and people uniformly denied that any special behavior was required. It sometimes happens that children are brought into contact with one of the mother's or father's brothers or sisters in the course of the types of residence cycles which are presently to be described, yet no consistent cultural pattern with respect to either the father's or the mother's side could be discerned.

The first ascending generation kin terminology faithfully represents the social situation engendered by bilocal residence after marriage, in that both sides of the first ascending generation are generally classified equally as "mothers" and "fathers." This residence pattern tends to give persons a random chance of associating with aunts or uncles of either the father's or mother's side. When such an association is prolonged for any length of time, the qualities of a parent-child relationship are maintained. Reflecting the less intense nature of uncle-nephew relations is the fact that uncles and aunts uniformly refer to nephews and nieces with the more general term *kúchwara* (child) rather than with the more specific son and daughter terms (*nó, marára*, etc.).

For brothers and sisters the relative age distinctions present in the kinship terminology reflect a degree of sociological reality, but one which probably was of much greater significance in the past than at present. In large families, older brothers and older sisters are theoretically looked up to and sought for advice; they share an important part of the child rearing role with the parents.

Probably due to long association in childhood, sibling bonds are the strongest set of family ties among these Tarahumara, especially those between siblings of the same sex. I spoke earlier of how children care for fields, or for goats, and how they sleep together by the corrals. Boys of a family also frequently "run the ball" together, or play *cuatro* (a throwing game with stones, similar in concept to horseshoes). Many times sets of brothers compete as teams in these games. Sibling solidarity built up in such cooperative ways persists through life.

Brothers often take up residence together. There were seven cases of joint residence of brothers in a sample of 46 residences from the area studied (both *Pagótame* and *Gentile*). Siblings also generally stick together in disputes, whether residing together or not. Sisters and brothers try to help each other in general: make sure their siblings get their share of *tesgüino* at *tesgüinadas*. They also look after each other's personal property when they are drunk.

The Tarahumara have a culturally prescribed obligation to share food with neighbors or relatives in need, but the obligation to share other goods refers to family members only, and especially to siblings. Consequently, when a man gets a new bolt of cloth, or acquires some piece of equipment such as a knife or a sash, his enjoyment of his new possession may be short lived if his brothers find out about it. He is not supposed to complain if they open his storehouse and remove something, or borrow one of his animals which they find wandering around the hills grazing. I have seen this kind of behavior lead to a good deal of smoldering resentment and repressed hostility which, however, was never allowed to culminate in aggressive actions, even at *tesgüinadas*.

Ambivalent and hostile feelings are also often aroused when, due to the *tesgüino* pattern, one's brothers may have had sexual intercourse with one's wife before marriage. Furthermore, after marriage, the brothers are privileged to enter into a joking play relationship with her which has a strong sexual component, and which occasionally does culminate in intercourse. But in spite of this ambivalent quality, I found no instances of serious violence between brothers. Resentment of such behavior was sometimes expressed privately, however.

Cousins are called by sibling terms and behavior with them is patterned upon sibling norms as outlined above, with the qualification that it is weaker. At this genealogical distance, the sibling-like ties are often not enough to prevent open conflict. Sharing and cooperative behavior are much less common between cousins than between siblings perhaps because cousins tend to live too distant from one another to associate on an everyday basis.

Husband-Wife Relationships

The ideal Tarahumara wife is one who "knows how to work well." This implies a willingness to perform her duties as well as

Family

the knowledge of performance. She is not "fierce" and not promiscuous at *tesgüinadas*, especially with Mestizos. Besides these qualities of character, physical attractiveness is important, with youth, plumpness, and regular features as the most desired qualities. Concepts of beauty often play an important part in mate selection because, with regard to the other criteria, most women are equal. They are familiar with feminine tasks and are imbued with the value of industriousness from childhood onward. Since women often initiate courtship, the possibility of voluntarily choosing a mate at *tesgüinadas* increases the importance of physical attractiveness. On the other side, adequacy in male tasks, youth, physical vigor, wealth, slimness of body build, and lack of pugnaciousness are the attributes most admired by women.

The relationship between marital partners is one of relative equality. Each has individual property rights and either may initiate sexual behavior. The knowledge that one's spouse may leave at any time reflects and helps maintain this equality; it also contributes to the high amount of ambivalence and jealousy characteristic of both sexes. Though public physical contact is not prevalent except at *tesgüinadas* (where it most often takes place between members of the same sex), a good deal of affection may be observed between spouses. On visiting a *rancho* in the morning, it is not uncommon to see a man and woman lying affectionately side by side in the sun beside their house before it is time to begin the daily tasks. Often a woman is seen combing her husband's hair with a pine cone, or picking lice from his scalp. However, the overt jealousy and possessiveness often exhibited at *tesgüinadas* indicates both the anxiety surrounding the tenuous marital bond and the ambivalence about it engendered by the permissive drinking norms.

In daily life, tolerance, respect, and affection seem to be the most often expressed qualities of marriage relationships, and hostile emotions are usually repressed until released by the atmosphere of the *tesgüinada*. It is under these specially defined conditions that such events occur as the cases of husbands beating and occasionally even murdering their wives. However, on those fairly rare occasions when sorcery is attributed to people close by, it is frequently a husband accusing his wife or vice versa. Thus, Valencio Pisáchi disclosed to us that his enemy, Seledonio, probably had given peyote to one of the latter's former wives who had died, and I previously described the older woman from Rabó who is reputed to have laid to rest two former husbands by her powers of sorcery.

Evidence for the quality and fragility of the marital relationship is also found in the extension of the sermon-giving pattern as a major method of settling marital disputes. The *siríame,* or other respected man, is frequently called upon to speak to an erring wife. Less often he is petitioned by a woman to counsel a husband. This indicates that though women have many rights in this society, they are subordinate in this sphere. Occasionally in cases of marital discord, recourse to an official trial before community officials is resorted to. Here the grievance can be aired, the "sermon" is more public and binding and a fine may even be imposed. Such legal recourse is much more typical of *Pagótome* communities than it is of the *Gentiles*.

The legal concept of divorce does not exist but *de facto* divorce is fairly common. A person of either sex may become so dissatisfied with their spouse's behavior that he or she either neglects expected tasks until the other becomes disgruntled and leaves, or runs off with another partner at a *tesgüinada*. The marital situation in these Tarahumara communities is a tenuous one, but if the union survives its trial period and persists through the vicissitudes of raising a family, it is often marked by confidence, respect, and familiarity. These sentiments are connoted by the terms *rijimára* (affectionate companion), *wírame* (old lady) and *ochérame* (old man), rather than the sexually charged *upíra-kunára* terms of youth and the joking relationships.

The Joking Relationships

The strongly institutionalized joking relationships which exist among the Tarahumara are of special interest because of their important role in social behavior. Though such relationships are found in many societies of the world, there seems to be nothing comparable to them in northern Mexico, and perhaps in all of Middle America (see Kennedy 1970, for fuller discussion and theoretical analysis).

The joking relationships of a male are with the following two sets of relatives: his male and female in-laws of the same generation, regardless of the type of connection, and all female grandparents and classificatory grandparents. The pattern of female joking relationships is the same with the sexes reversed. The joking relationships of an individual thus embrace quite a number of people since even spouses of cousins once removed may engage him or her in boisterous joking and horseplay if motivated to do so.

For a man, all women called wife (*upíra*) and grandmother (*ushú*) are in this relationship with him, as are all men called brother-in-law (*chiéri* or *muchímari*), or grandfather (*aparóche*). A woman may joke with males called husband (*kunára*) or grandfather (*aparóche*) and women called sister-in-law (*ripóri*) or grandmother (*ushú*). Informants were unanimous in stating that the behavior expected in alternate-generation joking relationships is exactly the same as for the in-law roles, but in my observation they were usually less intense, and less likely to lead to behavioral conflict.

At all of the forty-nine *tesgüinadas*, both *Gentile* and *Pagótome* which I attended, some form of the behavior now to be described was witnessed. Joking relationship behavior may be described as a kind of sexual horseplay, often rough and physical, and usually involving taunts and insults. The only opportunity, and the only approved time for this kind of play is at *tesgüinadas*. The same people meeting one another while sober do not behave in this manner, though occasionally a humorous remark referring to them may be made, which livens up the situation. Early in my research I found that an unerring way to break the ice with a group of Tarahumaras was to call one of them *muchímari* or *chiéri*. This always provokes laughter because it conjures up prevalent memories of hundreds of *tesgüinadas*.

Between males and females the prescribed joking roles often take the form of burlesque courtship. The woman sometimes takes the lead by striking her joking partner from behind or by trying to lift his loincloth, all the while making suggestive remarks. A more boisterous female (or a more inebriated one) occasionally will try to rip off the clothes of her *kunára*, or to wrestle him to the floor. Sometimes a loud insulting interchange of progressively more lewd remarks is made, all quite amusing to the onlookers.

The male partner too, may aggressively initiate such play, and on one occasion, I witnessed a drunken youth of about seventeen grab a woman of at least forty-five around the breasts and roughly throw her down. The disgruntled woman, who escaped as soon as was expedient, was his classificatory *upíra*.

From a psychological point of view one of the more unusual characteristics of the Tarahumara joking relationships is the behavior of joking relatives of the same sex. These relationships on the surface have a strongly homosexual character. From some of the descriptions of typical *tesgüinadas* in Chapter 4, it will be remembered how the interplay may take the form of a contest where two men taunt each other with threats or offers of anal intercourse. Wrestling is common and one may take the other down and assume the position of coitus. Sometimes such indignities provoke fighting and injury; more frequently the vanquished man passively acquiesces to his role or responds with laughter. The quality of the response usually depends upon the degrees of drunkenness and the state of relations between the partners. The permissiveness of the joking relationship may be used as an opportunity to bully another person or vent hostility under the guise of an approved type of interaction.

Such joking behavior may take a more mild form; the *chiéri* perhaps grasps the *muchímari* from behind and both stagger around the room laughing and simulating intercourse. There are numerous jokes about anal intercourse and acted-out simulations of it. It is interesting to note that all informants denied that any actual homosexual behavior occurs in these joking relationships, and I never uncovered any evidence of its occurrence. One informant explained that he would be afraid of his *chiéri* if people actually did such things.

One of the more interesting characteristics of the Tarahumara joking relationships is the fact that the grandparent-grandchild (*aparóchi, ushú*) relationships have sexual qualities similar to those between joking partners of the same generation. Frequently the play is less rough-and-tumble but not invariably so. As we have seen, members of these alternate generations may engage in quite boisterous behavior at times. Though the *ripóri* (or *ripómera*) relationship of female sisters-in-law has the same general connotations as the male *chiéri-muchímari* relationship, its expression in behavior is rarer and milder. The most violent homosexual-like play among women was observed between granddaughters and grandmothers (see Chapter 4).

Other important features of the joking relationships are their role prescriptions at death. As described in Chapter 5, in Inápuchi it is these relatives, particularly the in-laws, who are responsible for handling the burial arrangements and the death fiestas. In effect, a person's nonconsanguineally related age mates take over from the close lineal relatives at this difficult period. If there are no close affinal joking relatives nearby, the tasks are taken over by grandparents or grandchildren, those forming the vertical axis of the joking relationship pattern. These joking relatives must also carry out a ritual burlesque at the later death fiestas. They approach the simulated body of the deceased, kick at it, and make lewd gestures and jokes, just as they did in life. Joking relatives are exempt from the deadly anger which the departing soul directs towards its immediate family.

Marriage

To the *Gentiles* of Inápuchi, marriage is largely a matter of personal choice, subject, of course, to the rules of incest. Incest prohibitions are extended to all traceable blood relatives on both sides, and this often forces a person to go great distances for a partner or to wait several years. The sanctioned permissiveness of the *tesgüinada* seems functional in alleviating the tensions resulting from these conditions. By comparison with the *Gentiles,* the marriage customs in *Pagótome* Aboreáchi are much more formalized. There the *mayóri* has as his major role the contracting of matches in various parts of the pueblo. A father of either an eligible daughter or son generally asks the *mayóri* to find a mate for his child, and the official may spend considerable time and effort in effecting a union agreeable to both families. The *mayóri* also sometimes performs a ceremony which vaguely resembles Catholic ritual to formalize the union. Even where such formalization takes place matches are often dissolved after a short time if the pair do not find each other congenial. However, cases were reported in which first objections were overridden by force. *Soldados* (lesser *mayóri*) were sent to drag back a resisting woman, who had fled.

In Inápuchi, out of thirty marriages on which data were obtainable, ten males and seven females had been married two or more times, and four men had been married three times. None of these unions were solemnized by any ritual procedures. A marriage is accepted as legitimate when it endures long enough to be "recognized."

In Yehuachíque (a *Pagótome rancho*) five males and three females of twenty-one married couples had been married more than once. It should be noted, however, that such frequencies are more reflective of the toll of death than they are indicative of the brittleness of marriage. In both communities, most of those who now have mates other than their first ones took them after the deaths of previous partners. In Inápuchi, only three of the males who had new wives had "divorced" their old ones by announcing the split in a *tesgüinada.* Two of these three had deserted wives who are still in the area and who are now married to other husbands. These remarriages account for two of the women mentioned above who had more than one spouse.

The stated ideal is to find a spouse of about the same age, but the practical situation demands a great deal of compromise. Many women in this area are older than their husbands, though the reverse is also found. In Inápuchi two men were married to women more than twenty years older than themselves. However, the age distribution of marriage partners was somewhat random, indicating that age is not a critical determinant of choice. A person takes what is available in most instances, especially for a second or third spouse.

In all of Aboreáchi pueblo, including the *Gentile* area, I found only three cases of polygyny. Each of these involved two wives and one husband, and in one case the women were sisters. Polygyny is not the preferred pattern, but it is permitted. It is too infrequent to be regarded as culturally significant, though it would appear to be a functional custom under conditions of such low population density in such a rigorous environment. In the two cases I personally observed, the second wife appeared to be slightly mentally retarded, and she was utilized primarily for goat herding.

Second marriages in Inápuchi depend entirely upon expediency. Occasionally, a widower marries his first wife's sister, but if this happens it is because the two are well acquainted and like one another. There is no custom of sororate under which marriage to a sister of a deceased spouse would be the rule. Since the wife's sister is a nonrelative, she is simply one of the few convenient matches a widower can make. Brother-sister exchange also is not a preferential marriage custom among these Tarahumara. There was one case of two brothers married to two sisters, but again this was said to be a result of nothing more than nearby availability of desirable girls in the right age bracket who did not stand in prohibited degrees of kinship.

Residence

The following points summarize the essentials of the Tarahumara post-marital residence pattern:

• Residence after marriage in Inápuchi is dictated by convenience of economic resources rather than by a "rule" of residence.

•The residence group is continually changing in composition through an annual cycle of combination and split of its component nuclear families. It may be "extended" or "nuclear" at different times of the year.

•This group changes its form from generation to generation, going from nuclear to extended, and back, as members are born, die, or as they leave and enter by marriage.

These observations indicate the arbitrariness which would be involved in making a residence classification at any particular time. For example, if we classify the Tarahumara families at one time of the year, some of them would have a nuclear form or "matrilocal" pattern, while at another they would be "extended" and "patrilocal." The frequencies of types also vary according to the temporal "cycles of domestic groups," i.e., the ways families grow, split and amalgamate through time.

Case 1: Ignacio and his brother Pedro, each with his wife and two children in a house at *rancho* Inápuchi. This may be classified as a fraternal joint family. However, in the past year Ignacio, his wife, and children twice spent about one month in the house of Julio Rynárachi. Julio is Ignacio's father-in-law. Pedro and his family also spent three months at Rynárachi in the house of Polinario, his father-in-law, during the season of hunger. Therefore, during these periods, the households of Julio and Polinario were augmented in a matrilocal (or uxorilocal) manner. It must be noted that Polinario already had a grandson by one of his other married-out daughters staying with him.

Besides these shifts of residence, all of the above occupied separate caves in the gorge during the winter (approximately three months). Here we may note some complications arising from physical distances. Pedro and Ignacio's winter caves were only about 100 yards apart so that a great deal of visiting and interaction was carried on between the two families. Polinario and Julio were more separated from each other and also from Ignacio and Pedro. During this season, then the individual nuclear families were thrown into more immediate contact with members of other *ranchos* by the combination of the winter mobility pattern in such a broken topography and the fortunes of traditional inheritance.

Now let us consider what is entailed in generational changes. Up until four years ago the parents of Ignacio and Polinario were still alive and lived with their two married sons in the same household. If we had classified the household at that time, we should have had to call it patrilocal (virilocal), while now it is joint-fraternal. At the same time, upon the death of Julio or Polinario either Ignacio or Pedro will move from Inápuchi to take up permanent residence in Rynárachi to farm his wife's inherited land. Both Julio and Polinario are quite aged by Tarahumara standards. The joint family will soon again break up, with one of its components taking up matrilocal (uxorilocal) residence.

Case 2: Jesús with his wife and stepson live in a house alone on Inápuchi *rancho*. About fifty yards from Jesús' house is another house in which live his aged mother and his younger unmarried brother Ramón. About a half mile away live the two older brothers of Jesús and Mauricio (or Celia, the *hombre-mujer*) and Martín. These are three discrete living units, yet they are united by kinship. Each unit works land separately and stores its produce separately, yet they generally make *tesgüino* as a unit, and share a number of activities. For example, they herd their separately owned animals together, and alternately assume the responsibility of caring for them. Sometimes each of the three units eats its meals separately, sometimes they all eat together, and on occasion two of the units eat together. The old mother makes most of the blankets for the whole group. In winter Jesús and family along with Ramón and their mother, occupy one cave, while Mauricio and Martín occupy another one. An aspect of this family's residence is that occasionally Jesús is absent for one or two weeks at a time in order to work a field in Chawichíque (three hours away) where his wife has inherited a field. He takes his own nuclear family with him on these trips. The following illustrates the generational cycle.

Case 3: The first stage in the cycle of the family of Seledonio Inápuchi was one of augmentation. When María, Seledonio's mother, was a young woman, she married Pablo Quírare who came to live with her on Inápuchi in a matrilocal living arrangement. This family lived in Inápuchi, while their son, Seledonio, and their three daughters grew to adulthood. When Seledonio married, he brought his first bride from Charérachi to Inápuchi because there was more land there. He lived in the parental household and thus was living patrilocally. The final growth of the augmentation stage, besides the additions resulting from the birth of children to Seledonio, occurred when one of his sisters married and brought her spouse from Quírare to Inápuchi. They began rearing a family in a house about 300 yards away from the parental residence. This family was living neolocally if viewed from the perspective of household residence, but matrilocally by criteria of socio-economic functions.

For several years then, Pablo and María formed the nucleus of an extended family which was composed of themselves and two teenage daughters, their son and his elementary family, and the older daughter and her family. This group, occupying three houses within hailing distance on the same *rancho*, cooperated economically in many activities.

The second stage of the domestic cycle was one of fission. Later the two younger daughters married the brothers and moved with them to Uarárari to form a patrilocal joint-fraternal family. Shortly thereafter the father died and the mother went to live with Rodrigo Uarárari who had just lost his second wife. She therefore went to live patrilocally, at the same time rejoining her two youngest daughters who were living nearby.

The nucleus of the original extended family disintegrated and the present stage is again one of augmentation. Seledonio lives in his father's house with his new nuclear family, while his oldest sister with her husband and their nuclear family live some 300 yards away. Both of these groups farm land formerly worked by the parents. When the children of these two families mature, the inevitable consequences of marriage and death will again augment and disperse them in a similar but unpredictable fashion. Chance factors of death, birth, personality, strength, and economic opportunities at any potential spouses's *rancho* will determine the outcome.

Though I will not describe it in detail, winter descent to the canyon has entailed for this group of related families an annual cycle of residence group split analogous to Cases 1 and 2. These three cases are representative of Tarahumara family cycles in this region. The basic components of residence are the nuclear families which separate and combine into augmented living and cooperating units for various periods throughout the yearly cycle. These become fragmented by death and out marriage, only to augment again upon the growth and marriage of children. If the community is observed at any particular point in time, the number of matrilocal, fraternal-joint, patrilocal, and nuclear families shows a completely different pattern from that at another time of the year or from a time a few years earlier or later.

The important fact is that for the vast proportion of the time, the "new" home residence for a cohabiting couple and their family is on the same *rancho* as that of his or her parents. Given the ecology of small *ranchos*, this means that unstable augmented families of varying compositions are created, which cooperate together and perform many activities as units.

Conclusion

The Tarahumara present us with an elaborate kin terminology with slight importance in the structuring of relationships. Kin terms are little used in social encounters or for reference, and there are no reinforcing effects on the forms of social groups. It is evident that the patterns of kinship and family behavior as well as the minimal importance of kin terminology are strongly conditioned by Tarahumara adaptations to the Sierra environment.

The bilateral mode of reckoning kin, the open choice for post-marital residence, the freedom of choice in the selection of mates, the flexibility of marriage patterns and the individuated character of children's roles are among the features in the domain of kinship and the family most closely tied to Tarahumara ecology. These matters will be reviewed in the concluding chapter.

CHAPTER 7

LEADERSHIP, STATUS RANKING, & SOCIAL CONTROL

Political structure is rudimentary in form and diffuse in quality among the *Gentiles* of Inápuchi, and the existing set of officials is much smaller than those found in *Pagótome* Tarahumara pueblos (Bennett and Zingg, 1935:201-207; Fried, 1952). Inápuchi officials have comparatively less power, and this, in turn is correlated with less formalism and symbolism associated with their offices. This means that individuals in the Inápuchi community have more personal independence and freedom from control by others than do their *Pagótome* neighbors. In fact, they resemble peoples at the hunting and gathering level in this respect.

Territorial boundaries within which the *Gentile* officials have jurisdiction are hazy, and this contributes to the lack of power and to the minimal formality of their roles. The *Gentile* area has no official unity or set boundaries. It straddles the official pueblo (*ejido*) boundaries of Aboreáchi, Samachíque, and Yoquívo, and also borders on the *ejido* of Quírare, though most of the *Gentile ranchos* of this region technically lie within the boundaries of Aboreáchi pueblo. This is given official recognition at important pueblo-wide meetings of Aboreáchi by the assignment of a special seat for the *Gentile siríame* along with the high pueblo officials.

Some *ranchos* on the peripheries of the *Gentile* region do not recognize the governor, or *siríame*, who is recognized by the majority of nonchristians. Disputes among these few isolates are settled among themselves. There are also a few *Pagótome ranchos* within the territory occupied primarily by *Gentiles*.

In spite of many subcultural differences observable to an outsider, the *Gentiles* have no strong sense of being different from *Pagótome*, and on the peripheries of their area they participate in the *tesgüinadas* of *Pagótome* almost as often as they do in those of other *Gentiles*. The *Gentiles* of Inápuchi area do not explicitly define themselves as a named group, and they are not distinguished by rigorous social or geographic boundaries, but they do have a definite sense of relationship with the other *Gentile ranchos*.

In this situation of ambiguous boundaries the small degree of community unity which exists among *Gentiles* seems related to three conditions: •nonbaptism, a shared tradition of rejection of Christianity •a relatively high rate of endogamy, and ties of kinship and affiliation occasioned by this endogamy •recognition of the *Gentile* leader and other officials for at least *some* purposes. The nonchristian Tarahumara do not have a centralized organization like those in the *Pagótome* communities, where a church with its other buildings forms a stable focus for both sacred rituals and secular community activities.

The Official Structure

In Inápuchi there is one principal official called *siríame*, who has two classes of duties. One of these is representation of the *Gentiles* residing within the boundaries of Aboreáchi at larger meetings of the pueblo, and the other relates to handling internal issues of governance among the *Gentiles*. In regard to the first set of duties, however, the *Gentile siríame* is seldom notified of important pueblo meetings unless they involve disputes between *Gentiles* and *Pagótome*. For example, he was not invited to the three most important pueblo meetings during the year of our residence.

The more important part of the *siríame* role is concerned with the organization of internal *Gentile* affairs. Within the Inápuchi area the *siríame* is expected to call and preside over all meetings for matters important to the group. For this he must see that *tesgüino* is provided. He must act as chief judge in trials for serious crimes. He must give "sermons" on appropriate occasions, stressing the cultural expectations for good behavior and the penalties for infractions, and finally, he must act as arbiter of small disputes or interpersonal problems.

In conjunction with these role obligations, the *siríame* has authority over the *warúala (capitán)* and two *sontársi*. These officials are supposed to catch criminal offenders and bring them in (the *capitán* has the additional responsibility for actually administering any lashes that may be required as punishment). These officials also carry messages for the *siríame*. This is an important communication role throughout the Tarahumara area because of the distances involved. A final duty of the *capitán* with his *soldados*, is to "police" *tesgüinadas*—to warn people who are becoming belligerent or sexually promiscuous to desist, or in the final extreme to arrest them. This is a rare extremity and generally involves locking the culprits in a grain house until morning. The *sontársi* also have responsibility for keeping small children away from the drinking areas of *tesgüinadas*.

The full set of officials for the *Gentile* community really amounts to a single leader, or chief, with his assistants. However, in Inápuchi the chief is a leader whose functions are minimal, whose assistants are few, and whose power is negligible. When the authority of the *siríame* is called for, the decision in most cases is actually made by agreement among a group of adult males.

One other minor official role among the *Gentiles* that should be mentioned is that of *chokéame*, or race organizer. Races are not easy to organize because of the distances involved, and difficulties in getting a consensus as to time, participants, and place. During a race the *chokéame* has responsibility of handling the betting, for having proper kicking balls made, and so forth. The position does not confer prestige or power, and it is a rotating responsibility, activated at sporadic times during only a part of the year. The position of *chokéame* stands apart from the official hierarchy since it has no connection with disputes or community authority (see Appendix).

The comparisons in Table 1 indicate the differences in formal status positions between the *Pagótome* and *Gentile* areas of Aboreáchi pueblo. This comparison clearly demonstrates the relative lack and unimportance of official roles in Inápuchi, other than the position of *siríame*.

Table 1—Comparison of Official Statuses

Inápuchi[1] *(Gentiles)*	Aboreáchi (*Pagótome*)
(siríame)	*(siríame) gobernador* of whole pueblo
	teniénte[2] —assistant *siríame*
	nirárli (general) a councilor position occupied by former *siríames*
	alacánte —judge
(warúala) capitán	*capitán grande* (*warúala*)—head policing officer
	capitánes chiquitos (4)[3]—policing assistants
	oliwáshi (2)—guards and watchmen
(sontársi) soldados (2)	*soldados* (*sontársi*) (12)—policing assistants
	mayóri grande—marriage official with semi-formal social control duties
	mayóri chiquitos (11)—same as *mayóri grande*
	*comisario ejidál**
	*comisario policía**
	(*These were newly created officials after *ejidoization*—they do not sit with traditional officials in pueblo meetings)

– –

chokéame	*chokéames*—racing organizers
	tenánches—fiesta givers (3)
	chapeyókos—*matachíne* organizers (5)

[1]Duties of Inápuchi officers described in body of chapter. The Aboreáchi officers down to the *comisarios* are listed in the order in which they sit around the church patio in a semicircle for large meetings (*juntas*).

[2]At a large *junta* in Aboreáchi, the *Gentile siríame* has the right to sit in third position—between the *teniénte* and the *general*.

[3]Numbers in parentheses indicate number of officials in that capacity.

Social Ranking and Leadership

Regarding status ranking, the tendency among writers on the Tarahumara has been to accept as fact the Indian's statement: "All of us are equal," a generalization which appears validated by a general lack of symbolization of overt status differences. However, what emerge from our data are strong motivations toward status achievement, and a system of achieved informal leadership roles which underlies and often bypasses the rudimentary official structure. The more formalized and complex official system typical of Tarahumara pueblos is present in *Pagótome* Aboreáchi, but it is apparent that the same motivations for achievement of status also exist in Inápuchi.

While there are connections between influence, prestige, and official position in the Inápuchi area, these connections are weak, and this seems related to the relative lack of functions and power inherent in their conceptions of official status. A man needs a fairly high social ranking to attain the position of *siríame*, but he who attains that status is not necessarily the man of highest ranking. On the other hand, high social ranking is necessary for leadership, yet social leadership is not always associated with official position. To clarify this let us examine the relationships of the important elements: social ranking, prestige, influence, official status, and leadership.

It has been stated that these Tarahumara are egalitarian in orientation. Their emphasis upon personal and family independence is reflected in the lack of actual authority or power vested in the *siríame*, the elected official leader. No member of the community has power to coerce others, but there are men who are respected, who organize group activities, and who occasionally influence decisions affecting most of the *Gentiles*. These men are leaders regardless of whether their leadership is sanctioned by official status. On the other hand, all of the desired qualities of leadership may or may not be possessed by the designated officials, though they must possess some of them.

It should be clear that there are no social or economic strata among the Tarahumara, yet important differences in ranking do exist. Neither social ranking nor leadership is inherited by birth. Both are dependent upon personal qualities and wealth, and these two criteria go together; that is, positions of prestige and influence tend to be achieved rather than ascribed.

Earlier I described the process by which wealth is built up and the forces within the economic system which inhibit massive accumulation. The attainment of wealth is a slow process usually taking the better part of a man's lifetime. Limitations on the means of acquiring land, dependency on the older generation, the minimal use of money in the system, and the slow increment of animal herds in the rugged environment, all work to slow any quick amassing of fortune. In a relatively static, low energy economy like that of the Tarahumara, conditions, customs and varying events such as bad years for the crops, channeling of surplus corn into *tesgüino* making, splitting of resources by equal inheritance, and exploitation by Mestizos all play their parts in maintaining a general low economic level. While a certain amount of luck may occasionally make a difference (as for example inheritance of good land, large herds, or acquiring access to large fields by marriage), a rise in status depends largely on qualities of initiative, intelligence, and hard work. Wealth does not automatically confer authority, but those who have positions of prestige and influence are always fairly high on the scale of wealth.

Under these conditions, youth is not commensurate with leadership, and between ages 35 and 50 a qualified man usually begins to play important roles in decision making. If, by this age a person is well off, his good fortune is usually attributed to wisdom and initiative, and generally a true correlation exists between these personal qualities and wealth.

People moving up the prestige ladder may pass through several stages after adulthood and marriage. The man destined to become a successful leader will usually cultivate every available bit of ground, even if it means making long journeys to his wife's parents' *rancho*. He will accumulate a large herd of goats and several cattle through judicious trading and careful tending and he will begin early to hold *tesgüinadas* of his own. When he is given a minor position such as *sontársi*, *sakéame* (assistant *chokéame*) or later *waruála*, he will execute his role with initiative. He may also begin to feel that he has some *owerúame* powers. If this occurs he will then begin to dream about people's sicknesses and perhaps will assist an older curer in larger curing fiestas. Skills as a supernatural specialist are not necessary to leadership, but they benefit the ambitious. As we have seen, curing credentials in themselves provide a separate avenue of social mobility.

When a man is perceived as being inclined to leadership he may find himself requested to give sermons when the *tesgüino* is flowing. If he becomes a person of substance and is aggressive in the ways described he will rise, for these are the qualities of the influential man. A reputation for such personal attributes is built up over the years concomitantly with wealth, which, in turn, is taken as one sign of having such attributes.

In the Aboreáchi *Pagótome* area, the trajectory of the age-status climb is even clearer than it is in Inápuchi because of the many different specialized official and ceremonial statuses which constitute their system. There, young men begin as *soldados* and may gain a special kind of prestige as community runners or as *matachíne* and *fariséo* dancers. As they become older, the more competent ones may pass through the offices of *mayóri* and *capitáne chiquito*, and some may be appointed assistant *chapeyókos*. If they build reputations in the characteristics described for Inápuchi, they may eventually be chosen to fill the higher offices of *teniénte, alacánte,* and *capitán*. The major officials of the community (i.e., the *gobernador, general* and *mayóri grande*) are all experienced, established men. The highest ceremonial positions (*owerúame* and *sawéame*) are also filled by older men. *Chapeyókos* and *chokéames* generally are older also.

Young Tarahumara men are seldom leaders, but age in itself is not the critical criterion; in neither the *Gentile* nor the *Pagótome* areas are extremely old men found in any position of authority. It takes considerable time to develop substance and build a reputation, but after a certain point men feel that they have done their duty, and the physical vigor thought to be requisite for leadership becomes attenuated. The leader must be able to drink, speak, and work forcefully.

The interplay of the different elements entering into prestige may be illustrated by a brief description of some high and low ranked individuals in the community of Inápuchi. The method by which the ranking was determined was by an anthropological variation of the sociogram, along with observation of the interaction quality between the individuals involved. Differential participation and invitations to *tesgüinadas* was tabulated and in the context of other interview questions, people were asked who were the most influential men in the area and why. This method was checked by having men rank individuals to whom they would go for *kórima* in time of famine.

Seledonio Inápuchi was considered by everyone interviewed to be the most influential man in the *Gentile* region. He was about 40 to 45 years of age and had been married three times, his first two wives having died. His family consisted of a young wife (about 20 years old) and two small children (six and two years). He was considered wise in council, and did not fight at *tesgüinadas* unless attacked.

Seledonio was also wealthy by Tarahumara standards. He produced one and a half corn houses of maize during the year of the study (one corn house is considered sufficient for his family) plus a surplus of beans and potatoes. He was known to have sold five *decalitros* of beans and ten *decalitros* of potatoes (indicating a surplus), besides supporting two people in *kórima* positions for several months, and he was often sought for smaller gifts of *kórima*. His herd consisted of 115 goats, nine sheep, four oxen, and two cows. This was the highest number of animals owned by any men in the *Gentile* area. People came from as far as Aboreáchi and Quírare to attend his *tesgüinadas*. Another manifestation of his substance was that he owned two accordions valued at one young bull each.

He had ceremonial skills and sacred power. He was not yet a full-fledged or full time curing specialist, but he was asked fairly often by sick people of the region to attempt a cure by sending his soul out in dreams. Additionally, Seledonio performed many minor rituals at the *rancho* fiestas (see Chapter 4).

He also was a good organizer, and frequently took the initiative in making *tesgüino*. When a large curing ceremony approached, he sent boys to the *barranca* for the "medicines," and arranged to make *tesgüino* cooperatively. Seledonio was himself invited "very far" for *tesgüino*. During my stay, jealousy of his popularity precipitated several physical attacks upon him by a less popular member of the community. The combination of qualities described made Seledonio Inápuchi very influential even though he was not a powerful orator in the Tarahumara tradition, and he had not yet held the position of *siríame*.

Rodrigo Uarárari, about fifty years of age, was the *Gentile siríame* of the area and had held this position for eight years. He too was married to his third wife, but because of the early deaths of all ten children born to him, he had no heirs. Rodrigo was known for his wisdom and decorum, and he had long been considered a "strong speaker." His wealth consisted of about 95 goats and five sheep, but he had no cattle. His fields were, however, quite large, and he produced one and a half grain houses of corn in the year of the study. He also sold about ten *decalitros* of beans, and sold about thirty pesos worth of peaches to *Chavóchis*. The amounts he harvested were especially indicative of wealth since he had no heirs. Rodrigo also had two people from Sumárachi working for him as *peones* off and on during the preceding year. Out of personal preference he made *tesgüino* less often than either Seledonio Inápuchi or Seledonio Uarárari, though his *tesgüinadas* often were large and he was invited quite far. For example, he occasionally drank as far away as Aboreáchi. He had no shamanistic power, but he sometimes performed as *sawéame*. Rodrigo's prestige was lower than that of Seledonio Inápuchi, even though he was officially *siríame* of the *Gentiles*, and was so recognized by his seating position among the pueblo officials at the *ejido* meetings at Aboreáchi.

Patricio Inápuchi, who was about 29 years of age, had considerable oratorical ability. He should be contrasted with Seledonio Inápuchi on this attribute, since in spite of his skill, at this age he lacked many of the other requisite qualifications for high ranking. For example, he still lacked complete jurisdiction over his own land. He cultivated the fields of his father-in-law. His own father's land was in Awírachi and was being worked by his older brother and by his father. Physically, Patricio was the strongest man in the area, and he possessed great vitality and energy. However, he ordinarily did not take initiative in affairs outside of his own family, except in his occasional role as *chokéame* for races. His economic situation was tied up with that of his old

Aspiring leader

father-in-law, Dionicio Inápuchi who, though more than 70 years old, had not relinquished his land to his daughter. Since there were no other heirs, Patricio stood to benefit at his father-in-law's death by his wife's inheritance of Dionicio's herd of 87 goats and sheep and two head of cattle. Patricio had no sacred power, but he was the *capitán* (*warúala*) for the area. Because of his oratorical capacity he was also often called upon to speak at *tesgüinadas*. Patricio appeared to be an important leader in the making.

Dionicio Inápuchi, the father-in-law of Patricio was an example of a person with age and wealth, but who lacked the other qualities for Tarahumara leadership. Dionicio had never been *siríame* or even *warúala*, though he was he oldest man in the area. He worked hard, was one of the wealthiest men on Inápuchi, and had a reputation for not making trouble. On the other hand, he had never been regarded as wise, nor had he sought leadership for himself. He made *tesgüino* regularly, but did not organize other group activities. His fairly large herd of animals and ample productive fields were to pass into control of Patricio Inápuchi at his death because the latter had married his only daughter. Dionicio had no ability as a curer and did not even perform as a *sawéame*.

Valencio Pisáchi was a man of about 50 who had never held more than minor official positions. His prestige was generally low. He had seven children, which he had difficulty supporting. He is the person referred to, who had descended rather than ascended on the economic scale. Over the years he dissipated most of the wealth which he had inherited from his father, and because of his laziness he allowed his wife's fields to be taken over by others (see later discussion of land disputes). Valencio frequently made trouble at *tesgüinadas*, and he was not invited often to drinking parties at Inápuchi because of his long-standing land dispute with Román Inápuchi. He claimed curing power but was not respected as an *owerúame*. Valencio's main failings were laziness and failure to build up a reputation for wisdom. He held few *tesgüinadas*, and was unable to speak "strongly."

Juan-Tasio was another low ranking person. He was about 30 years old and had a wife and two small children. He was especially known as being *we parú* or inclined toward aggression at *tesgüinadas*. He was slight of build but despite this he frequently attacked others. He became fairly wealthy from early inheritance when Román killed his father about a year prior to the study. He inherited 40 goats, three cows, and acquired five burros. He produced one grain house of corn in the preceding year and a surplus of beans. However, he produced only three sacks of potatoes, and the amount of his wheat was also negligible. Juan-Tasio was not often invited to *tesgüinadas* outside of the plateau of Inápuchi, and he did not make *tesgüino* often. On one occasion when *tesgüino* was made at several houses for cooperative hoeing, the fields of the others were hoed first, while Juan-Tasio's were left undone. Only a few of the people even went to his house to drink *tesgüino*. When drunk, Juan-Tasio claimed to be able to cure, but no one came to him for help. Due largely to his aggressiveness and lack of other valued character traits, Juan-Tasio lived a more socially isolated and frustrated life than most of the other Indians in the area.

These examples illustrate the prestige range found in the *Gentile* region. Status differences are not marked by distinctions of housing or dress, except perhaps for the comparatively newer cloth used for the garments of the wealthy. Men of influence are not deferred to with any particular forms of speech, but they are more frequently honored by having an *olla* of beer dedicated to them at *tesgüinadas*, and by being served first.

Influence

It is more appropriate to speak of influence among the Tarahumara than of "power" or "authority," for leadership is weak, unstable, and always dependent more upon personal assertiveness and reputation than upon other qualities. It is little symbolized or fixed in clearly marked and authoritative official roles, and this makes for an aura of ambiguity regarding men's rankings. Social mobility is limited in comparison with modern industrial societies, but it nevertheless occurs and is important. The ambitious, as well as the very influential, sometimes attempt to signal their social aspirations and to demonstrate their positions to others. I have already mentioned how some items of industrial manufacture such as accordions, beads, and bright cloth aid in fulfilling these symbolic functions, and how the *tesgüinada* operates as a prestige showcase.

Persons of importance often attempt to demonstrate their influence when arriving at a *rancho* where *a tesgüinada* is going on by leading several other men into the festivities. If possible such an individual makes a dramatic entrance, proudly leading a single file of men. Such an entrance indicates to those present that he commands the backing of *soldados* (supporters). Upon entering the gathering, such a leader goes up to the ceremonial patio, and followed by each *soldado* in turn, crosses himself and turns around counterclockwise near each of the four sides of the ceremonial table. He then greets the host and accepts three proffered gourds of *tesgüino*. His followers do likewise. This somewhat decorous procedure is, of course, witnessed by the other people, who depending upon the stages of drinking, are usually sitting or standing or lying around the area in various clusters and pairs. Such a form of self-presentation seems related to the fact that, owing to the geographical spread of households and to the indefiniteness of leadership roles, a man's influence weakens in proportion to the distance from his home *rancho*. Even though he may be recognized as an official, an observable affirmation of support bolsters his confidence and visually demonstrates to others his attainment of some degree of higher ranking.

The weakening of prestige and influence relative to physical distance may be illustrated by the case of Rodrigo Uarárari, the *siríame* of the Inápuchi area. At his own *rancho* of Uarárari, Rodrigo is the acknowledged leader, though Seledonio Uarárari aspires to challenge that leadership. On the Inápuchi *rancho* itself however, and in several other *ranchos* on that side of the *Gentile* area, Rodrigo's influence is definitely second to that of Seledonio Inápuchi. On the other hand, Rodrigo is most influential at the *rancho* of Sumárachi, which is south of Uarárari. Of all the *rancho* leaders, Seledonio Inápuchi is the most respected on more *Gentile* *ranchos*, even though Rodrigo of Uarárari is still the acknowledged *siríame*.

Despite the relative lack of legitimate power associated with it, the title of *siríame* is not without significance, but possession of it is only one of the methods by which a man gains and demonstrates his influence. This incident will illustrate:

At a *tesgüinada* at Uarárari, a dispute broke out between Seledonio Uarárari and Seledonio Inápuchi. They were drunk and arguing vociferously, almost coming to blows. The dispute concerned who was to be the next *siríame* for the area. Each was claiming to be the better suited. Finally, when a fight seemed about to start, the quieter (but actually more influential) Seledonio Inápuchi gave in to his more assertive and boisterous opponent. He came over to me, the outsider, and publicly announced that Seledonio Uarárari would make a very fine *siríame*.

This example illustrates how initiative and self-assertiveness play a part in attaining status. The outcome did not immediately change anything since Rodrigo Uarárai was present and it was understood that he would be *siríame* for some time yet. It was clear, however, that after eight years in office, his position was challenged. New men of wealth and prestige were rising and asserting themselves. Thus, it is apparent that the position of *siríame* does have prestige importance, even if it gives little authority and has no power or wealth connotations.

The same basic factors are operating in *Pagótome* communities, but there are complications which I can only suggest briefly in order to indicate their contrast with the *Gentile* situation. One major difference is that the more complex and formal set of offices and duties in Aboreáchi lend more authority and prestige to officials by virtue of position alone.

Further advanced acculturation to Mexican culture as well as a more suitable area for animals brings about a situation in Aboreáchi where wealth is more easily amassed. Thus, there are some men there who are far richer than anyone in Inápuchi. These men may have several persons working for them at times. Furthermore, in the *Pagótome* area, the *teniénte*, the *general*, and the *alacánte*, all are regarded as almost equal in authority to the *gobernador*, and as a group these four make most of the more important pueblo decisions. They may be assisted by the *warúala* and the *mayóri grande* who, although they have more specialized and less important duties, are still regarded as authorities.

The popularization of the horse and horsemanship is another factor which has been added to the prestige equation in Aboreáchi, as are the much more prevalent use of money, and the greater use of manufactured clothing. In addition to these elements, the new roles of *comisario ejidal, comisario de policía,* and school teacher, all imposed by the state of Chihuahua, have introduced other criteria for prestige, which would not be fully assessable without an independent study of the *Pagótome* community. The socio-political situation of the *Gentiles* in Inápuchi is much closer to the type of socio-political organization which must have prevailed in the Sierra in aboriginal times.

Social Control–The Framework of Values

In the absence of strongly institutionalized authority and a formalized legal system, the problem arises as to how the conformity necessary for viable social life is achieved. The Tarahumara have a few basic rules, rooted in major value orientations. These are internalized and serve as a framework of constraints upon the actions of the individualistic Tarahumara people. As in all societies people who violate community norms and engage in conflicts are controlled by standardized means. However, in comparison with most groups, Tarahumara social control is minimally punitive. The concept of retribution is weak.

Responses to deviance in this part of the Sierra have a unique character due to the quality of social life engendered by the pattern of isolated agricultural-herding and the *tesgüino* complex. The most unusual and significant cultural condition influencing the social control system is that most breaches of moral rules, as well as the legal acts to redress them, take place in the context of the *tesgüinada.* But before examining this it is well to be aware of some more general value premises which are implicit in the social rules.

Individual Independence and Equality

The idea that each individual has a right to determine his own course of action without interference from others is a pervading theme of Tarahumara behavior. A person is taught the right way to do things in his childhood, but he is rarely forced to do things against his will. The child learns self-reliance and independence at an early age. As we have seen, he spends his first two to three years in complete dependence, much of it on his mother's back. Then, despite the dangers of the rugged terrain, from the age of five or six a significant change occurs, and he is allowed to wander great distances alone. At ages seven and eight, members of both sexes are spending long hours herding animals, and by 11 or 12 they may sometimes even stay out all night away from the *rancho*. After about age six, children of all ages frequently are left at home to care for the fields and animals while the parents attend distant *tesgüinadas*. From the age of ten upwards, the child is excluded from the house where the parents sleep at night. All of these conditions seem related to the development of a typical character in which self-reliance, independence, individuality, taciturnity, as well as shyness and graceful dignity, are marked.

Respect of the wishes and needs of others is a dominant attitude among the Tarahumara of Inápuchi and Aboreáchi. It is seen in the sanctions against parents using corporal punishment on their children. Striking a child is believed to produce "fright" which may cause sickness and death. The premises of independence and equality are reflected in the rules of visiting etiquette which require the visitor to sit some distance from the house and wait patiently until he is greeted by the inhabitants. The independence-equality orientation also is manifest in much of the behavior noted earlier; in the voluntary, noncohesive character of group activities, the egalitarian ethic, the relative social equality of the sexes, the freedom to choose and leave a spouse, the minimal nature of institutionalized leadership, the role of achievement in gaining and exercising influence, the unwillingness to press legal claims, the permissive attitudes toward deviants, and the immunity from prosecution enjoyed by sorcerers.

Nonviolence

Closely related to independence-equality is an orientation which may best be named nonviolence. The Tarahumara have for centuries been known as a peaceful group. There were, of course, early uprisings and killings of priests in the seventeenth century, but despite the much greater size of the tribe than any of their near neighbors, since the beginning of the eighteenth century there has been no more than a few isolated cases of violent resistance among them. They are known as *muy pacíficos* (very peaceful) by the Mestizos, who contrast them with the Tepehuánes to the south, the Yáqui to the west, and the Apache who raided this part of Mexico in the nineteenth century. These other groups are considered to be *muy bravos* (very fierce), in comparison with the jovial, drinking "Tarahumaritos." In my experience in the Sierra I never learned of a single case of a Tarahumara assaulting a Mestizo, though many instances of the reverse were reported, nor did I find any cases recorded in the literature after the Jesuit period. Furthermore, a Tarahumara never attacks another Indian unless under the influence of alcohol. Even during drinking, very little serious violence occurs in comparison with the situation in the contiguous Mestizo culture, where shootings are common and interfamily feuds go on for years.

This value orientation of nonviolence can also be noted in the lack of feuds resulting in death or serious injury. Of course, no people are exempt from quarrels, but it is remarkable that there is a lack of the persisting group conflicts so common in many groups at this socio-economic level. This condition appears related to the isolation from frequent contact and the structural condition of overlapping social ties, as much as to the nonviolent value orientation, but the latter is not without considerable influence.

The dominant Tarahumara response in threatening situations is withdrawal. Children, for example, sometimes run away to relatives for days if threatened by their parents. Withdrawal has also been the major response to the ever increasing migration of Mestizos into their territory, and it also characterizes all situations of social friction outside the special case of the *tesgüinada*. That is a different world, where other norms apply.

Materialism and Practicality

The Tarahumara of Inápuchi and Aboreáchi show little interest in questions of history, philosophy, or theology. Their "time orientation" is definitely the present. This is borne out not only by a stated indifference concerning past events but by the absence of continuity in kinship groupings, the lack of family names, and the lack of any but the most rudimentary of origin myths.

I earlier referred to the minimal degree of theological elaboration here, and mentioned how ritual is stressed while myth and doctrine are negligible. Most of what can be termed utilitarian ritual involves very specific actions pertaining to "curing" of fields, animals, or children; attempts to prevent disasters as well as to counteract the pervasive fear projections of world destruction.

There are no signs of mysticism or self-transcendental states, and there are no cults of the dead. Spirits and ghosts are believed to exist but they are associated with sickness, death, and disaster, and the attitude toward them is one of fear and pragmatism. Tarahumara rituals are techniques which are designed to produce effects in *this* world.

The utilitarian emphasis of these people may also be inferred from their relative lack of attention to arts, crafts, or architecture. Artistic and handicraft work centers in three pursuits; weaving of blankets and sashes, the making of several musical instruments and the fabrication of such utilitarian items as clay jars, baskets, and hand-sewn clothing. The last mentioned items are notable for their minimum of decoration and the limited variety of their styles. The woven blankets are also not elaborate, their decoration usually consisting of one or two thin stripes at each end of an otherwise blank expanse of brown or off-white. The belts, which are worn by both men and women, are quite beautiful. In contrast to the stark simplicity of most items, they sometimes have fairly intricate geometric designs in three or four colors.

Perhaps the most intense aesthetic expression of these Tarahumaras is their music. This appears simple and repetitive, yet it has some subtleties to the knowledgeable listener. The instruments which they now make are the violin, guitar, rattle, Easter drum, and flute. With the exception of the flute, considerable time and skill are required in making all of these instruments, even though by standards of Western technology they may appear to have been fashioned quickly. Occasionally, one finds an instrument very well made, with some carved embellishment.

I have described how houses are simply constructed of logs or stone with no nails or mortar. Though the Tarahumara grain storage house is well constructed, the elaboration of architectural form and style in general is minimal by any comparative standard.

The *Pagótome* Tarahumara communities have a whole set of Western-derived aesthetic items not possessed by the *Gentiles*. Most of these items have been transformed to conform with Indian concepts which are connected with the sets of ceremonies carried out during the Christmas period and at Holy Week. Decorated Easter paraphernalia used by the *Pagótome* includes crosses, pine arches with wreaths, flowers woven from dasylirion, Judas figures carved of wood or constructed of grass, painted drums, decorated lances and swords, and crude body painting (see López, 1972).

Pagótome items receiving some aesthetic attention are those associated with Christmas, though they are often used at other times as well. For example, there are the costumes of the *matachíne* dancers. The *corona* is a crown made of mirrors, pieces of tin cans, cardboard and colored crepe paper. Formerly, *coronas* incorporated feathers and animal tails (Lumholtz, 1902:354). Other *matachíne* items requiring a degree of workmanship are the dancers' *palmas*, wands and rattles, and the carved wooden masks of the *chapeyókos*. The bright clothing of the *matachínes* is now created from bandannas and manufactured cloth.

Of course, standards of style and quality exist in many activities, and aesthetic satisfaction is evident in some of them. For example, I have described how certain women are semi-specialists in making *tesgüino ollas* and baskets, as others are of blankets and sashes. The Indians can instantly identify the part of the Sierra which a person comes from by the cut of the loincloth or shirt, and the type of headband, blanket and sash he wears. A sense of style is certainly present, but in comparison with most cultures, the Tarahumara have not refined these crafts, and devote little attention to such pursuits. The artistic aspect of life in this region is relatively unelaborated.

More Specific Values

At a lower level of abstraction than the general value orientations described above are a number of more overtly recognized Tarahumara values, which are similar to those of many other groups. Principal among these are wisdom, industriousness, wealth, initiative in organizing activities, and self-control. Such are the qualities of men of highest status. Physical skills such as running are also highly prized, as is oratorical ability, called "speaking strongly."

SOCIAL CONTROL—THE LEGAL SYSTEM

We are now prepared to examine the types of offenses considered important by the *Gentiles*, their relative seriousness and frequency, and the kinds of attitudes and sanctions which are involved. The offenses are considered in the order of their seriousness.

Murder

As in most other cultures, killing another person is the most grave criminal offense among the Tarahumara of this region. It is the only crime considered serious enough to invoke authority from outside the community. The stated rule is that murderers of both Inápuchi and Aboreáchi be taken by a group of men to Mexican authorities in Bajisóchi, from whence they can be transported to jail in the *municipio* at Batopilas. The frequent result is that they are kept several months and then, if they can scrape up some form of compensation for the authorities, they are released. A man from Rynárachi who had killed his wife three years prior to the study was set free after three months when he bribed the officials with two yokes of oxen and thirty goats. He returned to his *rancho* and remained there until his death by disease about a year later. However, the following case reveals that even though murder is the most serious offense, the Tarahumara view of it is quite different from our own.

The Case of Román Inápuchi

About a year previous to the study, Román of Inápuchi *rancho* killed the father of Juan-Tasio at a *tesgüinada* by bashing his head with a rock. The men present held a meeting the following morning to decide what to do. Rodrigo Uarárari (*siríame*) dispatched Seledonio to trick Román into coming over by telling him he would help him escape or help pay for his release from the authorities. When Román came to the house of Dionicio with Seledonio he was seized by the *sontársi*, Patricio and Valencio, and taken to Bajisóchi where he was turned over to the authorities. Two days later Román escaped from the shed in Bajisóchi where he was being held waiting to be taken to jail in Batopilas. He returned to his house in Inápuchi. The Mexicans showed no more interest in the case and sent no one after him.

At first he tried to avoid the other people of the *rancho* except for his wife and children. For several months he stayed out very late with the goats every day and did not attend *tesgüinadas*. Finally, he began attending sporadically, and at the time of the study he was present at most of them. None of the people did anything further about his offense. They all said he was a fine person who was not entirely responsible for the murder because he was drunk at the time. Juan-Tasio, the man whose father was killed, now gets along fine with Román (according to other members of the community and personal observation). Román still tends to get somewhat violent at *tesgüinadas* but so do some others, and his behavior is not considered to be particularly out of line (see Chapter 3). He is not thought to be a different type of individual because of his crime, though several informants stated that he will go down to the underground world of *Diablo* after death.

Serious Injury Due to Aggression

This is a rare crime, and may bring about mobilized group sanctions, but it does not require any appeal to Mexican authorities. The following two cases are the only ones I was able to elicit from informants. The second occurred outside the *Gentile* community, but its repercussions were felt inside it.

The Case of Juan-Tasio and Jesús

In the course of a *tesgüinada*, Juan-Tasio and Jesús who stand in a classificatory brother-in-law (joking) relationship began taunting one another in the traditionally approved way (see Chapter 6). It started to get serious when Juan-Tasio accused Jesús of "using his" wife. They began wrestling in earnest and the slighter Juan-Tasio got Jesús down and was choking him. By the time they were separated, Jesús was unconscious and though he recovered, he could not talk for a week thereafter. At the next *tesgüinada*, there was much discussion of what should be done about this incident. Rodrigo Uarárari, the *siríame*, gave a sermon about the wickedness of such violent conduct and the men present finally got together and decided to punish Juan-Tasio. They made him sit on the ground before them, and Rodrigo lectured him on his bad behavior, then fined him one goat for his action, which was paid to Jesús immediately. Since that time, Juan-Tasio has gotten into several other fights, but none have been serious enough to arouse the people to invoke formal sanctions. An important punishment imposed upon him for his persistent aggressiveness has been an informal ban on inviting him to *tesgüinadas* outside of the *rancho* of Inápuchi.

The Case of Armando

In a *tesgüinada* at Basigóchi *rancho* Armando became drunk and accused his wife of having intercourse with another man. He pulled out his knife and stabbed her in the abdomen causing her

225

to bleed profusely. Thinking he had killed her, he ran away down into the *barranca* to hide. Meanwhile, a doctor from the Instituto Nacional was called. After several hours he arrived, and managed to save the woman's life. During the period of several days while the wife's life was still in danger the news about the incident spread throughout the Sierra.

I happened to be in Inápuchi at a large *tesgüinada* when one of the arriving men brought the news there. It caused a great stir of excitement, and Patricio, the *capitán* and best speechmaker of the area was urged by the older men present to gather all the people together for a sermon. In it he recounted the incident, spoke of how evil it was to attack others, and of how *sontársi* should be sent to help capture Armando. He spoke of how the Tarahumara should live in peace, and not fight or "use" the wives of others. The men present all concurred saying that this sort of thing was caused by women, and thanked Patricio for his strong words. However, no action was organized, and later in the evening I witnessed much behavior of the sort which must have provoked the incident (cases of adultery, and accusations and fights relating to them). About a week later, Armando finally heard the news of his wife's recovery. He came back and was reunited with her. Although the people were very upset over this incident, it was said that nothing was done because she recovered.

Theft

Stealing is an offense for which the culprits may be taken to the high authorities of Aboreáchi *ejido*, but up until the present time the *Gentiles* have not availed themselves of this recourse. All cases remembered by Inápuchi informants have been settled among the people of the *Gentile ranchos* themselves. Theft is not frequent, but it is relatively easy and there is considerable anxiety about it. It is one reason, in addition to animal care and field watching, for leaving children at home during *tesgüinadas*. Another kind of precaution revealing concern over theft is the tricky wooden lock used by many Indians for their storage house doors. Sometimes a man additionally puts a seal of white clay on his grain house lock so that it will be immediately apparent if it has been opened in his absence. The only important case of stealing in the Inápuchi area in the few years prior to the study was the following:

The Case of Rijónsi

Rijónsi is the wife of Román Inápuchi. She is about twenty years his senior and is known by everyone for her propensity to steal. For several years she had been stealing, and though people of Inápuchi had known who was doing it, they did nothing about it because she was not caught in the act. Rijónsi taught her young daughter to help her, and sometimes while most of the other members of the *rancho* were away drinking, these two would steal anything lying around, and even break into corn cribs. They stole cloth, beads, corn, knives, etc. Several times they were noticed with small goods of others. Finally, they were caught in a large theft when another daughter reported at a *tesgüinada* that her mother and sister were out stealing. Several *sontársi* were sent to catch them. They brought them back and a trial was held immediately at the *tesgüinada*.

Seledonio Inápuchi acted as judge since Rodrigo Uarárari was not present. Seledonio gave them a sermon. He sentenced Rijónsi to be taken to Aboreáchi to stand trial at the pueblo center, but she lay down on the trail in fear and resisted all efforts to move her. He then sentenced her to six whip lashes which were administered by the *capitán*. The daughter also received three lashes and mother and daughter were locked in Dionicio's corn crib for the night. They were made to return the stolen goods and were fined one goat. Rijónsi had not robbed anyone in the community for almost a year prior to our inquiries, though it is rumored that she recently had killed and eaten a cow belonging to a Mestizo rancher in the area.

Fighting and Adultery

At the beginning of most large *tesgüinadas* and all other fiestas, the *siríame* or another important man gives a "sermon" to the gathered people. Generally, this is an admonition to behave well while drinking. The people are cautioned not to fight or to engage in sexual intercourse with unmarried people or with the spouses of others. Stealing, gossip, and child care are also frequently mentioned. The speaker reminds the people not to pick up the headbands or sashes of others, and not to speak "badly" of anyone. (Sorcery as well as gossip is implied here). He tells them to keep children away from the drinking area, and occasionally gives a warning about behavior towards Mestizos—Tarahumaras should not cohabit with them or trust them. The principal concerns emphasized in these sermons are fighting and adultery.

Since fighting is frequent and adultery only a little less so, the frequency and emphasis of these admonitions seems in direct proportion to the actual occurrence of the prohibited acts during drinking parties. At most *tesgüinadas*, some kind of angry altercation ending in serious physical struggle occurs, and fighting and sexual suspicions are often linked. I estimate that between 50 and 70 percent of the fights are motivated by sexual jealousy.

Formal sanctions may theoretically be invoked against people who fight; in practice, even struggles which have resulted in bruises and cuts are forgotten the day after the *tesgüinada*, unless they result in serious injury. If asked about his fighting the next day, the person shrugs it off as due to *tesgüino*. Informal sanctions are brought to bear against persistent offenders by not inviting them to *tesgüinadas*; being deprived of this most valued form of social intercourse is effective punishment for most people.

The general *laissez-faire* orientation toward the actions of others is evident in the manner in which fights are handled. They are generally allowed to progress until blood actually flows or until one of the antagonists reaches for a weapon of some kind. This tendency to refrain from intervention is partly a result of the behavioral latitude allowed in joking relationships, and of the roughness which is considered normal in *tesgüinada* wrestling. It is also a manifestation of the "independence" orientation described earlier.

However, there are limits to this independence. If injury or murder appears imminent, friends and relatives often try to break up the conflict before serious casualties result. Each antagonist is then taken some distance away from the drinking area and some person of authority, or one who "talks well," is brought to lecture him in the traditional way. This serves to cool the combatants down, and the drinking resumes its affable atmosphere.

With regard to adultery and fornication the Tarahumara attitude is generally ambivalent. These actions are overtly forbidden, yet, in the general permissiveness of the *tesgüinada*, they are indulged in without apparent inhibition, and later there is no remorse. I never discovered a case of adultery outside the context of the drinking bout. In the ordinary course of life men joke about catching a woman at home alone, but women frequently run away if approached by a stranger, and a neighbor generally keeps his distance. On the contrary, the *tesgüinada* is known by all to be an opportunity for adventurous intercourse. Occasionally *tesgüinada* liaisons result in the loss of the spouse, and there were two recent cases of this among those living in Inápuchi. In both instances a fine of one goat was levied against the man who left his wife to live with another woman.

People are drawn to *tesgüinadas* because of the pre-eminent social and psychological needs satisfied by this institution. At the same time, it is recognized that there is some danger of losing one's mate. This is a relatively small danger, even though there is a gnawing knowledge that the spouse may cohabit with others. Still, the situation is ambivalent since the individual may anticipate having pleasurable extramarital activity himself. Because of such fears, some men are reported to go very infrequently to *tesgüinadas*. The number of fights motivated by jealousy indicates the psychocultural strain here.

No sanctions are normally brought to bear for adulterous behavior unless it results in the actual breakup of marriage. The unanimous opinion of informants was that *tesgüino* is to blame for this behavior, as it is for fighting. Such infractions are ascribed to the beer. Informants do not mention the underlying hostilities which sometimes exist, the aggressive impulses which people feel, or the permissive norms of the *tesgüinada* institution.

Property Damage

The offenses so far discussed, with the exception of thefts, occur almost exclusively in the context of the *tesgüinada*. Property damage, however, refers exclusively to damage done by animals to growing crops or to fences. If the owner can be proved guilty the penalty is equal repayment in kind. It is understood that authorities can be called upon in such cases, but no instances of such action were reported. In three remembered cases of animal damage to fields, an informal settlement was made of an amount of corn or beans equivalent to what was lost.

Disputes

The following case illustrates the minimal institutional means for settling disputes in the Inápuchi area. In the *Pagótome* part of

Aboreáchi pueblo the officials are vested with authority in such matters, and a new official, the *comisario ejidal*, is especially effective in providing clearcut abiding decisions. The *Gentiles* of Inápuchi never call upon *ejido* officials to settle a dispute. The difficulty in the following case arises from the ambiguity deriving from the norms of absolute individual inheritance and lifelong possession of land and the informal norm of advance inheritance.

The Case of Rodrigo

After the death of his third wife, Rodrigo Uarárari married María Inápuchi, who had recently become a widow. Rodrigo already had large fields and no children, but he wished to increase his planting by utilizing one of the fields of his new wife which was at Inápuchi *rancho*. For two years he cultivated both *ranchos*, but the traveling back and forth across the canyon between the *ranchos* of Uarárari and Inápuchi was so strenuous that he decided to let the land on Inápuchi lie fallow for a year. Two more years went by and it was still lying unused. Meanwhile, the sister of Seledonio Inápuchi had matured and married, bringing her husband to Inápuchi where she had a small field inherited from her dead father. It was hardly enough to support them and their two children, and seeing the fallow field of Rodrigo and María nearby, Seledonio's sister and husband began working it, justifying the action by saying that it was her rightful inheritance. This arrangement is most convenient for the young couple because this land adjoins their other field in Inápuchi. It is also not an illogical arrangement since Rodrigo Uarárari has large fields in Uarárari which more than satisfy his own subsistence needs and those of his present wife. Having no children of his own, he does not need land for the purpose of making his descendants secure. There is also some justification because Seledonio's sister *is* one of the legitimate heirs. However, this usurpation has bothered Rodrigo Uarárari for several years. He occasionally threatens to meet with the other officials to settle the dispute by invoking the inheritance rules, but he never does. It remains simply another of the persisting and unresolved points of tension in the community.

Other economic disputes arise which are not based upon conflicting property claims. As mentioned previously, fighting is particularly prohibited. *Tesgüinadas* provide an outlet for aggressive impulses through permitted means such as wrestling and aggressive sexual kinship roles, but often these get out of hand and genuine fights occur. Sexual jealousy often is the cause of aggressive actions, but economic jealousy is another source.

At *tesgüinadas* people sometimes make exaggerated claims of wealth which are countered by the bragging of others. These competitive cycles may result in threats to use peyote, or in physical aggression. Generally, such bursts of hostility come to naught; they are held to be the result of *tesgüino*, and they do not lead to persisting feuds. However, there are occasions when they eventuate in longer standing conflicts.

> Juan-Tasio is very jealous of Seledonio Inápuchi because of the latter's greater wealth and ceremonial prestige. Seledonio is invited "very far" whereas Juan-Tasio rarely is invited to other *ranchos* to drink. On several occasions he has not stopped with boasts that he is wealthier than Seledonio, but has physically attacked the latter at *tesgüinadas*. On one occasion which I witnessed, they injured one another's eyes and blood was running down both their faces. The next day Juan-Tasio came over and apologized to Seledonio.

Disputes of this type again illustrate the importance of prestige and wealth as important motivations in this economically low powered classless society with its egalitarian ethic.

Sexual Deviance

The *na'wi* or *hombre-mujer* (man-woman) Mauricio was a mature man of about 27 when it is said that he suddenly turned into a woman. At the time of the study he was about 40, and known for performing woman's work. He wore a costume intermediate between that of male and female and spoke with a forced high-pitched voice. Several strings of beads hung around his neck (most Tarahumara men no longer wear strings of beads, though it was typical earlier as shown in old photographs), and he draped a piece of cloth around his hips in a semblance of a skirt. In other words, Mauricio wore neither the male loincloth nor the full set of woman's skirts, but affected ambiguous dress. Mauricio was once married and has a teenage son, but at the time of our study he lived with a younger unmarried brother of about 25. Mauricio, who likes to be called Celia, frequents *tesgüinadas*, and when drunk, sometimes attempts to behave in an aggressive feminine manner toward men. He also engages in playful kinship behavior of a sexual nature with his classificatory granddaughters. According to Tarahumara belief, such people alternate their gender every month. However, during the entire period I was in the area this man consistently maintained a female role.

Most people had no explanation of why Mauricio behaved in this way. Some simply said that he wished to avoid men's work. One informant explained that Mauricio once wandered into a burial cave in the *barranca* where he encountered some magical poles set in the form of a blanket-weaving frame. Suddenly the poles came to life, seized him, and transformed him into a woman.

From a social control standpoint the salient fact is that even though recognized as deviant, Mauricio is accepted as he is. He is low in prestige, and despite his age he has no voice in important community affairs. Nevertheless, his nonconformist behavior is not censured except by slight ridicule. Informants laughed when I brought up his name, but they denied that he was in any way discriminated against. He is invited to *tesgüinadas* and takes an active part, although he usually does not participate in cooperative labor with the other men. Once, when he made a sexual advance to a man, he was gently repulsed in a dignified way. Though I never saw a sign of acquiescing to his desires, no anger was shown toward his behavior. The general attitude is that Mauricio has no control over his condition. In keeping with the Tarahumara value on individual freedom, the *hombre-mujer* is allowed to do as he likes so long as he allows others the same privileges.

Conclusion

There has been no development of any kind of strong political organization among the Tarahumara. This is probably due to the isolated and scattered character of the population which is the result of the unyielding ruggedness of their environment and the consequent need to be opportunistic in the use of economic resources. These ecological forces at the same time condition a strong sense of individuation and independence and the cultural tradition relating to these values in turn limits the Indians' willingness to submit to political coercion. Thus, the only major forces for social constraint are internalized attitudes; strongly held feelings of propriety prevent the normal expressions of aggressive

Hombre-Mujer (man-woman)

behavior or the assertion of power over others. These internalized restraints appear to create strong internal tensions which are repressed in the ordinary intercourse of daily life, but which are released in the special situation of the *tesgüinada*, resulting in the overt expressions of sexual acts and hostility. This often takes the form of humorous insults and horseplay of an essentially sexual character sanctioned by the concept of joking relationship between a variety of potential partners, but this joking occasionally flares into true conflict that results in verbal abuse, accusation and threats of sorcery, bloody fighting, and in one instance a violent murder. Thus, almost all rule breaking and nearly all acts of overt hostility take place within the context of the beer party.

Tarahumara beliefs and attitudes externalize these acts of interpersonal violence—they lay the blame for antisocial behavior on beer. Thus, it is possible for the Tarahumara to think of themselves both as equal and as gentle—and to be perceived as such by outsiders—because the antisocial acts are the result of something outside of human volition. They do not wonder why they are drawn to beer parties in the first place or why violence is so much a regular part of the beer drinking complex. These attitudes enable them to "forgive and forget" when the morning comes, to deny or at least to disregard outbursts of violence and to forgive what are, even by their standards, the most outrageous breaches in behavior.

The tensions found among the Tarahumara of Inápuchi revolve around two parameters that are denied. The first of these is sexuality. While in ordinary life a high level of moral propriety is preserved and impropriety is rarely given public expression, it is clear that aggression and sexuality lie under the peaceful surface of Tarahumara behavior. Second, while the people of Inápuchi consistently preserve a fiction of equality and do not admit to roles of differential prestige and power, there are among them many who are extremely jealous of status advancement and desirous of prestige. It is around these areas of sex and prestige that violence tends to occur in the context of beer drinking and this in turn gives evidence of the psychological reality that underlies the social facade of passivity, morality, and egalitarianism.

Despite the minimal institutionalized machinery for settling disputes in Inápuchi, there is a surprising lack of retaliatory attacks or direct reprisals for injuries. Those disputes which occur are between relatively unsupported individuals, and the ecologically determined overlapping system of cooperation results in split loyalties. This, along with the permissive institution of the *tesgüinada*, which enables violent impulses to be channeled off in a permitted manner, helps to account for the surprising lack of persisting enmities and feuds. Additionally, when it is realized that the major part of a person's time is spent in relative isolation and that the pattern of economic life with its limited goods and slow social mobility potential does not afford many opportunities for aggressive or deviant behavior, the relative lack of formal legal means for handling disputes becomes more understandable.

The sermon-giving method of social control, both as punishment and as warning, should be recalled here. Public shame is the most frequently invoked sanction against deviant behavior, and it is a most effective means of enforcing conformity among the Tarahumara. Fear of public humiliation creates powerful restraints, and the public whipping is an example of the shame sanction in extreme form.

One of the chief ways an important man or official influences behavior in favor of the traditional norms is through the advice-giving pattern at the personal as well as the public level. He may be called aside by a man at a *tesgüinada* to lecture his wife who does not stay home and perform her duties correctly, or he may be called upon to give a stiff reprimand to a youth who is acting improperly.

The effectiveness of this method is further evidence of the importance of the independence and nonviolent orientations among the Tarahumara. The individual is not threatened, but is remonstrated with. It is pointed out to him in a quiet, calm and rational manner that he is violating the norms he knows are correct. This is usually enough to deter further deviation, for at least the immediate situation. The behavior of the official or high ranking person toward the offender is gentle and nonviolent, much like the parent-child relationship in Tarahumara society. Resort to harsh measures of punishment such as whipping or locking the offender in a corn crib are made only under extreme provocation and community arousal. Even then, communal indignation does not continue at a high pitch. After the initial reaction against those who violate the rules, the tendency is to treat them as before. In the rugged Sierra, productive community members are valuable. No inherent evil or malevolence as persisting character traits are assumed, and the blame is placed primarily on beer.

CHAPTER 8

SHAPING FORCES OF TARAHUMARA SOCIAL LIFE

It is clear that the close relationship which the Tarahumara have with their environment—their ecology—has had a powerful influence on the formation of their particular kind of sociocultural life. However, it is also evident that knowledge of their habitat and its relationships to their modes of gaining a livelihood cannot account for many features of their society. Let us now review the most basic cultural-environmental relationships in Tarahumara social life (the cultural core), before tying in other features which are less directly connected with the ecology: features which are more peripheral and potentially more variable. However, many of these do show traces of the underlying ecological forces, but the connections are less clear.

It is useful to begin by asking just how precisely, and in what specific ways does the environment affect the socio-cultural organization of this group. The concept of the "cultural core" developed by Julian Steward provides a starting point:

> [Cultural core] ... The constellation of features which are most closely related to subsistence activities and economic arrangements. The core includes such social, political, and religious patterns as are empirically determined to be closely connected with these arrangements (1955:37).

Though the criteria for determining which patterns are "closely connected" or causative are not clearly specified by Steward, the problem does not seem so difficult in this case. Attributes of

Tarahumara living arrangements most closely associated with techno-environmental requirements are:

- the generally small size of population aggregates
- the comparatively great variations and fluctuations in size of these aggregates
- the comparatively wide dispersal of people (or the relatively great distance between aggregates, as measured by foot travel)
- the relatively high degree of spatial mobility

These four features are determined by the humanly difficult topographical features of the Sierra Madre mountains, as exploited by a technology of plow agriculture and herding, by influencing the amount and distribution of food supplies.

Let me summarize some of the data:

- The broken terrain coupled with occupation of the best land by members of an alien culture does not permit large groupings of co-residing Tarahumara.
- The spacing and locations of farming and habitation plots under a system of plow agriculture are determined by the sufficiency of arable land and by the availability of drinking water. These plots of land are distributed according to the chances afforded by topographical features. Therefore, in this environment they generally lie from 20 minutes to two hours apart by foot travel.
- The population of any given *rancho* thus generally varies in size with the amount of land available for plowing but it is also affected by marriages and inherited land in other *ranchos*.
- *Ranchos* vary in area, hence their populations vary in size from two to 100, but with a range of about 10 to 25 people (i.e., two to five households).
- Animals are essential for subsistence, but the climate, topography, and cultural techniques do not allow easy and close access to feed; distant grazing trips are required.
- Animals require some kind of winter adjustment because of their susceptibility to cold. Consequently, the most logical means of adjustment within Tarahumara technology is movement of the herd to warmer winter quarters.

Given the existing technology, the environment tends to produce fragmentation of large potentially cohesive groups by fragmentation of subsistence possibilities and economic requirements. This, in addition to the necessities for frequent movement, tends to prevent such large social groups from forming. Intensifying the environmental forces working against accumulation of land are the effects of the equal inheritance rules, which act to insure food for all, but entail greater mobility. Thus, these also militate against extended family solidarity. It is easy to see that such rules have survival value, though it would be an overstatement to say that they themselves were "determined" by the environment in a simple fashion.

This set of ecological factors does not provide the conditions necessary for the formation of unilineal kin groups or social units based upon common residence. In other societies where subsistence farming or herding are the basis of subsistence, it is often advantageous and "natural" to reside with or near parents because of assistance with maturation care and major tasks, along with inheritance probabilities. Extended families, clans, and lineages are the result. In the Tarahumara case, general land scarcity, differential distribution of resources, and differential family size make it necessary that a newly married couple have an open choice with regard to which of the parental *ranchos* will be selected for postmarital residence. Such a set of conditions does not encourage the consistent association of newly married couples with one parental family or the other, a situation which appears to be a precondition for the development of unilineal kin groups.

However, the processes favoring social fragmentation give us only a part of the picture. On the positive side, the network type of community structure developed by the Tarahumara is a natural adaptation to such a set of environmental conditions. The following set of interrelated statements enables us to account in large measure for the underlying network form which socially ties *ranchos* together in the *tesgüino* network system:

- There are pressures for economic cooperation, but the uncertainties of climate, and the requirements imposed by other important tasks such as herding, carrying of wood and water, coupled with the often small membership of the residence group which has been mentioned—these are not only small in actual size, but are frequently diminished by the dispersal of people to care for distant fields—make it difficult for the family group to accomplish larger tasks. Thus, conditions periodically occur which make it necessary to recruit extra help for the survival of some families. In such low population aggregates and given exposure to a number of debilitating diseases, high mortality randomly reduces the small work force. Under these conditions, the difficulties of the terrain render it impossible, even for individuals of good health and great stamina, to carry out all life-maintaining tasks at all necessary times.

• Needs for assistance are intensified by the ever present requirement of herding. If help were not secured at critical times, food supplies would be lost.

• Unpredictable and uncontrollable weather conditions, along with high frequencies of sicknesses create uncertain conditions which foster collective religious rituals. This is partially because the people in a larger area than any one *rancho* are warned of these threats at any given time. Thus, they seek reinforcement from others in the same situation in collective attempts to ward off the feared disasters of illness and famine. Economic considerations and common sense make it easier for a limited number of religious practitioners to handle common anxiety producing events collectively.

• There are many pressures, deriving from the universal interaction needs of human beings, to associate with larger groups than the family. Among these are: sexual desires, (coupled with the universal incest taboos), entertainment desires (driven by needs to escape boredom), needs for release of aggression, and needs for extrafamilial social control assistance. Such basic human motivations work together to produce general tendencies to gather in groups larger than the nuclear family.

Given the powerful universal conditions for social association, working in the context of the dispersed settlement pattern with its requirements for daily and seasonal movement, the network type of social structure which they created is highly adaptive. Since the fields of all Tarahumara families require the same kind and a similar amount of cooperative assistance, it is highly expedient that the labor force rotate from one *rancho* to another. Given this rotation, the adaptive processes of human pragmatic logic have led the Tarahumara to utilize the opportunities created by any social gathering for carrying out more than one group social function. Non-economic social activities have been adapted to coincide with the economic demands.

The overlapping character of the family-centered social networks with their shifting locales of group aggregation is a more practical solution than would be a fixed territorial group with rigid boundaries and a single fixed meeting place. A fixed grouping pattern in this precipitous environment would mean at least twice the amount of strenuous traveling for people on the peripheries. Some of them would have to travel to houses on the opposite side of their "community" area. A single meeting place for community affairs would also inevitably favor those living nearby at the expense of those at greater distances, while a rotating meeting place is fair to all. A fixed meeting place requires an enormously greater expenditure of energy for men, women, and children living far from the center.

If each social activity was specialized and had its own time and place, as is the case in many complex societies, the number of such activities would exceed the possibility of attendance. Economic requirements of daily life, seasonal moving, and often necessary movement to an in-law's *rancho* all act dynamically to weaken territorial bonds. Despite spectacular instances to the contrary, human beings usually try to minimize effort expended and to maximize their individual advantages. Under the conditions described here, the result of environmental conditions and human propensities and limitations, is the *tesgüino* network, a centrifugal household centered social system composed of many overlapping dyadic ties.

Such a simple case may provide some insight into some of the ways an environment may affect a social organization. Under certain conditions of economy, topography, and climate, we may discern how pressure may be exerted in predictable ways toward certain solutions of social organizational problems and to work against other forms. An extreme situation, like that of the Tarahumara, illustrates such dynamics clearly. Now if environment and economy can be seen to operate to generate the basic structure of Tarahumara social organization, we may now ask what effects the settlement pattern, and the social system which has developed in adaptation to it, may have upon *other* aspects of life and culture.

Though they never systematically analyzed it, most previous writers on this group mentioned the environment to account for many features of Tarahumara life, e.g., the monograph by Bennett and Zingg, emphasizes the effects of the scattered settlement pattern—the fact that individuals tend to have their interactions reduced to a minimum by the environmental restrictions. As I see it, some of these effects are:

• the relatively equal importance of the sexes in economic production
   • the flexibility of sex roles
   • the flexibility of work routines
   • the lack of economic specialization
   • the importance of individual initiative, as well as cooperation and voluntary action in group economic tasks
   • the practical emphasis and economic orientation of ritual
   • the norm of sharing food to prevent starvation
   • the relative roles of herd size, limitation, care and so forth, in wealth accumulation
   •the lack of economic classes

These characteristics of the social organization all have an aspect directly related to techno-environmental imperatives. Most of them are interrelated with the following sets of social and cultural features as well.

In the Political Realm
Leadership is weak and is constrained within a rudimentary official hierarchy. There is a relative lack of authority, an unclarity of role definition, and a reliance upon individual influence. These qualities are related to the lack of permanent cohesive social units and to the relative infrequency of needs for organizing activities. This group of interrelated features of governance, in turn, results from low population density, dispersal, and isolation. The relative lack of institutionalized means to resolve disputes also is plainly related to overlapping social affiliations. The absence of revenge as a means for settling disputes and the absence of feuding for redressing serious grievances relates to the overlapping nature of

cooperative social ties and the concomitant lack of cohesive groups above the nuclear family. The egalitarian, nonviolent value system cannot be said to be caused by the ecological circumstances of the Tarahumara, but it is consistent with it, and it can be postulated that once established, reinforces it, and is reinforced by it.

The Religious Realm

Ecological influence is clearly reflected in certain religious features of the society:

• Most rituals are concerned with palliation of fears arising from factors closely related to the uncertainties of ecological adaptation.

• Ritual is geared to the cycle of practical needs of men, fields, and animals. Due to lack of sufficient surplus in such an economy there is no organized hierarchy, and due to the individualism fostered under such a social system the recruitment to the role of *owerúame* is determined by self-selection.

• Temporal and spatial flexibility is also demanded by the distances between *ranchos*, and in the forms of ritual activities upon the defined needs of individuals and crops for curing. Thus, ceremonies generally involve relatively small numbers of people, and widely separated individuals make independent decisions about times and places of gathering (inviters and *owerúames*).

In the Realm of Kinship

• Residence, marriage, and the bilateral method of kin reckoning are related to ecological needs and requirements. *Ranchos* vary in size but on the whole they are too small to support enough people to form a survival group. Because surviving offspring vary in number, an inequitable distribution of scarce land and animals is created. Under customs of favored inheritance (such as primogeniture) which prevail in some societies, such environmental conditions would result in extinction for some members.

• Among the Tarahumara the equal inheritance rule reinforces the bilateral-bilocal pattern, and it too appears to be an outgrowth of ecological forces.

• Differential needs for manpower (e.g., a goat herder or harvesting help) occur for the same ecological reasons so that a newly married couple will live at the *rancho* where need or opportunity is greatest.

• The relatively important status of women (itself related to survival problems in the Sierra) further reinforces the randomness of postnuptial residence choice. This, in turn, creates a tendency for individuals to inherit rights to land in at least two *ranchos,* entailing further mobility, reinforcing the total pattern. The ecological system thus creates a dynamism favoring bilocality and bilaterality.

• The relative unimportance of terminology for kin outside the elementary family and the use of names instead to designate individuals reflects the ecologically imposed pattern of isolation.

• Both the stress upon generational terms in kinship classifications and the use of generalized child terms rather than specialized forms for nieces and nephews reflect the general sociological equivalence of people within these generations. These are related to physical remoteness and to the random association of people with the siblings of their fathers and mothers.

• The relative instability of marriage and the custom of voluntary mate selection are related to the relative economic equality of the sexes and to the associated equal inheritance rule, in addition to the environmentally influenced value of individualism.

It is reasonable to suggest that the isolation of households and the requisite pattern of independent action this fosters, serve as important determinants of some of the most characteristic Tarahumara attitudes and personality traits, especially the attitudes of independence and *laissez-faire*, practicality, social equality, and the shy personality structure. Others have pointed out that such features as haphazard house construction and poverty of material culture are resultants of the ecological pattern, especially of its mobility aspect. In turn, poor housing encourages winter moving, and this means less social stability and less accumulation of personal property.

This configuration of closely interdependent techno-environmental elements and sociocultural characteristics may be viewed as the "cultural core" in Steward's terms. In its basic essentials the core underlies both *Pagótome* and *Gentile* variations of Tarahumara culture, and with the same basic technical equipment it accounts for many of the similarities between them.

There is little in ecology and nothing in biology which can explain many of the *differences* between *Gentile* and *Pagótome* subcultures, however. These must be seen primarily as products of history. The simple fact is that the ancestors of the *Pagótome* accepted many aspects of seventeenth and eighteenth century Spanish Catholicism, and many features of Spanish community organization which those of the *Gentiles* did not. The reasons for acceptance or rejection are not entirely clear, but differences in the acceptance of these "diffused" ideas and practices have created significant differences in the lives of each group.

Nevertheless, the ecological imperatives, the "cultural core" of the Tarahumara system were very strong. The Catholic priests assiduously tried for more than two centuries to gather the Indians into centralized villages where they could be better educated (and controlled), but even in the *Pagótome* communities where they were most strong they were never able to achieve this. In this century the government has worked with a similar policy, but without success. The "pueblo" communities of today in Tarahumara country remain largely empty of population except for large ceremonial occasions or for Sunday *juntas*, when community business must be discussed or trials held. The logic of the herding-agricultural economy in the precipitous mountain environment has made it unfeasible to crowd into nucleated villages even if they had wanted to.

The fact that the Mexicans have created villages and towns in several parts of the region is the result of two other factors, in addition to their long European-derived tradition of village life. They occupied the best land by force, and this usually enabled them to procure full support from farmland near their dwellings. Additionally, they always have been connected, however tenuously, with the external support system of the national market economy and political system of Mexico. This relationship to the larger system has helped them maintain a dominant position with regard to the Indians, and has enabled even the poorest Mestizos to maintain a slightly more affluent life.

It is suggestive that many of the social structural features derived by the "Christian" Tarahumaras from the Spaniards appear to be devices which compensate for what might be called the social weaknesses of the basic ecologically consistent social system of the *Gentiles*. For example, for settling disputes, the official with recognized authority for the pueblo is clearly more functional. The *mayóri* system for matching eligible men and women also is obviously a more efficient system for getting potential partners together under conditions of population dispersal than is the *ad hoc* means used by the *Gentiles*. On the other hand, the ecological situation inhibited the acceptance of certain aspects of Spanish culture, such as centralized village structure. It obviously still operates beneath the surface in the *Pagótome* pueblos to produce a lack of intense pueblo unification in spite of the acceptance of Spanish group unifying mechanisms, including customs and norms of Sunday pueblo meeting attendance and an accepted ideal of pueblo unity.

It is now possible to see how important features of the Tarahumara personality structure and aspects of the *tesgüino* complex itself are related to the ecology. All accounts of these Indians comment upon their extreme shyness toward strangers and excessive restraint in the expression of affection among themselves. I have mentioned these traits in a number of contexts and have discussed the cultural-behavioral counterpart—the withdrawal pattern as an adaptation to Mexican encroachment and aggression against them. Along with shyness and inhibition of emotion go great patience, endurance, quietude, passivity and evasiveness. There is a calmness and lack of excitability, with a minimal use of gestures and of other body language while speaking. These all refer to a basic personality syndrome of introversion, in which shame is much more salient than guilt and where there is a tendency to choose flight over fight in threatening situations. Other characteristics of the syndrome are a general wariness, or cautiousness in interpersonal interaction, passivity, inner containment, inward resources, and dignity.

On the other hand, in the *tesgüinada* situation we frequently see metamorphoses in which people seem transformed into aggressive, joking, outgoing, loquacious beings. The often boisterous, extraverted, and sometimes aggressive and ambivalent personality traits which, in this context, come to the fore in many people are the opposite of the passivity, shyness and reserve exhibited under ordinary conditions.

This pattern of behavior, characterized by the eager reaching for the effects of alcohol, with its institutionalized support for reversing the day-to-day personality pattern, is certainly neither an inevitable nor a completely predictable consequence of the ecology. However, it is reasonable to assume that this degree of social isolation at once results in two conflicting character traits: a deep-seated need for social contact and an exceptional shyness. The *tesgüinada* institution offers the needed social contact and at the same time provides a patterned alternative to ordinary normative behavior. Both of these compensating functions are enhanced and excused by the intoxicating effects of the beer. It must be emphasized, however, that, whatever the psychological sources may be of the *tesgüinada* tradition of the Tarahumara, it in turn has its own behavioral consequences. We now turn to a consideration of these.

Effects of the Tesgüino Complex

It is clear that the alcoholic beverage *tesgüino* is associated with the economic, ceremonial, social control, and status systems, as well as with recreational activities of these Indians, and that it is regarded by them as their major incentive to gather in extrafamilial social activities. The satisfactions involved in communal drinking are great, but an examination of some "side effects" of this pattern clarifies other aspects of Tarahumara social life.

The quality of Tarahumara social interaction is colored by the involvement of drinking in almost all social activities. In contrast to many other societies where drinking is a custom, there is no temporal or spatial separation of formal and serious activities from those involving drinking and recreation. The resultant unique social quality stems from a combination of the universal chemical effects of alcohol on the human body and the cultural norms associated with drinking. At all extrafamilial social gatherings of the Inápuchi *Gentiles* these two sets of conditions uniformly create another set of characteristics which is distinctive of their social system.

Contrary to our own conflicting values about drinking, and in spite of 300 years of Catholic influence, the Tarahumara attach no shame to being drunk, and in fact, make drunkenness a matter of pride. After a *tesgüinada* people are proud to brag of their degrees of inebriation. The general result is that feelings of emotional release and the distortion of normal perception engendered by alcohol are associated with all religious, political, and economic activities. Thus, the attitude of respect and seriousness may be taken off of important matters, or at the other extreme, trivial events sometimes take on momentous importance.

These qualitative characteristics may be expressed by saying that regular intake of inebriating amounts of alcohol gives all extrafamilial social situations of the Tarahumara a distinctive atmosphere of increased sociability, accelerated activity, and intensified human closeness. "Society" itself is in effect "created" in association with shared alteration of perception. Group situations thus constitute a different reality from those of individualized daily activity. In the *tesgüinada* the norms and conditions of daily existence are temporarily suspended or modified. The contrast with everyday life created by the beer is heightened by a shared increase in the frequency and quality of social interaction, by the telescoping of social functions into a short span of time, and by their compression in space. Under the stimulus of crowding, the high frequency of interaction, and the altered states of consciousness produced by alcohol, actions tend to take on an exaggerated and intense character, memory is often impaired, and many of the daily operating rules are relaxed or reversed.

When a *tesgüinada* is held at their *rancho* the excluded children watch this forbidden, emotionally charged adult world from a distance. Unlike the normal situation in our own society, where children may occasionally see one of their parents or another adult highly intoxicated, all Tarahumara children witness a regular mass behavioral metamorphosis of all the adults they know. They can fully understand this only when they become regular participants after the age of about 14. It is no exaggeration to state that much of the meaning of Tarahumara social life is derived from the effects of *tesgüino* and the *tesgüinada*. Even a great percentage of dreams of the afterlife and the dead are concerned with *tesgüinadas*.

The qualities of extreme flexibility and uncertainty characterizing many aspects of Tarahumara social organization are basically ecological; the institutionalization of *tesgüino* drinking and its elevation to a position of sociocultural pre-eminence significantly increases the uncertainty and flexibility.

To deal with this phenomenon, the concepts of "costs" and "dysfunctions" are useful. Not all practices are equally beneficial to mankind simply because they exist; it would be ridiculous to argue that Nazism and cannibalism are equal to other political and economic systems in their social and human benefits. This leads to the inference that we must develop some kind of supercultural measuring stick which will enable us legitimately to transcend the bog of total cultural relativism, and the concepts of cost and dysfunction may serve as a beginning in this enterprise. Costs, as I conceive them, refer to practical losses, broadly economic, and threats to life and health. Dysfunctions are socially generated negative effects and losses, such as built-in conflict-generating customs, or institutions which change at differing rates, resulting in "culture lag" or becoming "out of phase."

Some obvious costs for Tarahumara society are things which have obviously negative consequences to health and life, many of which are recognized as deleterious by the Tarahumara themselves. The Indians realize that it is drunkenness which frequently causes the death of an infant when its mother drops it in the fire or, in a stupor, rolls over and crushes it, and that a Tarahumara doesn't injure or kill himself falling over a cliff unless he is stumbling home from a *tesgüinada* in the dark. According to informants both of these types of injury and death are common and they practically never occur except in connection with drinking.

Disease is also related to beer drinking. Since Tarahumara conceptions of sickness have a large supernatural component, they see no connection between infection and the common drinking gourd. On the contrary, they informed me that in addition to the necessity for using it in curing rituals, *tesgüino* has healing properties for many minor illnesses. This attitude seems directly related to the death rate, which is maintained at a high level by almost yearly epidemics of influenza, and high frequencies of pneumonia and tuberculosis. The common overexposure from sleeping along the trail on the way home from *tesgüinadas* on winter nights is seen as related to these, but the lure of *tesgüino* with its personal and social rewards serves to offset this knowledge. Also in the category of costs must be put much of the injury and death resulting from the fighting in *tesgüinadas*, especially since fighting is associated exclusively with drinking.

Another set of costs stems from the circumstance that the "*tesgüino* complex" has had an inhibiting effect upon social change and, thus, has been instrumental in maintaining the low subsistence level of Tarahumara culture. I am well aware of the dangers of such judgements, but on theoretical grounds, one would assume that, given their economic base, there would be a trend in the direction of more complexity of Tarahumara culture. However, my research indicated a general lack of interest in mythology and history, restriction of art to a few crafts, a makeshift quality to their houses despite cold weather and a simple technology based mainly on several basic tools of European origin. Yet the group has been in sporadic contact with the more complex Spanish–Mexican culture for more than 300 years. Since our theories assume that factors of surplus and diffusion are necessary conditions and sufficient causes of cultural development, it is reasonable to look for conditions which in specific situations may render such social developmental factors inoperative.

The fissive effects of the scattered and mobile settlement pattern were among the multiple and interdetermining ecological factors contributing to this cultural level and its particular shape. There also has been a transmitted attitude of fear of foreigners and consequent withdrawal from contact, a large wilderness into which they could retreat and the general poverty of the Mestizo culture with which they were in contact. The *tesgüino* complex has also played a significant part.

The inhibiting effect of institutionalized beer drinking on creative processes seems significant. It is true that creativity is essentially the product of individuals, yet to a large extent it flourishes and increases in environments where there is communication, interaction, and stimulation. In the Tarahumara situation, however, persons are either alone soberly carrying out daily tasks, or they are gathered together under the influence of alcohol. The depressant effects of alcohol are known to inhibit creative processes under most conditions, but additionally, in this case the norms developed for the *tesgüinada* are oriented toward release, sociability, and attainment of personal ends in the short time available. Such conditions militate against the exchange of ideas and creativity.

Another cost of the complex is the dissipation of the corn surplus in making beer. Despite the fact that the wealthier people tend to assume the responsibility for *tesgüinadas* more often and the undoubted nutrient value of the corn beer, the obligation to hold *tesgüinadas* imposes hardship on many people. They are aware that they may have to get into debt with Mestizos or even go hungry, yet a relatively high percentage of their precious corn must go into *tesgüino*.

A third growth-hindering cost is the amount of time devoted to the requirements of the *tesgüino* orientation. If an average figure of four to six times per year per family for making beer is correct, and if a man is reciprocally connected with 15 other households in a *tesgüino* network, he would potentially have the opportunity of getting drunk between 60 and 90 times per year. Actually, the number of potential *tesgüinadas* is slightly reduced by the custom wherein neighboring houses occasionally agree to make *tesgüino* at the same time, a custom increasing the possibility of making the intoxication complete. Allowing for such cooperative ventures and for the various reasons which often prevent attendance, I calculate that individuals attend at least 40-60 *tesgüinadas* per year, sometimes many more. Since beer parties generally last from 10 to 36 hours, with 15 to 20 being the average, a person will minimally spend about 750 hours or 50 fifteen-hour periods engaged in drinking behavior. Since a great deal of social business is actually being accomplished in these drinking periods, to calculate time loss, it is perhaps necessary to add the equal number of days which is takes to recover from the effects of drinking. After a *tesgüinada* a person frequently spends much of the next day inactivated, and a great many hours are spent in the long hikes across rough country to and from these drinking affairs. All this is aside from the considerable energy and time devoted to the preparation of *tesgüino* by the women. Taking these facts together, a conservative estimate is that the average Tarahumara spends at least 100 days per year directly concerned with *tesgüino*, and much of this time under its influence or feeling its aftereffects.

From the standpoint explained above, these effects of the *tesgüino* complex can legitimately be called costs, though from the traditional point of view of anthropology it might be argued that with the manifold functions of the complex, its "adjustive" value more than outweighs these effects. That the pattern is a viable response to the Tarahumara life situation which is very satisfying to the people and which has persisted for at least several centuries is evidence in favor of the functional view. However, it is possible to point to the retarding (or stabilizing) properties of such sets of customary practices from the standpoint of change and development, without making the assumption that such change is inherently "good" or "bad."

Besides being costly, the consequences of the *tesgüino* complex may be viewed as dysfunctional. For example, conformance to the norms of drinking behavior regularly places the Tarahumara individual in a socio-biochemical condition which leads him to violate other norms. A perhaps universal effect of large amounts of alcohol in the bloodstream is the partial breakdown of the internalized self-controls which have been built into the personality from childhood. Among the Tarahumara the effect is the regular transgression of their two most salient moral prohibitions—against fighting and against adultery. Despite a special group of officials (the *capitán* and *soldados*) who have responsibility to prevent such behavior at *tesgüinadas*, both aggression and adultery occur relatively frequently—and most never outside of *tesgüinadas*. On one level this is a case of a built-in conflict among norms, of culturally accepted but opposing demands on the individual. Persons ought to get as drunk as possible, but they should not fight or engage in sex relations with nonspouses, even though they are driven to do so when alcohol weakens their inhibitions.

A second type of dysfunction stemming from the institutionalization of beer drinking occurs when certain socially valued patterns of behavior are interfered with or short circuited by the consequences of the *tesgüino* complex. Examples of such dysfunctional short circuiting are the failure to complete tasks (such as hoeing or harvesting) for which a *tesgüinada* has been called, and failure to execute curing ceremonies regarded as important to crops and health. Those occasions when officials make journeys to distant *ranchos* but are completely sidetracked by *tesgüino* from the business at hand, and those when *owerúames* or native officials shirk their obligations to attend *tesgüinadas* are similar cases in point. In all such misfirings of purposive and culturally necessary activities, not only is the general anxiety attending such purposes intensified, but oftentimes a duplication of effort and expenditures of valuable corn are required.

Such failures are not uncommon accidents but frequent and expectable types of occurrences. They are structurally induced dysfunctions which add to the uncertainties of life to which the Tarahumara are accustomed. Resentment arises from the cooperative work failures, and frustration and time loss result from the sidetracking of officials. Informants said that if the crops should be poor after such a failure it would be because the proper ceremony had not been performed, though the men involved would not be punished for their failure. At least some of the time *tesgüino* may be anticipated to upset the best laid plans.

CONCLUSION

The modern cultural-ecological approach in anthropology arose in response to what is called the cultural–historical theory. As Julian Steward has commented:

> The cultural-historical approach is, however, one of relativism. Since cultural differences are not directly attributable to environmental differences and most certainly not to organic or racial differences, they are merely said to represent divergences in cultural history to reflect tendencies of societies to develop in unlike ways. Such tendencies are not explained. A distinctive pattern develops, it is said, and henceforth is the primary determinant of whether innovations are accepted. Environment is relegated to a purely secondary and passive role. It is considered prohibitive or permissive, but not creative. It allows man to carry on some kinds of activities and it prevents others. The origins of these activities are pushed back to a remote point in time or space, but they are not explained (1955:35).

He goes on to explain that his own concept of cultural ecology is not satisfied with such assumptions:

It differs from the relationship and neo-evolutionist conceptions of culture history in that *it introduces the local environment as the extracultural factor in the fruitless assumption that culture comes from culture* (italics added, ibid., 36).

Assuming the fundamental correctness of Steward's approach, the initial emphasis of this study was upon that most important *extracultural* factor, the environment. But once the potential importance of extracultural variables is realized, the *tesgüino* complex falls into place as another such influence. This complex is a social form which can be seen as an institutionalized response to the constraints imposed upon social life by the mountain ecology. However, once drinking was institutionalized, certain further effects followed, which are, to a degree, independent of culture. The extracultural feature of the *tesgüino* complex stems from the relatively uniform chemical reaction of the human body to alcohol.

The reasoning concerning the constellation of extracultural relationships which are clearly producing certain consequences in this case bears little resemblance to the formulations of the early environmental or racial determinists. For example, it is recognized that the action of the environment is only manifested through a set of cultural practices and beliefs (Forde, 1934:463), so that its effect is always "indirect" to a greater or lesser degree, depending upon the level of cultural development. The important problem is to assess the specific ways in which habitat conditions, or other uniformly acting forces, are dynamically causal. On the other extreme, we can analyze the means by which such forces may be neutralized or negated by culture and social organization. As Steward's work and the present study have shown, under certain sociocultural conditions a particular habitat has determinative (not just permissive) effects with regard to *some* features and qualities of socio-cultural life.

The indirect ways in which the environment and the ramifications of drinking affect and shape Tarahumara social organization are through such intervening variables as geographical mobility, randomization of settlement, dispersion of population, and creation of a behavioral environment radically different from daily life, all of which systematically influence the quality of important social acts. This is far different from saying that climate or topography has determined particular cultural features in a simple one-to-one manner. For example, connections were postulated between topography, economy, residence choice, bilocality, and bilateral kin reckoning, but no environmental explanation was adduced to explain why Tarahumara men call their older sister *kochí* and their younger one *wayé*. Nor was any attempt made to explain ecologically why men have three death fiestas while women have four.

It is evident that the isolation of the effects of extracultural influences, such as topography, institutionalized alcohol use, or endemic disease, is only helpful to explain the shape of social life in special cases. Even under the most extreme circumstances such factors are only a part of the complex multicausal sets of conditions which are responsible for the form of a sociocultural system. I agree with Steward in his reaction against totally historical explanations, yet it is clear that his rejection of the "fruitless assumption that culture comes from culture" is itself a counter reaction which goes too far. Steward himself actually never forgot the role of culture in his own empirical studies in "cultural ecology," even though some of his successors in the ecological field want to speak of "populations" and "ecosystems" in a manner much as if human communities were operating on a subhuman biological adaptational level.

In the case of the Tarahumara, the need to look to historical factors is most obvious when we try to account for almost any aspect of the socio-cultural system. For example, it is obvious that the present level of ecological adaptation typical of the group as a whole was largely dependent upon introductions from Spanish culture. The introduction of domestic animals, plow agricultural techniques, and fruit trees transformed a hunting-gathering-horticultural economy to one of agriculture-herding. Though little evidence is available about that period, obviously such changes had powerful and long-lasting repercussions upon the group. Instead of the more random and wide ranging search for game and edible plants with its effects on territoriality, a more regular temporal pattern and more stable and more limited territory were necessary for herding. Instead of hoe farms on tiny patches of even the most inaccessible hillsides, the plow, oxen, and goat manure made intensive farming of larger and more level plots the logical way to invest labor. Yet the potential of the smaller, more difficult plots, for the most part, was lost. It is easy to see how historical events have been critical to many aspects of ecological adaptation.

Furthermore, though it is evident that there is a congruence between the shy, nonaggressive personality typical of the Tarahumara and their cultural and ecological conditions, the role of history cannot be left out of the equation. In the first chapter of this book I mentioned that at least some of the constellation of traits of withdrawal, nonviolence, and passivity stem from the devastating military defeats and the continuing political and social domination imposed upon the Indians by the Spanish and Mexicans in the seventeenth and eighteenth centuries. This seems evident from the radical change, away from violent physical resistance which characterized their response in the first century of contact, to the quiet patterns which we find today. It seems clear that a whole new set of attitudes which has been consistent with the environmental and other conditions discussed above was planted in them during this early Colonial period. These attitudes have been perpetuated ever since.

A good case could be made that there is a basic *Indian* substratum of attitudes and traits of pre-Colombian origin, in Mexico, and probably the whole Western Hemisphere. Everywhere the Europeans encountered peoples who were characterized by dignified demeanor, restraint of emotions under ordinary conditions, taciturnity, and stoicism. These character traits often went along with unrestrained license on special occasions, unrestrained massacres of enemies, and so forth. I will not go into a long documentation of this here. I only want to call attention to the fact that though a consideration of ecology and the *tesgüinada* institution can tell us much, they cannot account for the entire picture. As with many other aspects of the culture, the basic Tarahumara character structure is rooted in an ancient cultural tradition.

These considerations underscore the importance of historical knowledge for understanding a social system, whenever such knowledge is available. Though history has not been emphasized in this book, I have tried to hold what we know of the past of this isolated people in mind at all times. The *Pagótome* have obviously been most profoundly influenced by Spanish culture, but the resisting *Gentiles* did not escape such influences. They accepted the same economic innovations that the *Pagótome* did, and their belief system was also affected. However, the fact that they early made the conscious choice to separate themselves from the encroaching culture was an historical choice, and the resulting effects of that choice could not have been predicted by any knowledge of ecology or other extra-cultural variables.

In recent years, historical events again have been exerting a profound influence upon the Tarahumara life-style and upon their modes of adapting to the environment. The Indians in the recent past achieved an adaptational equilibrium with their environment, which made reasonable adjustments to the gradual increase of Mestizos in their country. This balance is now being upset. The familiar pattern of the Third World is being re-enacted once again in the Sierra, and with the same disastrous results. Lumber and commercial interests have replaced the mining of the early period as the economic incentives for exploitation of the Indians and their native resources. These powerful interests now are accompanied by the inevitable influx of tourists into this wild, beautiful land.

These threatening forces are sometimes reinforced in many of their effects by the well intentioned programs of the government and the church. The introduction of modern medicine and education is changing the Indians' population balance, transforming the system of wants, and producing another exploitable class with no skills to sell at the bottom of the social ladder in northwest Mexico. The spread of commercial alcohol is disastrous in conjunction with native drinking patterns, and the shy and politically helpless Tarahumara have little recourse against the aggressive incursion of more powerful elements into their once isolated country.

With the development of modern transportation in the region there is no further sanctuary. The old pattern of withdrawal into the mountains will no longer adaptively serve cultural survival. Even the *Gentiles* hidden away in their canyons will soon be forced to contend with the onrushing tide of "civilization." In the face of these disruptions and imminent threats, the costs and dysfunctions built into their aboriginal life appear tame indeed.

It is futile to attempt to stem the tide of history, and nothing is gained by wishing for the preservation of imaginary aboriginal paradises, but the future looks bleak for these peaceful people. Must the Tarahumara travel the same tragic road already so well worn by other American Indian societies?

Appendix

Tarahumara Running

In pre-Colombian times virtually all of the tribes occupying western North America were great runners, and as Peter Nabokov has so well shown, many of them still preserve vital, but somewhat attenuated versions of their running traditions (Nabokov, 1981). The Tarahumara running tradition is especially interesting to us because it is so well preserved, and because it still plays such an important part in their culture. A knowledge of its workings can help us to understand how it must have been when running was a "way of life" for all of the tribes of the Greater Southwest.

The marvelous endurance feats of the Tarahumara, and the importance of running in their lives, have been extolled by nearly every observer who has been among them. Carl Lumholtz, the great Norwegian traveler who first documented the life of these Indians during the last decade of the nineteenth century, stated that their very name for themselves derives from their love of running:

> "This propensity for running is so great that the name of the tribe alludes to it. Tarahumara is a Spanish corruption of ralamari, the meaning of which, though somewhat obscure, may doubtless best be given as "footrunners" because "rala" certainly means foot" (1902:282).

Many journalists since then have seized upon the romantic notion of an entire tribe of foot racers, though modern scholars have not upheld Lumholtz's etymology of their name. Merrill finds that the word *Rarámuri* can refer to people in general, to all Native

Americans, to the Tarahumara tribe, as distinct from the Yáquis, Tepehuánes, etc., or to men as opposed to women (Merrill, 1980:78). Burgess, the foremost linguist of the Tarahumara language, feels that *ra* may come from the word for sun (*rayéna*) and that the best rendering of *Rarámuri* may be something like "Children of the Sun God" (1984: 54). Thus, the popular romantic notion that even the name of the tribe refers to running appears to be erroneous, but that, of course, does not detract from their running abilities, or their feats of stamina.

Fredrick Schwatka, a traveler who spent several months in the Sierra Madre in the late 1880s, was one of the first modern visitors to describe the incredible endurance feats of the Tarahumara:

> "It takes six or seven hours of fairly continuous climbing to make it, by muleback from the mine in a deep gulch to the "cumbra" or crest of the Barranca del Cobre, by a most difficult mountain trail, the ascent being five thousand to six thousand feet. It takes four hours to descend the same way. A message was sent from the "cumbra" by a Tarahumara foot runner to a person at the mine and an answer was received in an hour and twenty minutes, the same messenger carrying the letter both ways. ...Not a great many years ago the mail from Chihuahua to Batopilas was carried by a courier on his back, who made the distance over the Sierra Madre range, a good 250 miles and return, or a total of 500 miles in six days. Here he rested one day and repeated his trip, his contract being for weekly service. I could give a dozen other instances, but these are enough"(1893:202-5).

Lumholtz is the source for many of the statements and anecdotes which even now are used to describe Tarahumara running. For instance,

> "A man has been known to carry a letter in five days from Guasapares to Chihuahua and back, a distance of nearly 600 miles. ...they will run down a deer, following it for days through snow and rain, until the animal is cornered and easily shot with arrows, until it is overtaken utterly jaded and its hoofs falling off" (1902: 282).

From the latter part of the 19th century until the present time stories about the fantastic endurance and running abilities of the Tarahumara have continued to accumulate. Some of these accounts have attained mythical status but my own experience leads me to conclude that many of them reflect true observations. During my original fieldwork in 1959, I was living in a cave in a place called Agua Caliente, a small arroyo on the edge of the community of Inápuchi. One November afternoon I was inside the cave writing up some notes, when I heard excited voices and something crashing through the underbrush. I rushed out just in time to see two Tarahumaras clad only in loincloths hurling large stones at an animal they had cornered down by the creek. They laughed and shouted as they hammered it to death. As I approached I could see that it was a large antlered buck, the kind rarely seen in the Sierra these days. They told me that they had chased it since shortly after sunrise from a valley near Charérachi. I looked at my watch and it was 3:30 P.M. Their pride and elation seemed entirely understandable since they had been running across some of the most difficult terrain in the Sierra Madre for seven or eight hours and were not breathing much more heavily than usual. I was instantly relieved of my skepticism regarding what had seemed like an exaggerated claim: that these Indians can run a deer to exhaustion.

Since then I have often seen Tarahumaras carry 80 pound loads up precipitous trails all day long with a few brief rests. Thus, I also find quite credible the story about Alexander Shepherd, the famous manager of the great silver mine at Batopilas around the turn of the century. It is recounted how he used three teams of four Tarahumaras to haul an upright piano 185 miles across rough mountainous terrain, including descent into the immense Batopilas gorge. It took 15 days to accomplish this feat, after which they ran back to their highland community in three days (Nabokov, 1985).

By the 1920s news of the Tarahumara feats of endurance had reached the outside world and Tarahumara runners began to be transported to compete in various track competitions and exhibitions. The following is an account of a test put on by the Mexican government to showcase the abilities of their native populations.

"The race from Pachuca to Mexico City (100 km.)
Sunday, the seventh of November 1926, the Governor of the State of Hidalgo, at 3:05 A.M. gave letters to Tomás Zafiro, Leon

Sanmiguel, and Virgilio Espinosa containing a cordial greeting to the Governor to the Federal District, which were to be delivered by the winner at his arrival at the Stadium. Accompanying the runners were employees of the Ministry of Education, who were traveling in an autobus of The House of Indian Students, an ambulance of the Red Cross, and a traveling representative of the press. ...Anthropologists of the Department of Rural Schools made physiological observations along the way, taking advantage of brief moments in which they stopped to fix their huaraches, take *pinole* and water, etc. On reaching fifty six kilometers of the distance, Virgilio Espinosa could not continue on account of suffering from an external entorsis of the knee...The other runners continued without incident until reaching the Stadium, where they arrived at 12:42 P.M. that is nine hours, thirty seven minutes after starting, having run an average of eleven kilometers an hour and having lost a total of 30 minutes during ten brief stops to take their *pinole* and for other necessities. A few minutes after their arrival, they were examined and no symptoms of physical depression (fatigue) were found, but on the contrary they began again to run around the track" (Basauri, 1926:42).

This was apparently the first time that the Indians were taken out of their own familiar mountains and asked to perform according to the alien rules of the Euro-American athletic community. However, even though the Pachuca-Mexico City highway with the caravan of crowded motor vehicles was vastly different than their isolated canyon trails, they did amazingly well.

Tarahumara runners were soon brought to the United States in demonstrations similar to the 1926 event in Mexico. Running between San Antonio and Austin, Texas, two Tarahumaras made the distance of 89.4 miles in less than 15 hours. Another Tarahumara set a new record in the 51 mile race between Kansas City and Lawrence, Kansas. His time of 6 hours and 46 minutes broke the old record by more than an hour. These demonstrations took place in 1927 (McClellan, 1979:82).

Mexico entered several Tarahumaras in the Marathon in the 1928 Olympic Games at Amsterdam, where they finished well behind the leaders. They had paced themselves for the much longer races to which they were accustomed. It is also clear that they had very different motivations for running than did their international competitors. As we will see, their own kickball races involve extensive wagering, and community support. The runners kick a hard wooden ball along rocky mountain trails in races that may go all night long. They have a very different set of motivations from those of our own scientifically trained athletes, whose preoccupations are with speed and record breaking.

Due, no doubt, to the distractions created by the Great Depression and World War II, the remarkable athletes from the Sierra Madre were again forgotten by the industrialized world for more than two decades. Anthropologists Wendell Bennett and Robert Zingg described the culture of the Tarahumara, including their racing complex, in a somewhat obscure book issued in 1935, but it was not until the 1950s that sports journalists again turned their attentions to the exploits of such exotic "primitives." From that decade, up to the present time, articles have appeared regularly in sport, travel, or health magazines, recounting observations of this amazing isolated tribe of runners living up in the Mexican mountains. However, it was not until the 1990s that Tarahumara runners were again transported to compete in serious contests outside their native habitat.

In 1992, Richard Fisher of Tucson, Arizona, took a group of Tarahumara runners to compete in the ultramarathon named *The Leadville Trail 100*. This is a cross country race 100 miles in length. The course is all above 10,000 feet in elevation, and leads through the tough terrain of the Colorado Rockies. The Indians arrived only a day before the race. They were unfamiliar with the course, and they were disoriented from their long ride from Chihuahua. Thus, they became confused during the night portion of the race, lost their way, and dropped out.

Fisher resolved to try it again in 1993, and this time took more time to select better known runners. He also made sure they got to Leadville 10 days early, so that they could familiarize themselves with the race course. This time it was a different story. The 1993 race was won by 55 year old Victoriano Churro of Panaláchi, who set a new record, while the second and fifth places were also taken by Tarahumaras. Fisher also took a nine man team in 1994 and they had even better results in some ways. Not only did twenty-six year old Juan Herrera of Choguíta set another record in winning the race, but the Tarahumara team also finished in places 4 through 11.

More than 150 runners entered the contest but less than half of them managed to finish, and it seems remarkable that the entire Tarahumara team completed the full 100 miles. They ran in their traditional *huaraches*, cut from old truck tires, and drank only *pinole* mixed with water during the race. Their only training was the natural conditioning inherent in the course of their daily activities.

RARAJÍPARA—THE FOOT THROWING GAME

The Tarahumara love to run, and they have developed a form of long distance racing which is very much the same throughout their widespread territory. The most unique feature of their races is the fact that they must cover ultramarathon distances, while at the same time propelling a hard wooden ball ahead of them as they run.

The Tarahumara kickball race is now integral to their culture, as it was to the tribes around them, yet strangely, it seems that it came into the region rather recently. By examination of the Jesuit records, Pennington (1963:72-75) found that historically, the first mention of this type of race was in a letter from Padre Steffel in 1809. However, another Jesuit, Ratkay, had in 1683 described a Tarahumara game played with a rubber ball, which closely resembled the game played by the Aztecs and many other tribes. This was not a long distance running game, but one in which the players, naked except for leather protective belts, kicked a rubber ball around in an enclosed court. It is a mystery where and when the running game came from and how it completely displaced the rubber ball game in the space of slightly more than 100 years. Part of the answer to the latter question may be that the kickball race is so much more compatible with their life-style that its popularity swept the older Aztec game into extinction. The rubber ball game might itself have been a recent and unintegrated addition in this outlying "Chichimec" region of the empire. Research on these questions would be most welcome.

Types of Races Today

We can classify contemporary Tarahumara races into three types, based on size, complexity, and formality. The largest race that I observed, was a *rarajípara* put on between the Tarahumara community of Coloradas de la Virgen and the Tepehuáne community of Santa Rosa, both on the south side of the Barranca Sinforosa. For want of a better term we can call this kind of race the intertribal type. By no means did the race I attended involve the two tribes as whole units, but it did draw competitors from more than just the two adjacent pueblos on the Tarahumara-Tepehuáne boundary. At present this intertribal level of race is rare and probably is restricted to a few pueblos along the southern border of Tarahumara country. In the past such races were fairly common, and were held with groups of Pima, Guarojío and other tribes who bordered the Tarahumara. The intertribal race I witnessed was characterized by a larger crowd and more fanfare, and more formality than any other that I attended. For example, each community was represented by a corps of four drummers and two flutists who paraded and marched while the betting was being carried on. The race organizers were much more dramatic in their handling and announcing of the wagers, and there was more pre-race ritual than I have seen elsewhere. It was said that races of this magnitude might take anywhere from six months to two years to organize, making them rare and eagerly awaited.

The second type is the interpueblo level. These seldom involve whole pueblos, but rather are usually held between segments of two adjoining pueblos, that is, two groups of contiguous *ranchos* divided from one another by pueblo lines. When this type of race *is* between whole pueblos it may be of almost the same magnitude as the intertribal type. Similar races in terms of size and participation are those put on between segments of the same pueblo. This second type of race is the most frequent and popular kind because it is fairly easy to organize, and yet provides enough competition and brings together enough people from far enough distances to make it an exciting and diverting event.

The third type may be called the intracommunity race. These are spontaneously organized during drinking parties. They are very informal with little at stake with regard to the reputations of the runners or in the amounts of goods wagered. Some of the participants may run as far as fifteen or twenty miles on occasion, but the distances run are short by Tarahumara standards. Everyone participates, and there are no suspicions of witchcraft, such as are commonly experienced in larger more serious events. These contests are simply great fun. The reader may refer back to Chapter 5 for a description of one of them.

Women also have races *(ariwéta)* which are abbreviated versions of the men's contests, except that they use curved sticks to throw forward small padded hoops. Often they are held in conjunction with men's races.

Racing Season

The period of most intense racing activity corresponds rather closely with the growing season. The first part of this season is fraught with the anxieties attending the uncertainties surrounding the growing crops. However, this is counteracted to some extent by the euphoria experienced with the passing of winter, when people are often isolated in their winter habitations by the weather. The later part of this period corresponds with the seasonal rains. This is a time of increased social activity in general. It is the season of *tesgüinadas*. People begin to gather at one another's *ranchos* in a round of cooperative work parties through which the cooperative tasks of planting, weeding, timber cutting and hauling, harvesting, and fodder cutting are accomplished. At this time curing ceremonies are conducted, and large races organized.

Training and Equipment

Training for racing is not formalized or organized as it is in the industrialized world, but boys and girls from ages 5 or 6 run daily in the ceaseless tasks of herding the goats and other animals. They continue this "natural" training throughout life, not only by continuing to herd, but by traveling some of the considerable distances between *ranchos* at a trot, and by participating in the small informal races spontaneously organized at *tesgüinadas*. In my travels in the Sierras, on several occasions I have observed men 60 years of age or more in hot pursuit of an animal which had strayed too far from the herd. However, despite their generally fine condition the serious runners need several races behind them before they can compete without suffering soreness in their legs and chests. This is because the season starts immediately with races between 30 and 100 miles in length.

A ball (*komákali*) for each team is the most necessary piece of equipment for a race. These are carved from some hard wood on the day of the game, and are about the size and weight of an American baseball. Sometimes one of the *chokéames* paints a stripe on his team's ball to distinguish it from that of the opposing team. The rule is that the team whose ball which first crosses the line after the agreed upon number of laps is the winner of the game. During the race the ball is launched into the air with an action so swift that it appears to be kicked. The runner must stop suddenly, place his toes beneath the ball and fling it from 50 to 100 feet ahead, and he must do this without injuring his foot; hence, the contest is called *rarajípari,* or foot "throwing" game.

Other pieces of equipment are optional, or vary by region. For instance, a runner may or may not wear a rattling belt. One of these consists of a leather belt on which deer hooves have been strung with reed tubes on leather thongs. These belts were originally worn to infuse the runners with the speed of deer. Today they are said to be a good luck charm, and for keeping the runner awake. They also "sound good." Some boys now use strings of small metal bells instead of the traditional deer hooves. In some areas it is permissible for each of the main runners to carry a slender stick with which the ball can be flicked out of a cactus, thick bushes or a hole in the rocks. In other regions this is not allowed.

The most common racing attire is the simple loincloth, but Mexican denim pants and American-made tee shirts have become popular in places which are closest to urban influences. In some of the more transitional areas Mexican clothing has been adopted for everyday dress, but underneath, the traditional loincloth is worn as a kind of underwear which assists the individual to retain a sense of his Tarahumara identity. He strips down to this for racing. Sometimes runners begin a race in full Mexican dress, even wearing their *sombreros*; then they gradually discard these, along with excess shirts and pants, during the first lap. Typical footwear is a pair of sandals made from pieces cut from old automobile tires, which are lashed onto the foot with one long leather thong going between the first two toes and around the ankle. These are the same as those now universally worn by the Tarahumara for everyday activities. Some runners only wear one sandal for racing. In this case the kicking foot is left bare.

Rules

As I said, the first rule of the *rarajípari* is that the team whose ball crosses the finish first after completing the agreed upon number of laps (*vueltas*) wins. At least one runner must remain to bring the winning ball across the finish. He must have run the entire distance. An exception occurs when one teams drops out. Then, the leading team is awarded the victory. This is rare because of the obligations the runners have to those who have placed wagers on them.There is always a chance that the leading team may tire, that the *rarajípame* may injure his foot, etc.

The length of the race itself and of each *vuelta*, are agreed upon by the runners themselves with the mediation of race organizers (*chokéames*) from each side. For example, in a short race they might agree, after some haggling, to run 20 laps between certain landmarks. They do not conceive it in terms of precise units of either distance or time. Each race is thought of as a unique event, e.g., 20 or 30 laps, which might last up to one day and one night. Before the game, the *chokéames* must walk the course to agree on the landmarks marking the laps, and upon the stations for the men who have been appointed to watch for fouls: taking shortcuts, touching the ball with the hands, allowing others to kick it, etc.

The start and finish are often in a clearing which is the center of the course. For one *vuelta* or lap they run from the center to the end of the course and back, and then in the other direction to the end and back. In the central clearing, where the wagers (*tári*) are heaped up, piles of stones equivalent to the number of laps to be run are placed. These mark the start and finish, and as each team completes a lap, a stone is removed from its pile.

Another rule is that the runners cannot touch the ball with their hands, even if, as is frequently the case, the ball goes into an inaccessible place, such as a cactus patch, or a cleft in the rocks. This rule varies somewhat by locality. In some places the helpers, *riturúame* are allowed to retrieve the ball and place it for kicking, while in others the main runners are allowed to carry a long stick for this purpose.

The Preparatory Phase

In all races above the informal *tesgüinada* level a number of preliminary organizational activities must be performed. This is because people who ordinarily have little or no contact with one another must be brought together in competition. In every area there are men who have the role of *chokéame*. This position is usually assumed by self selection and tacit agreement of the adult males in an area that the individual is well suited for it. For very large events, the *siríame* of the pueblo may take charge, appointing as many as three regular race organizers to assist him. The *chokéames* have several assistants, called *sakéames*, whose specific tasks are handling the wagering process of the larger races.

The first step in organizing a race requires that a race organizer take the initiative by seeking out good runners and securing their agreements to run. Then he must travel to the rancho of another *chokéame* in order to extend a challenge. These race organizers are always older men who have personal acquaintance with their counterparts in other areas. The negotiations are generally quite secret. The *chokéames* may retire to a quiet spot in the middle of a corn field during a beer party, or they may arrive at night to avoid publicity. The principal points of discussion involve the organization of the race. However, one reason for the secrecy of these meetings is that, sometimes, in addition to the negotiations concerning the race, secret bets are made, and other shady arrangements carried out. The main points of negotiation supposedly only involve the place and date of the race, the number and length of the laps, and the number of runners.

When the *chokéames* return home they make trips around their own communities announcing the race, and they also begin spreading the word in as many *tesgüinadas* as possible. The older men of each community or group then put pressure on the best runners in their territory to prepare themselves for the competition. Preparation mainly requires abstention from sex and *tesgüino* for at least three days prior to the race, and a general readying of the mind. Runners also are obligated to report any foreboding dreams and they have an opportunity to secure any equipment they might need, such as a rattling belt. They must also get something ready to wager on themselves so as not to be suspected of skullduggery.

Because of the extreme dispersion of the Tarahumara settlement pattern, the people may begin gathering near the race course as many as three days prior to a large race. They usually camp in small family groups at one of the closest *ranchos* to the racing ground which are still within their own territory. While waiting they converse with friends, play games such as *cuatro* and *quince* and in general make the best of the opportunity to socialize. (*Cuatro* is a game somewhat like Horseshoes in which stones are tossed into small holes some 25 to 50 feet apart. *Quince* is a game resembling Parchisi). The night before an important race, special ceremonies may be held to "cure" the runners' legs. I did not observe any of these, but according to informants they resemble the initial part of the post-race ceremony which is described later.

On the morning of the race, further ceremonial acts are sometimes carried out by each side for protection and assurance of victory. The most elaborate of these that I observed was at the intertribal race between the Tepehuáne pueblo of Santa Rosa and the Tarahumara community of Coloradas:

> In the early dawn about ten Tarahumara families, along with me and my guides, gathered at the house of the head *chokéame* of the pueblo. A wooden cross draped with white muslin and beads had been set up in the cleared space in front of the house which perched on a small clearing about 50 feet above a stream. On the ground at the foot of the cross were a wooden ball of the type used in races, a ceremonial rattle, and a small jar of *tesgüino*. At a signal from the host, the people left the two fires in the yard where they had been huddled, and wrapped in their brown blankets, clustered shivering around the cross. Here, the old *owerúame*, the *chokéame* and the house owner performed a simple ritual before the sun rose. Each of the three took a turn leading a counterclockwise circuit around the draped cross shaking the ceremonial rattle, and dancing and chanting the *yúmari*. At each of the four directions they made a counterclockwise turn in place. Then *tesgüino* was ceremonially drunk by all those present after being dedicated to *Onorúame* by the old shaman. At this point, while a boy waved a white flag and another beat a drum, a young runner symbolically kicked the ball far up the hillside into the brush. At the conclusion of this ritual a gourd of warm *esquiáte* (parched corn ground with water) was passed around and, as the sun rose, the group began the hour and a half hike to the racing grounds.

Even if there are no such elaborate ceremonies, the racers drink cedar tea and ritually wash their legs in it on the morning of the race. This imparts strength and protection from sorcery, just as cedar smoke wards off evil from the animals in the yearly curing ceremonies. During the last few hours of the preparatory stage people continue filtering in from far and near to sit in small groups among the trees surrounding the clearing where the race is to begin.

The Betting Phase

The focus of greatest interest at a race is the placing and collection of wagers. This is an activity in which everyone may take part, and one which perhaps creates even more excitement and involvement than does the physical competition of the race itself. As Irigoyen Rascón and Palma Batista perceptively comment: "It is difficult to determine which is more important to the Tarahumara: their love for races or their love for gambling" (1985:90).

The racing course is usually centered in a clearing in the pines, often on the top of a ridge, but sometimes in a valley. The scene is animated and colorful. Many of the supporters for each side stand around in small groups in the clearing where the race is to begin. Mestizo men from the area conspicuously arrive on horseback, spurs jangling. For them too, the races put on by the Indians are among the few recreational opportunities in the isolated Sierra. One of them may have brought cigarettes to vend to the Tarahumara. Sometimes an enterprising Mestizo youth has purchased some brightly colored cloth which he knows will be attractive to the Indians. In some areas at the proper time of the year, a burro load of sugar cane or oranges brought up from the *barranca* can be sold in a couple of hours.

Two groups of men arrange themselves opposite one another in the center of the clearing, while back among the trees, clusters of women in embroidered white muslin dresses sit talking and sewing, their babies and children playing nearby. Groups of men in white loincloths and colored puffed-sleeved shirts dot the hillsides. Several teenaged boys are kicking a ball around the clearing, while in the nearby arroyo several herds of goats are being tended by bright-eyed young girls.

271

Under the watchful eyes of the two *chokéames*, the *sakéames* from each side act as brokers, handling each bet individually by matching it with one from the opposite side. Someone hands a roll of cloth to his *sakéame*, who takes it to a *sakéame* of the opposite side. The two men stretch it out to its full length and measure it off by folding it over in approximate one meter lengths. The opposing *sakéame* asks the watching members of his side for an equivalent piece. If no one comes forward with a comparable length of cloth or other equivalent, he tries to find its match further away, among the women. Eventually, a match is found and the two pieces are tied together, and placed on the stack (*tári*). In addition to pieces of new cloth, wagers typically include, large balls of hand spun yarn, bars of soap, flashlights, knives, peso bills, bows and arrows, strings of beads, etc. Many stories are told of rich men wagering goats, and even cattle, but, according to my observations, large bets of this kind are exceptional these days. However, in a very large race the total value of the bets may reach the equivalence of several hundred American dollars. The *tári* has a colorful aspect since cloth is the most popular betting good. The *sakéames* must have exceptional memories, for the bets are not recorded (Irigoyen Rascón and Palma Batista, 1985).

Technically the wagers are not placed upon individual runners but upon the teams. However, even though it is a team matter, the qualities of the various runners are known and discussed. If a new runner is brought in who has never run in the area before, people are reluctant to bet at first. Some runners have built up reputations for stamina and courage, which may have the same deterring effect.

The wagering goes on for at least two or three hours prior to the race. It is not closed before the start, but continues during the first two laps. People believe they can tell how the racers will do by observing their appearance after they have run the course a couple of times. Everyone keenly observes who bets how much and the excitement builds. Speculations and rumors abound. Certain men claim to have inside knowledge about the condition or mood of the runners, or that sorcery has been worked. Gossip and joking are rampant.

Just before the race, the *chokéames* and several of the older and respected men from each side take the runners aside into the woods. Here they make last minute inquiries about their condition and their willingness to run. They inquire as to whether they have had any portentous dreams, and whether they have abstained from drinking and sexual activities. If a runner has dreamed of a skull, for example, defeat would be inevitable. The runners joke among themselves. One might say that he feels so confident that he going to bet a bull or a yoke of oxen on himself. His counterpart may reply that he will not only wager a yoke of oxen, but will add his blanket to the bet. Everyone laughs nervously. The old men have been preparing some new balls and they select a freshly carved one for each team.

When all the arrangements are satisfactory to both sides, the runners are offered some *pinole* and are led to the betting area, where they sit down in front of the gathered people. Each, in turn offers a wager on his own team. They must convince the crowd that everything is aboveboard, that each runner will do his best.

The Running Phase

In many areas the race itself does not begin until early afternoon. The teams have from two to eight main runners (*rarajípame* or *júmame*), each of which has an assistant (*riturúame*). Sometimes the start may be made by one runner from each side kicking to his assistant, who is waiting 30 or 40 yards down the course. More often it is signalled by the *chokéames*, who throw out the two balls to the waiting runners.

In larger interpueblo races each team is often accompanied by a flag bearer for the first circuit of the course. In the Aboreáchi region this is done only when the course has never been used by the two groups before. The flag bearers in this case are for the purpose of officially marking the route. The flags are squares of white muslin cloth or red bandannas attached to sticks. In the large Tarahumara-Tepehuáne race which I witnessed, not only flag bearers, but also drummers followed the runners on the first lap.

At first there may be as many as 20 runners crowded together, but soon differences in terrain, differential abilities, etc., stretch them out over a considerable distance. They mostly remain in two main groups but slower runners plod along behind. The air is filled with shouting, as those behind warn the runners ahead that the ball is coming down. It seems a miracle that someone is

Runners pass the central clearing

not killed. The referees from both sides are stationed at various places along the course, and they run along with the teams for some distance to make sure no fouls are committed. They encourage their own runners, urging them forward.

In a long race the assistant runners may hurl the ball as long as they can and then may drop out. A very common sight is to see an eliminated runner hobbling along with a toe bleeding from kicking stones or cacti.

Some *rarajípame* run steadily and slowly at the rear of their team, husbanding their strength. They may hardly kick the ball until the first half is over. At the end, however, when the field has thinned, these stronger runners, who have been pacing themselves, often come into their own and bring the ball across the finish.

The last lap is the most exciting part of the race because most of the spectators participate, helping their team on to victory. Everyone who can run now excitedly rushes in, and even Mestizo boys sometimes run several miles. These "helpers" urge the official racers on with shouts of encouragement, *"wé sapúka!"* (hurry up!) *"wériga! wériga!"* (faster! faster!). Sometimes they pick up the ball with their hands and place it in a better position for kicking. The helpers may not kick the ball or run with it, and they drop out when they get tired. Women participate as eagerly as men, either by placing the ball or by running along beside the runners holding out gourds of *pinole* or herb tea to give them strength.

All this support provides a tremendous psychological lift to the runners. The scene becomes increasingly animated and exciting. The observers in the central clearing hear many voices raised in intense chant faintly in the distance. It gradually becomes louder as the leading team with its crowd of supporters approaches, and fades again as they pass the central clearing into the woods beyond. By this time the teams are often fairly far apart, and the second team may now be heard approaching.

Post-race phase

With the exception of the all-night races found in a few areas, the average contest lasts all afternoon and into the evening— between five to eight hours. When the victorious ball has crossed the finish line, attention immediately centers on distributing the winnings. The supporters of the losing team quickly desert the scene. Some start home in the dark, but more often they go to the house of a friend or relative, where *tesgüino* may be waiting. The winners must wait to collect their bets. The *sakéames* hold up each bet and call out the name of the winner. They must remember as many as 100 individual bets, but if memory fails, the bettor stands ready to claim his winnings.

One notable feature at the end of a race is the lack of attention paid the winning runner. Often he is left alone after his great physical effort, while everyone concentrates upon collecting their winnings. There are no back-slappings or hurrahs, although spectators who have won large amounts are later expected to pay a token of appreciation to the winning runners (usually a peso to each). This is especially demanded of Mestizos.

After a race the people may or may not gather for a *tesgüinada* depending upon the circumstances, and they sometimes perform further rituals pertaining to racing. At Samachíque, I observed a

275

Runner carries damaged sandal; his opponent launches the ball

post-race ceremony somewhat similar to the pre-race ritual at Coloradas, which was described earlier:

> Late in the evening after the race, at the house of one of the *chokéames*, I noticed that three large jars of beer had been placed by the side of the house. There was a fire burning in the yard and people were gathered in small groups all around the house. At approximately 9:00 P.M. I could make out some kind of activity over on the darkened porch area, so I edged my way through the crowd to investigate. An old man, barely distinguishable in the darkness, sat on the porch with his back to the wall. On his right was large clay jar of *tesgüino* and on his left, a bucket of cedar tea. A man nearby informed me that the *owerúame* was performing a *misa* (mass) on the legs of the winning runners. One at a time they approached and put one leg up on a small block of wood in front of the practitioner. He rubbed the legs of each with the cedar tea and said some ritual words to heal the pain and to impart strength in future races. He then gave the racer a staff which he held in one hand while he crossed himself with the other and turned in place counterclockwise. At each of

276

the four directions he stopped to repeat this ceremony. Not only was this performed for each runner, but some of the older men who had run along with them for the last two laps requested that the *owerúame* treat them as well.

Afterwards, six men lighted torches of pitch-pine from the fire, and arranged themselves in two lines leading down into the corn field in front of the house. One of the runners then ritually kicked the ball down the avenue made by the lighted torches. He did this three times. After the first two kicks the ball was retrieved by a boy, but after the third one, the kicker himself ran down between the torches and returned the ball to the starting point.

Following this, the *chokéame* (our host), made a short speech to the gathering, exhorting them to drink peacefully. The three *ollas* of beer were then each ritually dedicated by an important man who afterwards acted as server to the people now crowding around him. Each guest received three gourd-dips and the beer was soon exhausted. Within an hour the torches could be seen moving off into the night as the people made their way to another household, where more *ollas* of *tesgüino* were awaiting them.

In other races no drinking or ceremony follows. On one occasion the runners from one side with their families camped near the race course. They drank some *pinole*, wrapped themselves in their blankets and went to sleep. In the morning all returned to their distant homes. There is no required pattern.

Sorcery of racing

Lumholtz reported that when he was in the Tarahumara country, a race was never considered won by natural means because the losers always claimed to have been bewitched (1902:288). Many fears, and some practices of sorcery still surround Tarahumara racing. Most of the ritual precautions before a race, particularly the washing of the legs with cedar tea, are for warding off evil projected by the opposing side. Runners approaching a distant racing area exhibit anxiety concerning what a *sukurúame* from the other side may be able to do if they camp too near. I did not encounter the idea that all races are lost by evil magic, but I found that many of the older men whom I queried on the point claimed that the reason they had been forced to stop their racing careers was that they had been sorcerized. Frequent topics of conversation at ordinary *tesgüinadas* are the great races of the past. Men brag of their exploits, and the amounts which were bet upon them. In three distinct areas of the Tarahumara country I encountered the idea of men being struck down by evil magic in their last race. They recounted how they had managed to fall across the finish line writhing with pain in their legs and chest, yet they won the race. After that they had never been able to run again as *rarajípame*.

There are many methods of creating such supernatural havoc. Most of them are performed by either a shaman (*owerúame*) or a sorcerer (*sukurúame*), but some techniques may be utilized by any opponent. One method is to place a piece of a certain red colored wood in the path where the runners will pass. This is said to bring about a pain in the stomach and an excruciating inability to urinate. This wood can only be secured in the deep *barranca*, as it does not grow in the highlands.

Another means of sabotage is to make a small bet for one side publicly, but then secretly to place a larger bet on the other team. The cheater then runs along as a supporter who places the ball for the side on whom he has openly wagered. The evil is done by carrying salt in the hand used to place the ball for the runner to kick. This causes the ball to become heavier and heavier for the main runner, eventually forcing that team to drop far behind and out of the race.

The most deadly method of general sorcery in the Aboreáchi area and one which may be directed also against runners, is the use of peyote (*híkuli*) by a shaman or sorcerer. *Híkuli* is greatly feared. In this western canyon part of the region it is not eaten knowingly or taken into the body in any way, except by sorcerers and shamans. It is considered to be a powerful spirit which can "see" a person at a great distance and do him harm. It is also thought that it may be fed to a person after grinding it up and secretly putting it into his food or *tesgüino*. Ordinarily, if a person touches peyote he will waste away and die in about a year, but sometimes this deadly plant may strike more suddenly, as in a race.

Lumholtz reported that in his day, the leg bones of the dead might be dug up and buried near the track to induce fatigue, and that black magic ceremonies against opposing runners were performed at burial places (1902:284). These practices were apparently unknown in the areas I observed, where it was said that no one would dare to desecrate the dead in this way.

Many other secret charms both for protection and evil are said to be used in racing. Often they are some kind of rare plant from the *barranca,* such as a kind of small shiny red berry which I was able to observe one runner carrying in his clothing. "A muscle cramp is said to be caused by a spell cast on a runner. Stomachaches and sleepiness are also attributed to sorcery, and it is thought that smoking certain herbs and exhaling the smoke into a runner's face may suffice to put him to sleep. Another favorite [trick] is putting a drug that causes diarrhea or severe abdominal cramping in the *pinole* of one of the runners" (Irigoyen Rascón and Palma Batista, 1985:91).

This Worldly Chicanery

Much to my surprise I discovered that fixed races are not uncommon among the Tarahumara. This first came to my attention when I travelled with one of the runners from Aboreáchi to the racing ground at Bakórachi for a race with a group of nearby *ranchos* of Norogáchi pueblo. We camped in the trees some distance from the race course. On our arrival in late afternoon of the day prior to the race, the opposing *chokéame,* who lived nearby, was waiting for us at the campground. Our own *chokéame* approached him alone, and the two retired for a secret conference. That evening, after dark, our *chokéame* returned bearing several cloth bundles. My friend the runner was elated, saying this meant we would win. Surprised, I pressed him further and learned that the bundles contained secret wagers sent over by people of the other side to be wagered without their own people's knowledge. On occasion this may be done if the reputation of the runners on one side is very great. *Chokéames* and runners themselves also sometimes purposely arrange a loss. Occasionally, the runners are paid to lose by wealthy men of the opposing side.

Before a race scheduled on October 26, 1960, one runner told me he was going to lose because he had been "bought" by the other side. They already had sent money to him and would find more to bet secretly against his side. Part of this would go to him as secret winnings. He showed some guilt about this, but he said the action was justified because his father and the chief *chokéame* had "ordered" him to do it. He thought he might net about 100 pesos worth of material, which is quite a substantial amount in a region where most Indians never see that much cash at one time.

Theoretically, one may be fined severely by the pueblo authorities if such activities are discovered, but guilt is almost impossible to prove. I was told of a large race two years earlier which two runners from Yehuachíque had conspired to lose. There was some suspicion and much dissatisfaction at the time, but nothing was done because these were the finest runners in the area, and no actual proof was brought forward. The truth gradually leaked out in *tesgüinadas* through the intermingling of people from different *ranchos* near the pueblo borders. It is common knowledge that such things may occur, but people generally place their faith in their *chokéames*, or in their own abilities to divine or discover who the winner might be.

These illicit practices are not recently developed phenomena. Bennett and Zingg observed that "If the runners do not place bets, the people are afraid, and they too refrain from betting" (1935:338). Earlier, Lumholtz noted that, "It may even happen that some dishonest fellow will pay to the best runner of one party a cow if he lets the other fellow win" (1902:289).

The Social Role of Racing

Racing is more than a game to the Tarahumara. Obviously it is a pleasant diversion, but additionally it is an economic activity, a force for social cohesion, an institutionalized channel for aggression, and a socially constructed means for celebrating the importance of the physical fitness required in this difficult environment. It may be objected that this evaluation is self-evident since in many cultures games and sports have similar significance. The major difference in the Tarahumara case lies in the fact that there are very few institutions in the culture which perform these functions. Thus, from a comparative standpoint, racing appears more socially vital than similar activities in most other cultures. To clarify I suggest that, if this institution were removed from Tarahumara life, the cultural imbalance resulting would be much greater than if some sporting activity were dropped from our own complex culture, where many alternative institutions and complexes would keep the overall structure more intact. The negligible impact of the American baseball strike of 1994-5 is some evidence for such a judgement.

Racing occupies much of the thoughts of men and women because it provides one of the rare opportunities for economic gain and because there are few other opportunities for large scale group interaction. Also, not only does racing offer a means for prestige gain for runners and an opportunity for the *chokéames* to voluntarily assume temporary authority roles, but it is surrounded by sorcery and ritual, indicating that it is a cultural focus of anxiety and high interest.

Yet there is something paradoxical about Tarahumara racing. Bennett and Zingg call it a "socializing force of minor import," and relegate their description of it to a residual chapter on games and sports (1935:330, 335-41). I do not believe that assigning such a trivial role to the Tarahumara racing complex is justified. Let us look at some of the reasons for re-evaluating the role of racing in this society, and then consider some of the factors which might cause us to underestimate these.

It is apparent that the races should promote social integration. Few activities in Tarahumara life require the degree of sustained interdependence of roles found in the race. To put on a race requires that an organization of activities related to a group goal be activated for several days. It also entails a number of interlocking cooperative activities on the basis of age. The elders make arrangements, care for the runners, prepare equipment, and act as teachers and supernatural protectors. The youths enact the rigorous role of runners, who are responsible for the economic welfare of their friends and relatives. Both men and women involved in the actual running must subordinate personal desires for sex and *tesgüino* for the good of the group, and allow themselves, at least temporarily, to be under the direction of the elders.

Most of the people participate in the betting, and since those from one side all bet on the same team, they win or lose as a unit. They are all either euphoric winners or depressed losers together, and this should tend to strengthen in-group bonds among them.

However, perhaps the greatest solidarity is created by, and reflected in the total group involvement in the actual physical attempts of individuals to aid their own side to win.

Races are a means of interpueblo communication, and interaction. The Tarahumara have no political organization above the level of the pueblo, and there is also no system of regional markets or other institutionalized means of bringing about interpueblo interaction. Pueblos are also largely endogamous, and the attitude of people towards the members of neighboring pueblos is one of reserve and distrust. Many people have never visited the pueblo center of any neighboring pueblo. Both the large interpueblo races, and those between subsegments of neighboring pueblos may be viewed as weak and intermittent economic institutions. A quasi-market structure is created by the interchange of goods through wagering and the other attendant peripheral exchange activities. This is not an efficient economic institution since there is no immediate exchange (except for small Mestizo vendors) minimal profits, and no livelihoods derived from racing. Nevertheless, more goods change hands at one time in this way than in any other single economic activity of the Tarahumara. It is certainly true too, that the major interest of the people in the race is in the betting and expectation of economic gain. The long haggling activities and public display of desired goods are as exciting as the running itself.

It should be pointed out that the economic importance of racing is increased by the lack of developed economic institutions and opportunities in the culture. Most ordinary economic transactions are occasional barters of animals for food (maize or beans) and infrequent contacts with Mestizo traders and store keepers. Since money is still in very limited use among the Tarahumara, these latter contacts are infrequent and usually involve payment in kind or the engenderment of debt. The race provides a means of acquiring goods without the heavy-hanging implications of such debt. It also provides an economic showcase for people who, in the isolated course of their daily lives, seldom have an opportunity to see so many desired items on display. It should be pointed out that food and animals rarely appear in the actual betting, which is ordinarily limited to items which, if lost, will not threaten existence in a subsistence economy.

Another point bearing upon the role of racing in Tarahumara society is its psychological function in the release of aggression. One of the strongest social norms is that relating to nonaggression. Yet hostilities and persisting enmities occur, and the racing complex provides one indirect means by which they may be expressed. I first was made aware of this when a certain runner from Yehuachíque gloated over beating another man with whom he had a long-standing enmity, in an intrapueblo race. The latter was a high pueblo official (*teniénte*) who, unlike the informant, possessed more capability for leadership than for running. The aggressive emotions of both men were sublimated and channeled through culturally approved nonviolent methods: political and judicial discrimination by the official, and racing by the informant. Several other cases of a similar type came to my attention.

It seems clear that some of the repressed hostility people have as a result of the strong prohibitions against aggression, is projected against the relatively unknown members of other pueblos in inter-pueblo races. Moreover, the fear of sorcery exhibited by runners undoubtedly is paralleled by some overt acts of magical aggression. While I never witnessed any of these, I was assured by many that they do occur. The economic gain and loss involved could also be expected to motivate sorcery in places where the belief is held that such behavior is common and effective. The competition of the running and betting, in themselves, also appear to serve the function of diverting aggression outside the pattern of everyday interaction and channeling it in a culturally acceptable way. This explanation takes on more plausibility in view of the extreme lengths to which the Tarahumara typically go to avoid conflict situations.

It is apparent that racing plays a more important role in Tarahumara life than has been recognized. Yet, on balance, it is necessary to point out that to some extent, the social functions of the activity remain largely unrealized. Races are not frequent and thus their functions are not often performed. It is this condition which makes it difficult to understand the role of the race in Tarahumara culture. This is both a result and a reflection of the character of the Tarahumara social system, a system characterized by great flexibility in the performance of activities. This is related to the demands imposed by a maize-agricultural herding economy in a mountainous region. There is a necessity for situational adaptation and mobility, with a consequent lack of cohesive or large scale territorial or kinship groupings. This social system as "centrifugal" in that it is composed of a vast net of small bilateral family and *rancho* groupings. These are bound together in overlapping household centered networks by bonds of cooperative labor, kinship, ritual participation, and mutual aid, which are defined and symbolized by beer drinking reciprocities.

A most important quality of the network form of social organization is its overlapping and interlocking character, which means that the set of people with which any individual family interacts varies from that of all other families to a greater or lesser extent. There are no clear-cut enduring group boundaries of either a territorial or social nature.

Superimposed upon this ecologically dependent basic system in all but the *Gentile* communities is the pueblo political organization introduced by the Spanish, headed by the *siríame* (*gobernador*) and a panel of officials. Integration at the pueblo level is weak and any individual's most frequent and important social contacts are carried out in the context of the diffuse and flexible *rancho* networks.

The race, too, reflects these characteristics. Of great importance are the pervading qualities of indeterminacy and individual choice with regard to both time, place, and performance or non-performance of activities. All of the social roles involved are characterized by self-selection. The organizing roles of *chokéames*, the roles of the runners themselves to a large extent and group attendance, are dependent upon the initiative of the actors. There is no fixed calendar of racing and no fixed place, though certain areas are favored. What this means is that people of two different areas must be interested and organized with regard to a time and place which is set by *chokéames*, and must be advertised by word of mouth. The larger the scope of the race, the more difficult it is to coordinate the activities of the scattered people.

I have already spoken of the *tesgüinada* system of cooperative work and ceremony, characterized by individual arrangements and voluntary attendance. If the planning of one of these coincides with a race, there may be competing motivation for attendance. Besides cooperative labor obligations, other activities may also claim a person's time and effort at the time of a race: a journey to a Mestizo store in a distant part of the pueblo, a deal regarding an animal, etc. There is always the pressure of caring for the animals, requiring that most households leave at least one person behind. Fields must also be protected from marauding animals during the growing season.

For a large interpueblo race problems of distance limit attendance. A suitable ground must be chosen which is intermediate between two pueblos. Given the great scatter of the settlement pattern, this means that many people will have to travel from the far side of the pueblo sometimes involving as much as four to eight hours of continuous foot travel.

These conditions make the larger interpueblo race a rarity requiring organization far in advance by the *gobernador* of the pueblo. When it is realized that in the opposing pueblo the same kinds of randomness, freedom, and uncertainty obtain, it is obvious that the difficulties of organization and attendance become compounded. The smaller race between some members of two pueblos is the much more practical event, but these also have great variability of both personnel and attendance. For example, a given *chokéame* may go in any direction to find opponents. Usually, he knows several other *chokéames* in different areas, any of which may contact him. Much too, depends upon the availability of good runners. Some areas may lack men with racing ability for several years at a time, while others are oversupplied. One purpose of the smaller intrapueblo *tesgüinada* races is to determine who is capable, and to get runners in shape for the larger contests.

Individualism and self-determination correlated with the lack of strong group affiliation are further demonstrated in the not infrequent case that one or another of the runners does not appear as he has agreed. I was surprised to find that on several occasions, well known runners found it necessary to withdraw on the very day of a race. Some of these reported having had a bad dream, but more than once it was clear that the runner had chosen to take care of a routine transaction which could well have been handled on another day. No anger is expressed towards these men since independence and the right to individual choice are among the strongest values of the culture.

The effects of the network type of social system are also seen in the startling frequency of "fixed" races, a situation which indicates weak commitments to the group one represents. The economic self-interest which may take precedence over group allegiance, also reflects the independence orientation which, in turn, stems from ecological and social influences. The fact that the organization of races is dependent upon individual initiative, that runners vary in number in any particular area from period to period, that attendance is voluntary, that racers may cheat without sanction, or withdraw without notice, all reflect great flexibility in the racing complex. This is consistent with other Tarahumara patterns and is more evidence for the interpretations of their social system in this book. The race has an important place in that system, though this importance undoubtedly varies by subregion of the extensive Tarahumara country.

BIBLIOGRAPHY

An introductory guide to the Tarahumara literature

Arrieta, O. *Acculturation and the National Integration of the Tarahumara Indians of Northern Mexico.* Ph.D. dissertation, University of Arizona, 1984. An interesting study of culture change in Samachíque.

Ascher, R. and Clune, F. "Waterfall Cave, Southern Chihuahua, Mexico." *American Antiquity,* (1960) 26:270-274. One of the few archaeological references on the Tarahumara.

Balke, B. and Snow, C. "Anthropological and Physiological Observations on Tarahumara Endurance Runners." *American Journal of Physical Anthropology,* (1965) 23:293-301.

Basauri, C. "The Resistance of the Tarahumaras." *Mexican Folkways,* (1926) Vol. 5, No. 2.

Beals, R. "The Comparative Ethnology of Northern Mexico before 1750." *Ibero-Americana,* (1932) II:92-226.

Bennett, W. and Zingg, R. *The Tarahumara.* Chicago: University of Chicago Press, 1935. A basic reference.

Birdsell, J. "A Basic Demographic Unit." *Current Anthropology,* (1973), 14:337-56.

Brambila, D. S.J., *Diccionario: Rarámuri-Castellano* (Tarahumar). Mexico: Buena Prensa, 1986.

Burgess, D. "Western Tarahumara," In, *Southern Uto-Aztecan Grammatical Sketches, Studies in Uto-Aztecan Grammar*, ed. R. Longacker, Summer Institute of Linguistics, Publications in Linguistics No. 56, Vol. 4. Arlington: Summer Institute of Linguistics and University of Texas at Arlington, 1984.

Burgess, D. and Schwalkwijk. B. (eds.) *Tarahumara*. Edición Privada de Chrysler de México, 1985 (English and Spanish). Limited edition. Magnificent photographs by Schwalkwijk. A fine set of folktales collected and translated by Burgess, a good essay by Luiz González Rodríguez, and a poem by Alfonso Reyes.

Burleson, B. and Riskind, D. *Backcountry Mexico: A Traveler's Guide and Phrase Book*. Austin: University of Texas Press, 1986. Useful aid in Tarahumara country.

Bye, R. Jr. "Hallucinogenic Plants of the Tarahumara," *Journal of Ethnopharmacology*, (1979) 1:23-48.

Conklin, H. "An ethnoecological approach to shifting agriculture." In, *The Transactions of the New York Academy of Sciences*, (1954) Ser. 2, 17:133-42.

De Velasco Rivero, P. *Danzar o Morir*. México: Ediciones CRT, 1983. Scholarly analysis of Tarahumara religion.

Dunne, P. *Early Jesuit Missions in Tarahumara*. Berkeley: University of California Press, 1948.

Edgerton, R. "Cultural" vs. "Psychological" Factors in the Expression of Values, Attitudes, and Personality Characteristics." *American Anthropologist*, (1965) 67:442-447.

Fisher, R. and Verplancken, L. S.J., *Mexico's Copper Canyon*. Tucson: Sunracer Publications, 1994. Excellent guide.

Fontana, B. "Tarahumara: Runners of the West." *Arizona Highways*, May, 1979a.

Fontana, B. and Schafer, J. *Tarahumara: Where Night Is The Day of the Moon*. Flagstaff: Northland Press, 1979b. Fine account of visits to Tarahumara communities on the Concho river. Historical and ethnographic information. Excellent photographs.

Fontana, B. and Teiwes, H. *The Material World Of The Tarahumara.* Tucson: Arizona State Museum, University of Arizona, 1979c.

Forde, C. *Habitat, Economy and Society.* New York: Dutton and Co., 1934.

Frake, C. "Cultural Ecology and Ethnography." *American Anthropologist,* (1962) 64:53-60.

Fried, J. *Ideal Norms and Social Control in Tarahumara Society.* Ph.D. dissertation, Yale University, 1952.

Fried, J. "The Relation of Ideal Norms to Actual Behavior in Tarahumara Society." *Southwestern Journal of Anthropology,* (1953) 9:286-95. Illustrates flexibility in Tarahumara social behavior.

Gajdusek, D. "The Sierra Tarahumara." *The Geographical Review,* (1953) 43:15-38.

Goldschmidt, W. *Man's Way.* New York: Holt and Co., 1959.

Goldschmidt, W. "Theory and Strategy in the Study of Cultural Adaptability." *American Anthropologist,* (1965) 67:402-08.

Graham, M. *Rarámuri Residential Site Structure: an Ethnoarchaeological Approach to Settlement Organization.* Ph.D. Dissertation, Dept. of Anthropology, University of New Mexico, 1989. Important analysis of site use and patterns of movement.

Groom, D. "Cardiovascular Observations on the Tarahumara Indian Runners—The Modern Spartans." *American Heart Journal,* (1971) 304-318.

Irigoyen Rascón, F. and Palma Batista, J. "Rarajípari: the kick-ball race of the Tarahumara Indians." *Annals of Sports Medicine,* (1985) Vol. 2, No. 2, 79-94. By an M.D. who worked at Cerocáui and Norogáchi. Batista is a Tarahumara Indian.

Kennedy, J. "Tesgüino Complex: The role of beer in Tarahumara Culture." *American Anthropologist,* (1963) 65:620-40.

Kennedy, J. "La Carrera de bola Tarahumara y su significación." *América Indígena,* (1969) 29:17-42.

Kennedy, J. *Inápuchi: Una Comunidad Tarahumara Gentil*. México: Instituto Indigenista Interamericano, 1970.

Kennedy, J. and López, R. *Semana Santa in the Sierra Tarahumara: A Comparative Study in Three Communities*. Los Angeles: U.C.L.A. Museum of Cultural History, 1978.

Kennedy, J. "Bonds of laughter among the Tarahumara Indians." In, *The Social Anthropology of Latin America*, eds. W. Goldschmidt and H. Hoijer. Latin American Studies Center, U.C.L.A., 1970. Description of joking relationship behavior, with theoretical discussion.

Kennedy, J. *Tarahumara*. New York: Chelsea House Publishers, 1990. Written for high school level readers.

Levi, J. *Pillars of the Sky: The Genealogy of Ethnic Identity among the Rarámuri-Simaróni (Tarahumara-Gentiles) of Northwest Mexico*. Ph.D. Dissertation, Harvard University, 1993. Excellent study of ethnicity in a Tarahumara Gentile community.

López, R. "Tarahumara Ritual Aesthetic Manifestations." *The Kiva*, (1972) 37:207-23.

Lumholtz, C. *Unknown Mexico. Vol. 1*. New York: Scribner's and Sons, 1902. A basic resource.

McClellan, B. "The World's Toughest Runners." *Runner's World*, October 1979.

Merrill, W. "Thinking and Drinking: a Rarámuri Interpretation." In, *The Nature and Status of Ethnobotany*, ed. R. Ford. Ann Arbor: University of Michigan, Museum of Anthropology, Anthropological Paper 676, 1978.

Merrill, W. "Tarahumara Social Organization, Political Organization, and Religion." In, A. Ortiz, ed. *Southwest*, Vol. 10, 290-305, Handbook of North American Indians. Washington, D.C.: Smithsonian Institution Press, 1983a.

Merrill, W. "God's Saviours in the Sierra Madre." *Natural History*, (1983b) 3:59-66. Fine description of Easter.

Merrill, W. *Rarámuri Souls: Knowledge and Social Process in Northern Mexico.* Washington D. C.: Smithsonian Institution Press, 1988. Excellent analysis of knowledge, and its transmission.

Murdock, G. *Social Structure.* New York: Macmillan Co., 1949.

Nabokov, P. *Indian Running: Native American History and Religion.* Santa Fe, New Mexico: Ancient City Press, 1987.

Ocampo, M., S.J. *Historia de la Misión Tarahumara (1900-1950).* México: Buena Prensa, S.A., 1950. Account of Jesuits return.

Pastron, A. *Aspects of Witchcraft and Shamanism in a Tarahumara Indian Community of Northern Mexico.* Ph.D. Dissertation, University of California, Berkeley, 1977.

Pennington, C. *The Tarahumar of Mexico.* Salt Lake City: University of Utah Press, 1963. Focuses on material culture.

Pennington, C. *The Tepehuán of Chihuahua.* Salt Lake City: University of Utah Press, 1969. Material culture of northern Tepehuáne.

Pennington, C. "La Carrera de bola entre los Tarahumaras de México: Un Problema de Difusión." *América Indígena,* Vol. 30, 1970.

Plancarte, F. *El Problema Indígena Tarahumara.* Memorias del Instituto Nacional Indigenista #5, 1954. By first director of I.N.I. station in the area. Emphasizes social justice.

Roca, P. *Spanish Jesuit Churches in Mexico's Tarahumara.* Tucson: University of Arizona, 1979.

Schwatka, F. *In the Land of the Cave and Cliff Dwellers.* New York: Cassel Publishers, 1893.

Sheridan, T. and Naylor, T. eds. *Rarámuri: A Tarahumara Colonial Chronicle 1607-1791.* Flagstaff: Northland Press, 1979.

Slaney, F. *Death and "Otherness" in Tarahumara Ritual.* Ph.D. dissertation, Départment d'anthropologie, Université Laval, Quebéc, 1991. Throws new light on Tarahumara religion.

Spicer, E. *Cycles of Conquest*. Tucson: University of Arizona Press, 1962. The basic historical reference for northwest Mexico.

Spicer, E. "Northwest Mexico: Introduction." In, R. Wauchope, ed. *Handbook of Middle American Indians, Vol. 8, Ethnology Part II*, Austin: University of Texas Press, 1969.

Steward, J. *Theory of Culture Change*. Urbana: University of Illinois Press, 1955.

Tamayo, J. *Atlas Geográfico General de México*, 1945.

Williams, K. "The Tarahumara Race for Cultural Survival." In, *Mexico's Copper Canyon*, eds. R. Fisher and L. Verplancken, 1994.

Zingg, R. "The Genuine and Spurious Values in Tarahumara Culture." *American Anthropologist*, (1942) 44:78-92.

INDEX

About the Author

John G. Kennedy is Professor Emeritus of Anthropology and Psychiatry at the University of California at Los Angeles, where he taught for 25 years. His Ph.D. research was a cultural ecological study of the Tarahumara Indians. He has written four books on them (one with Raúl López), as well as a number of journal articles.

In 1962-65 he taught at the American University in Cairo and did research on social change among the Egyptian Nubians, who were being relocated as a consequence of the construction of the high dam at Aswan. He continued his interest in the Middle East and in 1974-76 directed a Medical Anthropological project in North Yemen studying the social and medical effects of the nearly universal use of the stimulant drug *qat* in that country. His research in the Arab world was reported in several journal articles, and in the books: *Struggle for Change in a Nubian Village*, *Nubian Ceremonial Life*, and *The Flower of Paradise: The Institutionalized Use of the Drug Qat in North Yemen*.

He began making annual visits to the Sierra Madre again in 1987 and is preparing another book on the Tarahumara.